Scandals and Scoundrels

Scandals and Scoundrels

*Seven Cases That Shook
the Academy*

Ron Robin

UNIVERSITY OF CALIFORNIA PRESS

Berkeley   Los Angeles   London

University of California Press
Berkeley and Los Angeles, California

University of California Press, Ltd.
London, England

© 2004 by the Regents of the University of California

Library of Congress Cataloging-in-Publication Data
Robin, Ron Theodore.
  Scandals and scoundrels : seven cases that shook the academy / Ron Robin.
      p.   cm.
  Includes bibliographical references and index.
    ISBN 0-520-23578-9 (cloth : alk. paper)—ISBN
  0-520-24249-1 (pbk. : alk. paper)
    1. Plagiarism.   2. Impostors and imposture.   3. Learning
  and scholarship—Moral and ethical aspects.   I. Title.
  PN167.R63   2004
  174'.937873—dc22   2003024854

Manufactured in the United States of America
13 12 11 10 09 08 07 06 05 04
10 9 8 7 6 5 4 3 2 1

Printed on Ecobook 50, containing a minimum 50 percent
postconsumer waste, processed chlorine-free. The balance
contains virgin pulp, including 25 percent Forest Steward-
ship Council Certified for no old-growth tree cutting, processed either TCF or ECF. The paper is acid-free and meets
the minimum requirements of ANSI/NISO Z39.48–1992
(R 1997) *(Permanence of Paper).*

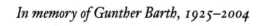

In memory of Gunther Barth, 1925–2004

CONTENTS

PREFACE AND ACKNOWLEDGMENTS

I am the confused beneficiary of tectonic shifts in American academia. The barricades of center and periphery that once marginalized scholars from outside the United States have mostly disappeared. A new awareness of diverse scholarly practices has benefited from technological advances offering instant electronic access to academic journals and intellectual exchanges. Yet, paradoxically, this expansive intellectual milieu is frustrating. Diversity has accelerated the splintering of the academic community into subgroups with little meaningful interaction or rapport. Moreover, accessibility has inundated intellectual precincts to such a degree that it has increased the invisibility of outsiders and newcomers.[1]

Diversity and improved access have also induced epistemological confusion. An expansive public space has, indeed, encouraged a refreshing airing of the mores and standards of the academic enterprise. At the same time, both the technical and the philosophical extensions of scholarly communication have increased dissonance and conflict. While contemporary academic discourse is intellectually egalitarian and electronically instant, it is also highly contentious, lacking in reflection or moderation, and often annoyingly self-righteous.[2] Diversity and uninhibited access to the major intellectual deliberations of the liberal arts have heightened conflict by exposing—and at times inventing—flaws in contemporary academic practices. Often the only discussions garnering broad attention in such crowded and cacophonous conditions are the provocative and intensely confrontational polemics about academic crimes and misdemeanors.

It is with these conflicting realities in mind that I attempt to explain the growing volume of academic scandals in the latter-day American academy. In the following pages I argue that the inflation in deviancy spectacles is more the result of changes in conventional modes of scholarly mediation than a sign of existential crisis. Deviancy debates and scandal are in themselves necessary vital signs of a vibrant intellectual body, delineating its rules and regulations through the creation of borders and margins. Increased visibility of scandals is the result of crucial technological and organizational shifts rather than some underlying intellectual declension.

Like many of my previous endeavors, this book began on the fringes of the Berkeley campus during coffee-saturated exchanges with Paul Flemer and Richard Hill. Along the way, I gained insight from David Hollinger, Marilyn Young, John Wiener, David Engerman, Steven Whitfield, Michael Burlingame, Yuval Yonai, Maoz Azaryahu, and Fania Oz-Zalzberger. I thank them all for their time and patience.

At the University of California Press, Naomi Schneider has been much more than an editor. She has guided this project from

its hesitant beginnings, offering along a tortuous way many crucial correctives. Her support and enthusiasm never wavered, even
when my spirits flagged. Erika Büky and Jacqueline Volin have
skillfully guided this book through a maze of production stages.
They joined forces with Andrew Frisardi in a relentless and unforgiving scanning of the text for errors and logical lapses. Joshua
Baron Cahn, my research assistant, appeared out of nowhere, offering much-needed advice and correctives.

Much of the writing occurred during summer respites at the
Roosevelt Study Center, in Middelburg, Holland. This wonderful intellectual sanctuary offered me the space, time, and financial
support to disengage myself from troubled surroundings. I am
deeply grateful for the understanding and generosity of the center's director, Cornelis (Kees) van Minnen, the unending patience
of Leontien Joosse, and the insight of Giles Scott-Smith, the center's resident postdoctoral fellow. I owe a special debt of gratitude
to Hans Krabberdam, the center's assistant director. Hans is a tol-
erant listener, a scholar, and a friend.

As for my debt to my family, words fail me. My partner in life,
Livi Wolff-Robin, and our children, Gal, Sivan, Noa, and Matan,
have humored me beyond the call of familial duty.

I wrote this book during a particularly grim period of my professional life. As dean of students at the most pluralistic university in Israel, I have spent the last few years confronting the af-
tershocks of three years of bloody conflict. In addition to my
routine tasks, I have witnessed grief, anger, and a loss of hope affecting the young citizens of my war-torn society. I have also had
the unenviable duty of consoling the families, friends, and peers
of students—Jews and Arabs—who lost their lives in tragic and violent circumstances. Our students' mature behavior under such

impossible circumstances has been a source of strength and inspiration.

I dedicate this book to the memory of Gunther Barth, inspirational teacher and humanist. With almost biblical patience, Gunther taught me the craft of writing and researching. He also taught me to be a concerned and socially responsible academic. In his life Gunther would have been annoyed by such ceremonial piety. I hope he will forgive me for aggravating him posthumously.

Scholarly Scandals: Why Do They Happen?

In 1956 the American historical establishment suffered an embarrassing moment when George Kennan published his inquest
of the infamous Sisson documents. This compilation of top-
secret reports, letters, and memoranda—purchased and circulated in 1918 by Edgar Sisson, a special representative of the
American Committee on Public Information stationed in Petro-
grad during the Great War—provided documentary evidence
that Russia's Bolshevik leaders were paid agents of the German
General Staff. Kennan pronounced the Sisson documents forgeries and, in the process, impugned leading members of the
American historical profession for aiding and abetting a major
case of intellectual fraud.[1]

Kennan's accusations focused in particular on J. Franklin
Jameson, former editor of the *American Historical Review*, and
Samuel Harper, professor of Russian language and institutions at
the University of Chicago. When called upon to examine Sisson's
collection, these two experts had found "no reason to doubt the

genuineness or authenticity of these . . . documents." Kennan maintained that the premise of German-Bolshevik collaboration was historically implausible and that the documents were patently fraudulent. In support of his belief, he offered persuasive technical evidence, ranging from the use of suspicious letterheads and seals, to language discrepancies, to the presence of defunct dating systems in the letters, to apparently forged signatures, and, most incriminating of all, evidence that the same typewriter had been used to prepare supposedly original documents emanating from different offices. On his predecessors, who had validated the documents in the heat of World War I, Kennan pronounced a harsh judgment: Jameson knew no Russian, and his role in the authentication of the Sisson documents had been one of "vulgar innocence." Samuel Harper was the willing victim of war hysteria. By Harper's own admission, "it was impossible for a university man not to make a contribution to the development of the war spirit, even if it involved the making of statements of a distinctly biased character."[2]

Such government-academic collusion was by no means a trivial matter; the historians' seal of approval had far-reaching ramifications. In early 1918, when the documents were certified and published, the Wilson administration was confronting wavering public support for American involvement in the war against Germany. Evidence of complicity between Germany and the pariah Bolshevik regime was an important weapon in the arsenal of public-opinion makers during this period.

Kennan's 1951 verdict was of contemporary significance as well. Published as the clouds of the Cold War settled over the United States, his investigation challenged the growing tendency in academia and government to conflate all forms of totalitarianism, in particular Nazism and Communism.³ Just as the 1918 scholarly acceptance of these forgeries raised unavoidable concerns over the role of academia in the shadow of war, Kennan's findings pinpointed the inherent dangers of a symbiotic relationship between the national-security state and the university. Even though his inquest was ostensibly aimed at clarifying an issue from the past, Kennan was obviously preoccupied with the military-intellectual complex of his own times. A mobilized academia, however noble the cause, was a self-defeating enterprise, he implied. The intrusion of ulterior political motives into the world of scholarship eroded cherished principles of objectivity and independence—the cornerstones of the modern Western university.

Despite such broad implications, Kennan's findings were greeted with public indifference. Irrespective of obvious ramifications for contemporary geopolitical arrangements, this professional uproar did not attract the attention of the mainstream media in the United States or elsewhere. The rituals of public soul-searching and censure that we associate with recent episodes of academic malfeasance were nonexistent at the time. From the moment of exposure and throughout the process of inquiry, the Sisson affair transpired in the restrictive social and intellectual surroundings of a clearly defined scholarly community. Upon completion of the unpleasant yet vital task of censoring the errant and pleading the profession's integrity, the affair disappeared from view.

For better or for worse, such restraining circumstances no longer characterize investigations of intellectual misconduct. Contemporary deliberations invariably cascade out of well-defined academic surroundings and scholarly journals. The "out-ing" of deviant scholars is now a veritable cottage industry and the source of incessant public controversy. The undertone of many of these exposés is that we are living in particularly decadent times and that some fundamental flaw permeates academia. Critics bemoan the cynical lack of integrity and the waning of professional ethics within the American university. As is often the case when a society is confronted by fears of rampant wrongdoing, there is a tendency to round up the usual suspects, who in most cases at present appear to be aligned with an allegedly powerful "linguistic left," where performance and appearance overshadow reality and truth.

My analysis in this book of an alleged climate of decline and error focuses on significant instances of hoax, plagiarism, and misrepresentation in the liberal arts, with special emphasis on history and anthropology. Both disciplines have captured public attention in part because of their contentious attempts to remap their cultural and intellectual terrain. For more than two decades, both history and anthropology have been involved in a destabilizing process of self-reflection, accompanied by acrimonious philosophical clashes between practitioners of different persuasions. As early as the 1970s, Elzbieta Sklodowska reminds us, the anthropologist Clifford Geertz and the historian Hayden White offered a then startling proclamation that the primary merchandise of historians and anthropologists was the production of self-reflexive texts. Both iconoclastic theorists urged an abandonment of what they considered to be the pretentious and elusive quest for scientific truth and proposed new paradigms of textual analysis.[4]

These changes have split the community of practicing historians into camps that share no meaningful common ground. Traditionalists, who claim the production of objective knowledge as the primary goal of the discipline, confront a powerful coalition of literary and social theorists, who dismiss such a concept as elusive, naïve, and fatally flawed. Controversies over whether history is a scientific enterprise or a subjective exercise—more reflective of the historian's ideological concerns than it is a verifiable version of the past—have challenged disciplinary standards, practices, and objectives. In open defiance of previously axiomatic assumptions, a visible and influential cohort of historians declares that "the past is not discovered or found," but rather is "created and represented by the historians as a text." The text is reportedly more revealing of the practicing historian and her culture than of a hopelessly irretrievable past.[5]

A similar valorization of relativity, suspicion of grand theory, and rejection of master narratives has affected mainstream anthropology. Contrary to the traditional paradigm of scientific ethnography, a powerful legion of practitioners has redefined the ethnographic practice "as a sort of creative writing rather than a scientific exercise."[6] Such destabilizing incursions exacerbated further the intellectual rifts that had already transformed most U.S. anthropology departments into a series of autonomous and mutually suspicious enclaves—archeology, biological anthropology, cultural anthropology—badly in need of some disciplinary guidelines.

The instability induced by the linguistic turn in both history and anthropology was, of course, potentially fertile ground for scandal and controversy. In periods of flux, standards are particularly vulnerable to incursions, disciplinary violations, and a variety of other intellectual challenges. Nevertheless, my point of departure is that, contrary to popular impressions, recent years have not been particularly rife with academic scandal. Acrimonious debates over wrongdoing are certainly more visible than they once were, but cases of deviancy are not necessarily rampant.[7]

The fundamental differences between contemporary deliberations and some of their antecedents are their visibility, their modes of presentation, and—most important—their avenues of dissemination. Latter-day scandals are media events. They are performances, staged and choreographed for mass spectatorship. The whistle-blowers, and occasionally the accused parties, deliberately go outside academic precincts to the public arena. Wide diffusion—academic and popular, global and local, conventional and digital—has affected our awareness of intellectual malfeasance, redrawn some of the distinctions between the legitimate and the aberrant, and altered the terms of the debates. The once clear internal procedures for identifying misrepresentation sometimes appear to lack coherence in such a porous intellectual environment. However, there is little to suggest that infractions are any more prevalent or disruptive than they have been in the past.

HISTORY

In order to understand the resonance, dissemination, and public exposure of recent deliberations on intellectual wrongdoing, I have focused on the briefs of seven highly charged debates, all of which are linked by significant common denominators. All seven cases involve prominent academic personalities; the crimes and misdemeanors of the rank-and-file remain, for the most part, hidden from public view. In all seven episodes, deliberations took place in the public domain and attracted attention well beyond the American academic community. In fact, the most striking attribute of these controversies is their visibility. They all moved rapidly from scholarly precincts to the front pages of the nation's major newspapers, periodicals, and electronic media, reaching the broad public especially via the Internet.

Plagiarism, the most common kind of scandal, attracts our attention when it involves luminaries. It therefore comes as no surprise that some of the historical profession's superstars have found themselves embroiled in plagiarism scandals, among them the historian Stephen Ambrose and the biographer-historian Stephen Oates. Both belonged to a small cohort of hybrid scholars: academics who dabble in popular culture and whose academic credentials bolster the sales of their books. Both enjoyed the benefits and suffered the consequences of their celebrity. The history guild's internal and informal networks of crisis management failed to function in the borderlands where academic writing and other literary pursuits intermingle.

The most fascinating attribute of these two plagiarism scandals was the fact that accusations of literary theft appeared to be a pretext for something else. In both cases, discussion tended to wander from deliberations on plagiarism to a more general critique of celebrity historians. In fact, animosity appeared to focus on their hybridity—the fusion and attendant confusion of an intellectual calling with a popular writing style—rather than the ostensible offense of purloined prose. Accusers implied that the main problem was not individual wrongdoing, but rather the threat of a mass-mediated form of historical writing in which mass-produced parts are conveyed along an assembly-line culture of remembering. Hybrid scholars such as Oates and Ambrose were guilty of producing boilerplate history, replete with sentimental and derivative storytelling and a frivolous dismissal of disciplined remembering. Plagiarism was not the central issue, but rather an example of the type of transgression that occurs when scholars cross the line dividing intellectual activity from sentimental boosterism. The recycling of the prose of others was, according to critics, an inevitable occurrence in a commodified historical enterprise. Such standardization of the historical imagination, which precludes complexity and instead offers facile hero-worshipping, was the cardinal sin of both Oates and Ambrose.

Another of the historical profession's great scandals of recent years occurred in the wake of the publication of Michael Bellesiles's prizewinning book *Arming America*. Bellesiles offered a provocative rebuttal of conventional chronological, social, and political interpretations of the roots of an American gun culture. Americans' infatuation with firearms, Bellesiles argued, was not rooted in the early American past. The vast majority of early Americans were neither enamored with nor hostile toward guns, which had little significance for their daily lives; rather, they were indifferent to them. Prior to the 1850s, he claimed, guns and gun culture were conspicuously absent from the American scene.

Bellesiles's study attracted widespread attention because of the challenge it posed to a common historical interpretation of the right to bear arms. According to Bellesiles, the concept of a well-armed and self-regulated citizenry during the formative years of the American body politic was not a historical fact, but a modern-day political construct. He bolstered his contention of a gun-free America with an impressive array of evidence. Both literary and statistical records indicated that only about 14 percent of American households during this period possessed firearms, over half of which were either broken or defective.

Almost overnight Bellesiles was inundated by irate amateur scholars—most of whom were associated with gun-rights organizations. Even though these amateur scholars were denied access to traditional scholarly precincts, they managed to place Bellesiles on the defensive by inundating Web sites as well as by skillfully manipulating the scandal-hungry media. Bellesiles's amateur rivals attacked in particular his study of statistical records, claiming that significant portions of these records were figments of his imagination. Numerous scholars subsequently validated these claims, as well as other lacunae, charging Bellesiles with carelessness or even pure fabrication. But on one major point opinion was unanimous: a significant portion of Bellesiles's statistical sources did not exist.

Bellesiles remained unrepentant, claiming that errors in a study of this magnitude were inevitable. His main contention was that a scholarly analysis of his study had spun out of control due to the transfer of the debate to the Internet. The anonymity of Web exchanges, he argued, enabled politically motivated laypersons to pose as experts, thereby undermining the conventional modes of scholarship. Bellesiles ranted against this digital trivialization of academic discourse and the attendant decline of the customary platforms for adjudicating scholarly disputes.

Bellesiles's identification of the Internet as his nemesis was accurate. It was indeed through the Internet that doubtful observers pressured the reluctant governing bodies of the historical profession to refrain from an instinctive protection of a card-carrying colleague and instead to address the uncomfortable concerns outside the protective walls of academia. Yet, in the final analysis, Bellesiles's downfall was the result of his obsessive urge to be relevant. The bright lights of public recognition had led

Bellesiles down the slippery slope of "presentism," the deliberate, willful, and in his case erroneous construction of the past as an explanatory device for contemporary reality. In tailoring the notion of a usable past to fit popular demand, Bellesiles demonstrated a casual attitude toward archival records. Instead of a historical investigation—anchored in verifiable documents and cognizant of the "the finality of the past"—Bellesiles chose a manipulative representation of the past as a reflection of present-day concerns.

Contemporary scandals of the historical profession are not limited to debates on the ethics of writing and research. An addiction to scandals in general, and a fascination with fallen gods in particular, has led to an intense scrutiny of the historian's public persona. Revelations concerning the private lives, personal flaws, and intimate weaknesses of the profession's stars—the select group of professional historians who have captured the attention of mass audiences—have found their way into the public domain. Joseph Ellis, winner of the Pulitzer Prize, historian of America's founding fathers, and TV's most coveted "presidential historian," is a tragic example of the liabilities of academic fame and fortune.

In June 2001, Ellis acknowledged that he had embellished his lectures and public interviews with a fabricated version of his own personal history, including an imaginary participation in the Vietnam War, a nonexistent activism in the civil rights cause of the 1960s, and other fictitious heroic acts. His personal experiences, Ellis habitually explained to his classes on Vietnam and American culture at Mount Holyoke College, had led him to become an active member of both the antiwar and civil rights movements.

Because Ellis had no apparent professional reason for embellishing his past, these revelations inevitably prompted a variety of psychological explications, including his alleged desire to be part of a defining moment in American history and his almost pathological identification with Thomas Jefferson, the "protean president," who constructed for himself a self-delusional persona of "many possibilities."

In fact, Ellis's embellishments were a reflection of issues far broader than any personality complex or an obsession with a defining historical moment. Ellis appeared to be reacting to the demands of his immediate audience, America's college-age youth, who craved the "real thing." His fictional involvement in Vietnam and other past events was a rhetorical device for persuading audiences to endorse his interpretation of the past. "Being there" provided an illusion of authenticity and an element of persuasion to captivate his student audience.

Ellis was responding to the siren song of "experiential" history, the learning of the past through "a sensuous form" such as the historical theme park, or the historical film laced with real or pseudoreal footage, and, of course, the direct encounter with the protagonist, the bearer of an authentic version of the past. In an age jaded by fiction that borders on memoir, the comments of a detached scholar, removed from events by both time and personal circumstance, lacked the immediacy sought by the public, which craved an eyewitness to "reality," even if the eyewitness account is invented. Simultaneously and somewhat paradoxically, we are attracted to the fake because, as the sociologist Sherry Turkle reminds us, the fake is often more exciting and compelling than the real.[8]

ANTHROPOLOGY

As with the history scandals surveyed here, the notoriety of anthropology scandals corresponds to the fame of the perpetrators. Accusations leveled against Margaret Mead—an anthropological icon, social reformer, and symbol of the revolution in sexual mores, gender relations, and child-nurturing practices in mid-century America—are representative of this tendency.

In 1983, Derek Freeman, a relatively unknown New Zealand anthropologist, became an instant media star with his sensationalist debunking of Mead's *Coming of Age in Samoa* (1928). Mead's book had addressed the heated nature-nurture controversy that still rages in American society. She argued that, unlike the "terrible teens" of Western youth—attributed by experts to raging hormones—Samoan youth came of age gently and stresslessly. Contrary to the dominant biological theories of adolescence, she claimed that the only explanation for such markedly different behavioral patterns was social environment—in particular, a relaxed attitude toward sex and the noncompetitive nature of Samoan society.

Contrary to Mead's findings, Freeman claimed that Samoan society exhibited none of the promiscuous tendencies that Mead had observed, and he argued that Samoan youth were as rebellious as their American peers. The Samoan society of Freeman's research was violent, sexually repressive, and as highly competitive as any Western society. Freeman stated that Mead's Samoa was radically different and manifestly false because of her blind adherence to the ideologically driven theory that human behavior was determined exclusively by culture. Mead's study of adolescence in Samoa was the result of a distortion—willful or otherwise—of the meager data she had collected. Moreover, Freeman argued that tales of sexual license, passed on to Mead by her youthful female informants, were merely an adolescent prank, and perhaps a projection of Mead's own sexual promiscuity.

Freeman's critics dismissed his findings as politically motivated, a reflection of a changing political climate in the West rather than an instance of superior scientific capabilities. Discontent with the revolution in values associated with Mead's text provided the necessary political motive for a deconstruction of her work. Freeman's critics also chastised his tabloid style of inquiry. He had exaggerated the role of sex and sexuality in Mead's study, they argued, and had peppered his exposé with revelations concerning Mead's own sexual behavior in order to attract media attention.

In the final analysis, supporters of both Mead and Freeman chose to ignore the effect of both anthropologists' distortion-creating interventions in Samoan culture. By the very act of their visible reporting on, and intervention in, Samoa, both Mead and Freeman had altered rather than merely documented the makings of a distant culture. Both sought to portray Samoa as a remnant of a pristine culture, relatively unspoiled by the forces of Western civilization. Both chose to understate their role as authoritative, imperious voices of the primitive other. Both detrimentally affected the Samoans' self-image and the framing of their culture in the public eye. During the heat of the battles of these anthropological titans, both Mead and Freeman, as well as their supporters, abandoned their status as objective observers of a distant people. Samoan culture elicited little interest beyond its role as an exotic counterpoint to American culture.

Debates over the anthropological profession's negative influence on the lives of its subjects rocked the academic establishment again in 1999 with the publication of Patrick Tierney's book *Darkness in El Dorado*. Tierney accused the recently deceased geneticist James Neel of aiding and abetting the spread of a deadly measles epidemic among the Yanomami, an indigenous people inhabiting the Amazon River basin spanning Brazil and Venezuela. He claimed that Neel had seized the opportunity of the outbreak of measles in order to conduct epidemiological experimentation, rather than attempting to contain the disease.

Tierney was particularly incensed with James Neel's protégé, the renowned University of California, Santa Barbara, anthropologist Napoleon Chagnon, whom Tierney accused of cynically hastening the decline and destruction of the Yanomami. For both ideological and pecuniary reasons, Chagnon had single-handedly disseminated the image of the Yanomami as the last remnant of a Stone Age "fierce people." His representations of a violent Yanomami boosted the appeal of his best-selling books but, at the same time, legitimized the aggressive and destructive actions of private individuals and host governments in Yanomami territory. While acknowledging that the Yanomami did indeed exhibit bellicose behavior, Tierney claimed that their recourse to violence was the result of Chagnon's intervention in, and deliberate disruption of, indigenous ways of life. Touting the Yanomami as the last untouched primitive society, Chagnon was committed to proving that warfare and inequality were the most significant factors in humankind's evolutionary separation from other primates. In so doing, he had induced fear and exploitation of this primitive and relatively gentle people.

Chagnon responded by accusing Tierney of fabricating images of the noble savage and fantasizing about pristine egalitarian social arrangements where they did not exist. Chagnon belonged to a cohort of theorists who believed that violence and warfare were highly successful evolutionary strategies, promoting positive genetic selection, complex habits of cooperation, and collective arrangements. Claims such as these mobilized the campaign to discredit Chagnon. His legitimization of warfare as a positive evolutionary form immune to civilizing forces challenged the relevance of investment in peace and conflict resolution, and, conversely, encouraged massive defense spending, gunboat diplomacy, and a Darwinian approach to international relations.

Tierney's accusations led to an unprecedented inquiry by an American Anthropological Association (AAA) task force into the alleged malpractice that had been documented in *Darkness in El Dorado*. The task force exonerated James Neel of genetic experimentation, while Chagnon was reprimanded for his allegedly unethical misrepresentation of his subjects. The AAA task force was also highly critical of Tierney's *Darkness in El Dorado*, the book that had ignited the controversy. They chastized him for his unfounded and sensationalist vilification of Neel and for his immoderate use of the media to spread half-truths in support of his antiscientific worldview.

Through a conscious process of dramatization and exaggeration, Tierney indeed had propelled the controversy from low-profile professional deliberations to the front pages of newspapers and magazines. Moreover, Tierney had skillfully and manipulatively employed the Internet to make his study more visible. Prior to the publication of the book, he had disseminated accusations and snippets of information and disinformation into cyberspace. Within days, e-mails accusing Neel and Chagnon of Nazi-like behavior ricocheted through cyberspace, with most anthropologists receiving each multiple copies of these messages from different sources.

The battle over the Yanomami was a political struggle mediated through anthropology; politics rather than science lay at the heart of the controversy. Placed within the context of the Cold War, critics implied that a dominant current in evolutionary genetics, sociobiology, and anthropology—as represented by Chagnon's anthropological practices—had served the cause of an intrusive American expansionism.

Political rifts between left and right, and the active role of anthropology in uncovering, hiding, revealing, or inventing exposés on the sufferings of indigenous people, were by no means novel. Some ten years prior to the Yanomami controversy, the field of anthropology was entangled in another major scandal concerning the plight of Latin America's indigenous inhabitants. Charges of ulterior ideological motives and politicized methodology affected the fortunes of the Nobel Peace Prize laureate Rigoberta Menchú, whose moving autobiography, *I, Rigoberta Menchú* (1984), broke through Western disinterest about the decimation of Guatemala's Maya.

Menchú's testimony brought to light one of the most horrific chapters of political violence in Latin America, impugning in the process American involvement in and acquiescence to the genocidal policies of Guatemala's military. In 1954, the CIA aided and abetted a coup against Jacobo Arbenz's reformist regime, replacing it with a repressive, yet comfortably anticommunist, military dictatorship. The ensuing civil war between American-backed security forces and a Cuban-backed guerrilla movement eventually "exploded into scorched earth counterinsurgency warfare and terror," with particularly grim consequences for Guatemala's

Maya peasants, who were caught in the crossfire.[9] By the time the peace accord was signed in 1996, about 150,000 Mayas had been killed, most of them victims of army brutality.

The adoption of Menchú's book as required reading in a host of core undergraduate courses in the United States unleashed a bitter reaction. Critics accused a left-leaning, self-hating American academia of willfully adopting a text riddled with inaccuracies in order to further a politicized agenda. These critics drew support from the anthropologist David Stoll, who charged that central portions of Menchú's autobiography were political embellishments that had little to do with the truth. Menchú was not the illiterate peasant girl she claimed to be, nor had she been present at a whole series of atrocities she claimed to have witnessed. She apparently invented the death of a brother who allegedly died of starvation, as well as numerous other incidents in her autobiography. Stoll approached such embellishments as evidence that Menchú's text was first and foremost a political manifesto written to support the cause of a Marxist guerrilla movement and framed to fit the prejudices of a sentimental liberal readership. Stoll argued that Menchú's text was not an authentic account of events, but rather a narrative constructed out of a compilation of different witnesses' accounts for manifestly political reasons.

At no point, however, did Stoll challenge the fundamental truth or the essential elements of the collective tragedy depicted in the book. He accepted as irrefutable that Menchú, her family, and her people were the victims of political violence, and that the Guatemalan army was responsible for unconscionable human rights violations, including the death of many members of Menchú's family. His aim, he explained, was not to refute all of this. Instead, he sought to rectify ideologically motivated distortions and fabrications that obscured the real meaning of the Maya tragedy.

Menchú, according to Stoll, had romanticized the guerrilla movement in Guatemala and in the process had transformed the complex internal struggle in Guatemala into a recognizable but false narrative of a war between Indians, backed by a popular guerrilla movement, and rapacious landowners, supported by American-backed state security forces. Stoll had challenged Menchú's testimony in order to subvert the "last-resort paradigm," the allegedly false assumption that masses of peasants had joined hands with the guerrillas simply to avoid starving to death. In fact, Stoll claimed that prior to guerrilla incursions the Maya had even been making modest gains, and that Guatemala's radical left had made a calculated decision to move the struggle from urban areas to the countryside for reasons that had little to do with the peasant predicament. In other words, the guerrillas had enlisted or duped the politically innocent peasants to serve as pawns in a larger cosmic class struggle.

Menchú and her advocates dismissed Stoll's accusations as a combination of ignorance and reactionary politics, aimed primarily at halting significant curriculum reform in the United States—in particular, the replacement of the tomes of Dead White Males with more relevant multicultural perspectives. Stoll stood accused of trivializing the meaning of *testimonio*—the literary format of Menchú's tale—which, advocates cautioned, was not to be confused with the report of a legal witness; neither, for that matter, was it an eyewitness account. For both literary and functional reasons, this mode of expression involved a certain amount of poetic license. Rendering testimony in oral cultures was a more complex performance than the legalist pledge to bear witness. According to Menchu's advocates the *testimonio* of indigenous people should not be mistaken for "truth-as-facts that must be empirically verifiable and objective." It was, rather, "a truth that can be more metaphoric in which individual voices may serve to represent not the experiences of the person speaking but the community at large."

Stoll responded by rejecting the very notion of multiple truths. He contended that Menchú's many misrepresentations were above and beyond the type of inconsistencies one might expect in this literary genre. As far as he was concerned, Menchú's story was not a classic testimony, but rather an attempt to cram a transparent political manifesto into a maudlin format. Stoll claimed that Menchú's most ardent supporters within academia were aware of the gaping discrepancies permeating her story, but they chose, for ideological reasons that had little to do with academic integrity, to ignore the cold, hard facts. He argued that the winds of multiculturalism and postmodernism that privileged multiple versions of "truth making" over empirically based, objective portrayals threatened the very foundation of scientific inquiry within the university. Moreover, as a politically involved person, he felt the need to dispel a dangerous romantic myth of third world guerrilla movements that had captivated the imagination of the educated classes in the Western world.

The specter of postmodernism, with its provocative mix of fact-finding and textual analysis, imagination and reality, informs the final scandal documented in this study, and moves the debate beyond the precincts of history and anthropology toward a more general inquest of the academic calling in latter-day America. In 1996 the cultural journal *Social Text* unwittingly published a hoax. The New York University physicist Alan Sokal managed to slip a parody into the journal's forum on the "science wars," the contentious interrogation of the sciences' claim of objectivity and unbiased knowledge-seeking. Sokal's article lampooned the style and clichés of cultural critics, and was peppered with outrageous claims and a hefty dose of nonsense. The point of this prank was to prove that adversaries of the scientific enterprise were ignorant of the field that they pretended to critique, and that paradigms of the "linguistic left" represented by the journal were riddled with anti-intellectual narcissism. Sokal argued that he had chosen a hoax because a more conventional exposition might have never penetrated the bastions of his adversaries. Moreover, in a world where media exposure was the ultimate objective, a gimmick was a means to attract the attention of the mainstream press.

By proving that nonscientists were at best incompetent to understand what scientists do, Sokal may have intended to purge, punish, and banish intellectual trespassers from his territory. Ironically, the technology of choice for disseminating the hoax achieved the converse. Following Sokal's inauguration of an elaborate Web site dedicated to the hoax, the Internet became the primary platform for challenging Sokal's own interpretation of the scandal. Transforming the debate to the Internet disrupted the conventional divisions between performers—Sokal and the editors of *Social Text*—and their audience. Web debates inevitably complicated narrow narratives of the hoax. Once moved to cyberspace, participation became unregulated, often in direct contradiction to previously authoritative and stable versions of events. Closure and control appeared impossible in the chaotic exchanges encompassing multiple, ever-changing sites and venues.

In an ironic ending to this saga, Sokal's own field of expertise produced a proverbial turning of the tables, when French twin brothers managed to insert into a peer-reviewed physics journal a series of articles later deemed by experts to be nothing more than gibberish. When pressed to clarify how such "nonsense" had evaded peer-review procedures, leading physicists explained that the brothers' work appeared vaguely profound and no one was prepared to say otherwise. One of the embarrassed editors added that, even in physics publications, reviewers were reluctant to acknowledge that they had failed to understand the work of their peers, especially if it contained the necessary buzzwords. The paper was like *Finnegan's Wake*, a bemused observer noted: it was "essentially impossible to read" yet accepted as insightful without question.[10]

THE ACADEMIC SCANDAL AND THE AGONIST IMPULSE

The incidents surveyed in this book appear to be significantly more serious than their precursors. Actually, they are not. The difference lies in their visibility, due in part to aggressive modes of presentation. The deviancy debates contained in this book all serve a cause larger than merely interrogating an isolated position or an individual perpetrator of wrongdoing. Such delving into core philosophical debates helps explain the hostile nature of these cases. But at the same time, they reveal a rise in gratuitous acrimony, irrelevant verbal abuse, and the demonization of adversaries, sometimes even at the expense of instituting long-term corrective procedures. In at least some of these cases, one could imagine other formats of crisis resolution than the academic equivalent of public executions that took place. Intimidating opponents and dispensing summary justice is not just an unfortunate side effect of a momentary flaring of tempers. The metaphorical bloodletting accompanying these disputes reflects an academic subculture trapped and disfigured by compulsive contentious disorders.

In part, this warping of the academic discourse is the result of our "argument culture," in which an attack-dog criticism appears to garner greater rewards than civil discussion.[11] "Agonism," a form of "programmed contentiousness," is the medium of choice for evaluating our students, assessing scholarship, and assigning intellectual accolades.[12] Agonism, according to the linguist Walter Ong, does not refer to the type of acrimonious clash of adversaries arising from differences in temperament. It is instead a habitual and fatal attraction to the most litigious manner possible of presenting an argument. "The way we train our students, conduct our classes and our research, and exchange ideas in meetings and in print are all driven by our ideological assumption that intellectual inquiry is a metaphorical battle," Deborah Tannen has asserted. "Following from that is a second assumption, that the best way to demonstrate intellectual prowess" is by aggressive and unrelenting litigation and a scorched-earth mentality which disregards personal issues and the future well-being of the field in question, all in the quest for victory.[13]

Closely related to such rampant agonism are the prevalent "hermeneutics of suspicion," a term coined by the philosopher Paul Ricoeur to describe the impulsive and sometimes irrelevant assignment of base motives to maverick ideas or accomplishments. At times, the Yale philosopher Seyla Benhabib explains, the hermeneutics of suspicion are driven by legitimate although controversial motives to discover the social and political underpinnings of grand theory. But all too often, we confront a "biographic" and deeply personal variation of the hermeneutics of suspicion with its "breathtakingly irrelevant" focus on the intimate lives of protagonists. As "citizens in a republic of voyeurs, we are intent on microscopic moralism, incapable of appreciating more gracefully the contradictions, tensions, and ragged edges of all lives, and unwilling to take ideas seriously, as something more than bandages for personal wounds." The pervasive cultural fascination with fallen gods and private lives, as well as the almost pornographic satisfaction derived from exposing the guilty, has impoverished academic discourse in general and the understanding of deviancy debates in particular. We "are too quick to conflate the biographical with the theoretical, the personal with the intellectual, and to dismiss the latter in the name of the former."[14]

THE MEDIUM AND THE MESSAGE

To complicate matters further, the fatal attraction to agonism and the personalization of conflict appear to be tailor-made for specific forms of mass mediation and dissemination. Both whistle-blowers and defendants intentionally frame arguments in accordance with media requirements, often as a means for circumventing deliberations within the conventional forums of the profession. Scandals exposed in public avoid complexity and ambiguity, and therefore foster the melodramatic. The scandal as a media event is driven by a blockbuster mentality: a sensationalist repetition of well-worn dramatic principles, such as the morality tale of pride leading to a fall. It draws on sensational language, polarized rhetoric, personalized conflict, and familiar mass-media images. Deliberations on academic wrongdoing are retooled to fit the media's interpretive frameworks.

The mass mediation of American intellectual disputes today is accompanied by a simultaneous, independent, and sometimes conflicting dissemination of information in cyberspace. While the mass media has traditionally been a predominantly one-way form of communication, with clear divides separating reader from writer, participant from spectator, the Internet has no such stable divisions. Cyberspace encourages instant participation and active rejoinder, and erodes the familiar trajectory of a handful of producers relaying information to a mostly passive audience. The blurring of distinctions between audience and authors, recipients and producers of information, disrupts the normal process of adjudication, challenges authoritative viewpoints, and precludes closure. The abundance of platforms and participants diminishes the authority of conventional gatekeepers. With the erosion of distinctions between expert and amateur, audience and participant, the terms of debate appear negotiable and under constant revision. The Internet is inherently subversive, open-ended, and disruptive.

Moreover, virtual deliberations have encouraged what Sherry Turkle and others have described as "disinhibition," the discarding of normative etiquette upon entering cyberspace.[15] A cursory glance at cyber deliberations of scandals suggests that restraints that exist in conventional forums of academic discourse, oral or written, disappear at the stroke of a keyboard. Given equal and immediate access, as well as a certain degree of anonymity, individuals express their opinions openly, defiantly, and often with animosity. Improved and accessible channels of communication are not necessarily an avenue for understanding. Quite the contrary; this type of instant pluralism sometimes increases dissonance and intensifies conflict. Cyber debates thrive on volume and speed, rather than persuasion and deliberation. Internet discourse is democratic, immediate, and accessible. It is, as well, spontaneous and often inflammatory.

To be sure, the instantaneous processing of events via mass media and the Internet sometime moves at crosscurrents. The Internet, with its deep memory and its attendant ability to maintain issues in the public eye, stands in contradistinction to the media's casual discarding of coverage due to considerations of audience fatigue. The mass media captures large and often heterogeneous audiences, while Internet forums are characterized by specialization and subgroups. Different concepts of space and time separate these two formats, as well. The mass media seeks closure, while cyberspace is comprised of open-ended links extending and expanding the range and scope of discourse. The two formats do not compete but rather complement each other. Taken together, they blur previous distinctions between the public and professional arenas, the local and the global, while empowering in the process new groups of participants, arbitrators, and rule makers.

At a theoretical level, my study of controversy suggests that the medium indeed is the message. This does not mean that the text is unimportant, but rather that the use of a particular medium dictates the terms of debate; it has a significant impact on the controversies' lifespans, their narrative structure, and their tone. Mass media and virtual communication are not only techniques for transmission and reception. The recourse to such platforms itself reflects fundamental changes in the status of professional gatekeepers, the rise of a new pluralism, and significant shifts in the geopolitics of academia. The mere use of a novel technology or mode of dissemination is at times more significant than the content of its messages.

The adjudication of intellectual deviancy has achieved un-precedented resonance because of the expansion of interpretive communities and the exposure of controversy by disparate com-municative formulas and disruptive technologies. The disinte-gration of barriers in academia—between academic fields and be-tween the academy and the rest of society—has unsettled concepts of role, identity, and community, while technology and modes of dissemination have blurred distinctions between judge and jury, audience and agent.

Yet, lest I be accused of technological determinism, I should note that the applications of these technologies have achieved res-onance because they are powered by prevailing cultural, *nontech-nological* forces—in particular a widespread discontent with aca-demic gatekeepers and the limitations they have imposed on the production of knowledge; a growing fascination with the limita-tions of objectivity in scientific inquiry; and a powerful public yearning for moral transparency, intellectual integrity, and stable standards in unsettled times.

Finally, I should note that this book is neither a detective story nor a narrative of the "university in ruins." Even though I have not purged my own views from the following chapters, I have little interest in passing definitive judgment. I leave such conclu-sions up to the reader. Instead I have approached these delibera-tions on wrongdoing as intriguing pretexts for airing and debat-ing some of the social, cultural, and political concerns of the academy. Hence, the cases analyzed here bring into focus some of the major intellectual issues of our times: the role of the public in-tellectual, applied versus theoretical research, the rift separating the sciences from textual disciplines, the geopolitics of knowledge production, and the contestation of borders in the adjacent fields of fact and fiction, to mention but a few. The episodes included here are, in essence, morality tales about nagging questions permeating the academic enterprise: Whom do we trust? What causes do we, as academics, celebrate or condemn, and why? What is the meaning of truth seeking within the university? What are the obligations of academic practitioners as opinion leaders? Some of the affairs related here may offer closure. But for the most part, I suspect that whatever clarification may be gained from the following intellectual autopsies will be counterpoised by the creation of additional, no less troubling, queries.

Scandals in History

ONE

Plagiarism and the Demise of Gatekeepers

In the fall of 1990, the career of the renowned historian and media star Stephen Oates spun out of control. Oates, a popular scholar both within academia and among the general public, was accused of multiple acts of plagiarism, the cardinal sin of the historical profession. His ordeal commenced at a scholarly conference, where fellow scholars accused him of incorporating the prose of others in his well-received biography of Abraham Lincoln. Well before the Lincoln scandal died down, Oates found himself confronted with charges of purloining prose in his biographies of William Faulkner and Martin Luther King, Jr., as well.[1]

Plagiarism scandals featuring academic luminaries have since struck regularly. In 2002 alone, two of history's most revered river gods were embroiled in plagiarism controversies. Pulitzer Prize–winner Doris Kearns Goodwin admitted that she had incorporated numerous portions of Lynne McTaggart's *Kathleen Kennedy: Her Life and Times* (1983) into her own book *The Fitzger-*

alds and the Kennedys (1987). Forced to resign from the Pulitzer Prize committee, as well from the *McNeil-Lehrer News Hour*, on which she had made regular appearances, Goodwin also acknowledged that she had paid McTaggart an undisclosed sum as part of an out-of-court settlement. Unforgiving columnists reminded Goodwin that in 1993, after she had settled with McTaggart, Goodwin had complained that author Joe McGinniss had used unattributed portions of *The Fitzgeralds and the Kennedys* in his book *The Last Brother* (1993).[2]

Goodwin's historic lapses and symbolic penance were swiftly overshadowed by revelations involving Stephen Ambrose, perhaps the nation's most renowned historian, and chronicler of the "Greatest Generation." In January 2002, Ambrose acknowledged the presence of several unattributed passages in some of his bestselling books. Pleas of innocent oversight rather than literary kleptomania by this national star did little to abate public fascination with his flaws. Unlike the Goodwin affair, which disappeared swiftly from the public eye, the Ambrose scandal remained on the public agenda even after the historian's untimely death. Ambrose's recycled prose attracted sensational public exposure in both professional journals and the mass media.[3]

Both the Oates and Ambrose crises had an unusually long life span and touched a host of issues above and beyond the charge of plagiarism. While ostensibly preoccupied with assessing evidence on literary wrongdoing, the condemnations and defense briefs in both incidents suggest that plagiarism is sometimes the pretext for debating issues of far greater cultural complexity. The charges leveled against these two renowned chroniclers of the American past were not narrow investigations of malfeasance. Other political and intellectual subtexts permeated the public deliberations.

THE CASE OF JOE HILL

The significance of recent accusations leveled at historians is sharpened when placed against the backdrop of previous scandals. Public exposure beyond the academic domain used to be rare. For the most part, academic scandals were not considered newsworthy. A case in point is the embarrassing ordeal of the popular historian Philip Foner. In 1971, the Cornell labor historian James Morris accused Foner of plagiarizing Morris's long-forgotten master's honors thesis on "Wobbly" labor organizer and working-class martyr Joe Hill. In an article published in *Labor History*, Morris claimed that more than a quarter of Foner's book *The Case of Joe Hill* (1965) was a verbatim or near-verbatim reproduction of his thesis, which he had deposited in the archives of the University of Michigan in 1963. "The longest passage of uninterrupted identical material is one of 101 lines beginning on page forty-four, and ending on page forty-six; there are other passages of almost equal length, and a great many of a paragraph or two. A single page is sometimes a mosaic put together from as many as four different pages of the Morris manuscript."[4] Morris identified as well sections where Foner had even copied his typing and spelling errors.

In addition to the reproduction of whole passages, Morris claimed that the "structure, sequential development, and overall content and size of the Foner book and the Morris manuscript bear a striking resemblance." He discovered no significant difference between the two works, aside from their respective conclusions: Morris had concluded despite flimsy evidence that Joe Hill had committed murder; Foner, conversely, preferred "to continue the left-wing legend of Joe Hill, as the honest working-class victim of bourgeois justice, the Mormon Church, and the copper trust."[5]

Responding to these accusations, an unapologetic Foner argued that his study differed from the Morris paper in its conclusions as well as in its more extensive use of sources. Moreover, he claimed to have completed all of his research and "practically all of the writing" before learning of Morris's manuscript. For his response to the incriminating evidence—more than thirty-one pages of identical or near-identical text—Foner chose a resounding silence. He offered no defense, thereby admitting, at least tacitly, his indiscretions. Nevertheless, he offered neither apology nor any expression of regret.

Despite being indicted in the pages of a major journal, Foner suffered no apparent repercussions. Having waited out the brief storm, Foner even continued publishing articles in *Labor History*. *The Case of Joe Hill* is still in print; Foner's ordeal is all but forgotten.[6]

Contemporary academic culture and politics may have contributed to the muted reactions to Foner's misdemeanors. Foner, an unrepentant communist, had been blacklisted as early as 1941. Prior to his hiring by Lincoln University in 1967, he had lived the life of a political pariah. Having once been victimized for the courage of his convictions, he was considered by many to be beyond reproach. Presumably seeking to disassociate themselves from the political indiscretions of the past, the readers of *Labor History* appeared willing to forgive and forget.

Moreover, Foner was (unjustly) considered to be a marginal intellectual figure within the historical profession at that time. Among an expanding cohort of historians espousing social science methodology and grand theory, Foner appeared to be a synthesizer who compiled existing narratives into voluminous chronicles. In a discipline bent on establishing itself as an objective scientific enterprise, Foner was transparently political. For his detractors, the additional charge of plagiarism merely confirmed their judgment. As a political untouchable and a minor intellectual figure, Foner was beyond sanction. Humiliation within the pages of a major journal appeared to be the only severe enough penalty.

The limited exposure of the Foner-Morris plagiarism controversy was, however, mostly the result of benign neglect. The humanities of the 1970s in general and a discipline such as history in particular were relatively self-contained and of limited interest to laypersons; internal controversies and adjudications were the concern of cognoscenti only. Thus shielded from the mass media by disinterest, and living on the margins of the academic establishment, Foner easily put the crisis behind him. Celebrity status and public interest—two indispensable prerequisites for transforming internal accusations of wrongdoing into public scandal—did not exist.

Recent plagiarism scandals underscore today's radically different trajectory for adjudicating wrongdoing in the academy. The contemporary historical profession is a popular and public enterprise, replete with history book-of-the-month clubs, a history cable channel, and an insatiable appetite for made-for-Hollywood historical films. The most conspicuous product of this exposure has been the rise of a new generation of media-savvy practitioners. These are hybrid historians, fusing academic and popular genres of history writing, and as such they enjoy both academic notoriety and public standing. They, in particular, have been at the center of the more tempestuous plagiarism debates.

The hybrid scholar has induced significant shifts in the rules and customs governing deviance among historians. Public exposure makes it impossible to dismiss controversies through informal procedures or an enforcement of rules that apply primarily to the purely academic scholar. Following the erasure of boundaries separating academic writing from other more public literary pursuits, the adjudication of deviance is now part of the public domain. Hybridity has rendered obsolete, then, informal and intimate procedures for handling wrongdoing among the guardians of the nation's past.

STEPHEN OATES AND THE ABRAHAM LINCOLN COTTAGE INDUSTRY

A typical instance of the opportunities and liabilities of hybrid history occurred in 1990, when the usually sedate annual conference of the Illinois Historical Society produced an academic tempest. During the course of this relatively obscure event, literary scholar Robert Bray and historian Cullom Davis accused renowned historian Stephen Oates of plundering and pillaging large portions of his best-selling biography, *With Malice to None: The Life of Abraham Lincoln* (1977). The source from which Oates drew was Benjamin Thomas's *Abraham Lincoln: A Biography* (1952). According to Bray and Collom, Stephen Oates had copied entire segments from Thomas's biography and employed scores of unattributed vignettes. Moreover, they argued, the structure and style of Oates's book and its predecessor were almost inseparable. Thomas's study served as a powerful template "informing the emulative strategy of Oates." At the very best, his accusers claimed, Oates had not written an original study of the "life" of

Lincoln, but instead a boilerplate hagiography of "'lives' previously composed."[7]

An indignant Oates responded, "Plagiarism means, and has meant, the verbatim lifting of whole sentences, paragraphs, and pages from another author's work and presenting them as one's own creation," adding that no such thing existed in his book. The semblance of identical or near-identical phrases were, he protested, the result of "the devious technique of editing passages from my biography and Benjamin Thomas's" in order to create an impression of grand theft, while in actual fact he had never come close to what he considered to be plagiarism as it is usually defined.

As for the repetition of vignettes and their sequences, Oates explained that Lincoln literature consists of a common body of folk knowledge that had accumulated for more than a century and is in the public domain. "If there are similarities between my book and Thomas's," he said, "it is because both biographies draw from that common text or body of writing and information."[8] Oates's department chairman at the University of Massachusetts, Robert E. Jones, agreed: "There are only so many ways you can talk about Lincoln's early life without saying something that has been said before: How many ways can you say that Abe Lincoln was born in a log cabin in Kentucky?"[9] Certain canonical events appear invariably in Lincoln biographies, often with little or no change in their language style and formation. Moreover, Oates's defenders contended that his book differed from the Thomas biography in both content and theory. "While Oates presents the Civil War president as a great statesman attuned to pressing problems of race relations and emancipation," Thomas focused upon the image of "Lincoln as the savior of democracy." Oates, as opposed to Thomas, also incorporated "Don B. Fehrenbacher's thesis . . . that there was no real hiatus between Lincoln's career in Illinois, and his later accomplishments in the country at large."[10]

Oates's adversaries acknowledged that they had discovered a multitude of snippets and phrases, rather than the wholesale purloining of sentences or paragraphs. Nevertheless, they saw this as evidence of an artful perpetrator who "slices his copying up into finer pieces" to hide its origins. The most damning evidence, according to accusers, was the conspicuous textual and sequential parallelisms, the repetition of narrative structure, and an "overdependence on Thomas's language."[11] Irrespective of Oates's protestations of innocence, they dismissed his Lincoln study as a "palimpsest, a text written over with the ghosts of countless earlier subtexts, a dimly visible haunting."[12]

In the midst of defending his Lincoln book, Oates was beset with a new batch of accusations. Leading the charge was Michael Burlingame of Connecticut College, who was aided and abetted by Walter Stewart and Ned Feder, two government employees of the National Institutes of Health (NIH) who had developed a software program for detecting plagiarism.[13] Burlingame claimed that Oates's lapses in the Lincoln biography were part of a larger pattern. Armed with the findings and testimony of the NIH plagiarism experts, Burlingame claimed that Oates's studies of Martin Luther King, Jr., and William Faulkner were similarly tainted. These revelations, Burlingame stated, "cast doubt on Oates's main defense: that he and the Lincoln biographer from whom he had plagiarized, Benjamin P. Thomas, consulted the same meager sources of information . . . and were thus bound to use similar language."[14]

For five years the Oates saga continued unabated. Called to defend himself before the American Historical Association for inappropriate conduct, Oates denied its jurisdiction. He argued that he was not a member of the organization—in itself a somewhat startling revelation—and therefore the AHA could not rule on his case. The intervention of government experts, employees of the National Institute of Diabetes and Digestive and Kidney Diseases of the NIH, provoked accusations of government regulation of the marketplace of ideas, a form of institutional "moral totalitarianism."

The most conspicuous aspect of Oates's case was the amount of public attention it commanded. For a year, pundits offered exhaustive analyses of the decline of standards, while a gleeful media followed the bungled attempts of official bodies to adjudicate the accusations. Meanwhile, a hapless Oates appeared trapped in the limelight.

Oates's most conspicuous failure was his aborted efforts to limit judgment on the issue to a jury of "true peers" of fellow Lincoln scholars. His attempt to question the credentials of his critics (such as Bray, who was a literary scholar and neither a historian nor a Lincoln expert), dismiss the opinions of novices (at the time of the accusations Michael Burlingame had yet to publish his study of Lincoln), or delegitimize the meddlings of laypeople (such as the NIH inventors of the "plagiarism detector") met with limited success. NIH employees Stewart and Feder were rebuked by their superiors and reassigned to fields closer to the NIH's ostensible mission.[15] However, Oates's much-touted assortment of Lincoln-scholar supporters suffered a setback when C. Vann Woodward and Robert Bruce, two of his most prominent allies, withdrew their support.

Oates's failure at damage control was partly the result of his own inconsistencies. To begin with, his self-proclaimed status as a Lincoln expert was debatable, to say the least. Oates had not dedicated his career to Lincolniana. His biography of Lincoln was merely part of a corpus of biographies on nineteenth-century cultural and political icons. Moreover, his rejection of the judgment of investigators outside his discipline smacked of insincerity, given the fact that he had denied the jurisdiction of professional historians as well.

But above all, Oates's tribulations were the result of poor timing. His contested practices came to light at a moment of institutional crisis within the historical profession. Experts who in the past had lived comfortably set apart from popularizers now felt threatened by the crumbling of the barrier that had separated academic from popular historical writing. The erosion of distinctions between highbrow and middlebrow triggered an attempt to enforce standards and resurrect borders between the norms of academic research and the practices of mass culture.

Oates stood accused of cheapening the role of the intellectual and the historian. In the writing of Oates, the historian was transformed from intellectual pacesetter into a middlebrow raconteur. The literary historian Louis Rubin, who had no doubts that Oates was a compiler of the work of others, was far more concerned with Oates's trivialization of the academic creed than with charges of plagiarism. In his review of Oates's Faulkner biography, Rubin dismissed him as a voyeuristic creator of pulp masquerading as an intellectual scholar. Oates's book, he claimed, was mostly a laundry list of Faulkner's "rather thwarted sexual experience" and sensationalist descriptions of his alcoholic binges. A testy Rubin added, "Faulkner's fiction is not ignored in the transaction; it is merely trivialized." Rubin wondered, "what is the point of literary biography, anyway, if not to illuminate the sources—historical, familial, geographical, social—of the author's literary imagination, and to interpret, as best possible, the ties between an author's life and what he or she wrote? One can find far more sensational, more inherently interesting and more prurient biographical data to write about in connection with personages other than authors, if that is one's object. Why bother with Faulkner?"[16]

Robert Bray, the literary scholar who first launched the accusation of plagiarism against Oates, acknowledged that, while the purloining of texts was indeed a gross misdeed, he was somewhat more concerned with Oates's theory and practice of writing. Oates, he stated, was not a biographer, but a casual mythographer given to inventing details to embellish his story. Oates, he argued, clairvoyantly revealed his protagonists' private emotions and even claimed to have access to their innermost thoughts. In what was perhaps the most candid explanation of his motives for his crusade, Bray said that Oates's cardinal sin was not plagiarism, but rather his presumptuous claim that he was both an imaginative artist and realist writer of history. As an artist he employed fiction or what he called "the techniques of dramatic narration and character development, of graphic scenes and telling quotations." At the same time, Oates claimed the solid ground of factual realism, by supposedly representing "the Lincoln who actually lived."[17] Somehow, Bray complained, Oates audaciously assumed that he could practice these two different strategies simultaneously without falsifying the historical record.

Even Oates's supporters could not suppress their misgivings about his rather simplistic manner of reconstructing the past. Eric

Foner, who was among the signers of the petition supporting Oates, gently chided his friend for "believing narrative should take precedence over analysis." Moreover, Foner complained, Oates's study of Martin Luther King pandered to a public yearning for superheroes. Oates facilely linked the triumphs of a complex "mass movement with a single individual." His King Lite "failed to delineate the conditions, apart from the appearance of a charismatic leader, that enabled America's African descendants to confront and overcome the legacy of slavery."[18]

Another ally, Andrew Delbanco, was equally dismayed with Oates's study of Clara Barton, the Civil War nurse and founder of the American Red Cross, *A Woman of Valor* (1994).[19] He complained that Oates had cavalierly dismissed the important issues of Barton's life and times—such as the role of war in hastening equality for women and "the terrible disproportion between the technology of killing and the technology of life-saving during the Civil War years." Oates preferred instead to detail—and mostly probably invent—the amorous rustlings of Barton's bedsheets. At one point, Delbanco observed, Oates stated that "Barton 'regarded menopause with relief, since it freed her from menstruation and the risk of pregnancy,' though in fact there is little evidence that she had much discomfort from the former or much risk of the latter . . . and later, when Clara witnesses her 'lover' being wounded, Mr. Oates presents her running toward him on the strafed beach, 'her tiny feet churning in the sand.' The fact is (as the author himself acknowledges in the references) that there is no clear evidence that she performed any such bullet-dodging rescue."[20]

Oates's books raised antagonism because of their hybrid nature. As a champion of mixed media, Oates riveted lay audiences and antagonized colleagues with his artful blending of argument with entertainment, of analysis with emotion. This formulaic merging eclipsed conventional historical scholarship by privileging the reassembling of cheap, remanufactured parts over the laboriously crafted original product of the academic scholar. Oates's main fault was his mixing of genres; plagiarism merely ratified the attendant dangers.

Oates's popular writings had made him a veritable media star. By contrast, his academic colleagues languished in obscurity and irrelevance. Oates flaunted the fact that he represented a new type of historian, who found conventional historical writing—a disciplined academic account of the past—irrelevant, and disassociated himself from academic historians. His colleagues could not but challenge what they considered to be the intrusion of a dangerous genre of derivative mythography and its attendant violation of the code of disciplined remembering. The very fact that Oates had gained such overwhelming success raised fears of the irrelevance and the fragility of the rules upheld by tradition-bound professional organizations in an age of media exposure and popular demand for mass-produced, easily digestible reconstructions of the past. Thus, it would appear that the accusations of plagiarism were not an end unto themselves, but represented an effort to purge a fusion and confusion of crafts that threatened the integrity of the academic guild.

The Oates case was never conclusively closed. The 1992 AHA finding, which many hoped would achieve some sort of resolution, was a curiously compromising document. The AHA avoided a verdict of plagiarism, but it did conclude that Oates's Lincoln book was "derivative of a 1952 book by Benjamin Thomas, and that Mr. Oates had failed to give Mr. Thomas sufficient attribution." Both sides publicly claimed victory and privately expressed frustration. Oates, who had previously denied the right of the AHA to censure a nonmember, was "delighted" that the AHA had made no finding of plagiarism, but he was "disappointed" that it "then rendered a 'finding' on an altogether different matter: what constitutes 'appropriate attribution of sources' in a work aimed at a general audience." Cullom Davis, by contrast, was "a little puzzled that plagiarism is not the specific judgment that they reach, even though it seems to be the spirit of their conclusion."[21]

Subsequent AHA rulings on accusations of plagiarism in Oates's biographies of Nat Turner and William Faulkner merely compounded disappointment on both sides. The AHA said it had found "no evidence that Stephen Oates committed plagiarism as it is conventionally understood," although there was "evidence in Mr. Oates' work of too great and too continuous dependence, even with attribution, on the structure, distinctive language, and rhetorical strategies of other scholars and sources." In its clearest statement on the controversy, the AHA declared that "Oates does not sufficiently distinguish between the use of conventional language or widely shared factual material and the borrowing of distinctive language and rhetorical strategies from the work of others."[22]

Oates expressed outrage, threatening to sue the AHA for "libel and conspiracy to libel," as well as denial of due process. The AHA, he maintained, had waged a "three-year vendetta against me," in the process of which it "invented a vague rule specifically for me and then faulted me for violating it."

In the final analysis, the Oates controversy merely faded away. The case was never resolved in favor of any of the parties, and professional organizations and the mass media lost interest, even

though the warring sides continued a campaign of mutual snip-
ing. Highly visible debates on plagiarism among hybrid historians did not, however, disappear from the public arena. New versions of the saga return every now and again, with new characters
but remarkably similar sequences of events.

STEPHEN AMBROSE

Oates's ordeal bears a striking resemblance to the recent trials and
tribulations of Stephen Ambrose, perhaps the most renowned
historian of America's recent past. Ambrose, whose work on
World War II has endowed him with superstar status, skipped the
perfunctory stage of uncomfortable revelations at a scholarly
conference or in the pages of a professional journal. The initial
exposé of his scandal appeared in the conservative magazine the
Weekly Standard. Its executive editor, Fred Barnes, pointed out
near-identical passages and phrases in Ambrose's *The Wild Blue:
The Men and Boys Who Flew the B-24s over Germany* (2001) and a
work of University of Pennsylvania scholar Thomas Childers,
*Wings of the Morning: The Story of the Last American Bomber Shot
Down over Germany in World War II* (1995). Barnes observed that
none of the many incriminating passages, sentences, and phrases
he had found were adorned "with quotation marks and ascribed
with quotation marks. . . . The only attribution Childers gets in
the *Wild Blue* is a mention in the bibliography and four footnotes."[23] Subsequent scrutiny of *The Wild Blue* revealed a similar
pattern of copying or near-identical paraphrasing from other
books, including Wesley Frank Craven and James Cates's multi-
volume study *The Army Air Forces in World War II* (1948–58),
Michael Sherry's *The Rise of American Air Power: The Creation of*

Armageddon (1987), Donald Currier's *50 Mission Crush* (1992),
George McGovern's *Grassroots: The Autobiography of George Mc-
Govern* (1977), and other books. Such revelations prompted the
question, "Did Ambrose write *Wild Blue*, or just edit it?"[24]

Forbes magazine discovered similar indiscretions in several of
Ambrose's other books. Ambrose's *Crazy Horse and Custer* (1975)
contained numerous near-identical and unattributed passages
from Jay Monaghan's *Custer: The Life of General George Armstrong
Custer* (1959). As in *The Wild Blue*, Ambrose footnoted the passages but skipped the use of quotation marks, thereby producing
the impression that "the cited work is a source for the information presented, not the actual words."[25] *Forbes* revealed as well that
Ambrose's *Citizen Soldiers* (1997) and *Nixon: Ruin and Recovery,
1973–1990* (1991), the third volume of his Nixon biography,
contained passages apparently derived from Robert Sam Anson's
Exile: The Unquiet Oblivion of Richard M. Nixon (1984). The military historian Joseph Balkoski was also "somewhat depressed"
upon reading Ambrose's *Citizen Soldiers*. "The writing seemed
very familiar, and much to my astonishment, it was my own," the
source being Balkoski's *Beyond the Beachhead* (1989). Ambrose,
Balkoski noted, "will footnote me, but the writing is either identical or subtly changed without using quotation marks."[26] A comparison between *Citizen Soldiers* and Harold Leinbaugh and John
Campbell's *Men of Company K* (1985) revealed a similar pattern.
In Ambrose's *Nothing Like It in the World* (2000), his study of the
construction of the first transcontinental railroad, he omitted acknowledging direct citations from David Lavender's *The Great
Persuader* (1970).[27]

Forbes's most sensational revelation was a scathing 1970 letter from Cornelius Ryan to Ambrose, "Ambrose's predecessor as America's favorite World War II chronicler" and the author of the best-selling *A Bridge Too Far* (1974) and *The Longest Day* (1959).[28] Ryan had discovered two uncited quotations from his own *The Last Battle* (1966) in Ambrose's study of Dwight Eisenhower, *The Supreme Commander* (1970). "The crowning indignity," Ryan wrote, "is that in his notes on sources . . . he [Ambrose] gives credit to—guess who? None other than his previous book." Adding insult to injury, Ryan complained that Ambrose had also garbled the citations in the process. An apologetic Ambrose promised to rectify the error in subsequent editions, but according to *Forbes* he never carried out his pledge.[29]

Critics argued that the Ryan exchange proved that Ambrose's inappropriate use of the words of others was neither limited to what he dismissed as "six or seven sentences in three or four of my books" nor made in haste while producing a popular historical account for the general public.[30] Instead, such practices were numerous and dated back to the very beginning of his scholarly career, when Ambrose was still a professor, well before he streamlined his operations into Stephen Ambrose Enterprises.[31]

Ambrose reacted swiftly to these criticisms. While acknowledging mistakes, he argued that his errors did not constitute plagiarism. Speaking through his publisher, Simon and Schuster, Ambrose belittled his omission of quotations marks as "a matter of methodology and not wrongdoing." Simon and Schuster publisher David Rosenthal added that Ambrose's deeds did not constitute plagiarism "because there is no effort to deceive," adding that "the material had been adequately footnoted."[32] All that was missing, he claimed, were quotation marks, which Ambrose considered superfluous. "I tell stories. . . . I don't discuss my documents. I discuss the story. . . . I am not writing a Ph.D. dissertation."[33]

In an apology of sorts, posted on his Web site, Ambrose made light of his transgressions with the help of a friend. Following a softly made acknowledgment of error, Ambrose appended a letter from George McGovern, the central figure and hero of *The Wild Blue*, who offered humor to belittle the slipups of this "superb historian," "gifted writer," and personal friend. "Like the rest of us, he [Ambrose] is not beyond an occasional mistake," wrote McGovern. "For example, his biography of Richard M. Nixon concluded that he deserved reelection in 1972. In my biased judgment, that was a more serious mistake than using a few sentences without attribution on what the ball turret of a B-24 looks like."[34]

Most of Ambrose's victims were not amused. Even though he had initially accepted Ambrose's apology, Thomas Childers publicly and prominently announced the removal of Ambrose's books from his courses, citing "disturbing" revelations of multiple charges of plagiarism, as well as Ambrose's disingenuous apology. David Lavender, another offended author, noted, "It is reaching a point where I'm beginning to get a little scornful of the man and a little jealous of his reputation which he does not deserve."[35]

Ambrose's ordeal aroused occasional murmurs of sympathy from academic colleagues. Eric Foner, the nephew of Philip Foner and a historian at Columbia University, reiterated the importance of footnotes and honest attributions. However, Foner did not "see anything malicious" in Ambrose's conduct. He attributed Ambrose's mistakes to uncharacteristic "sloppiness from speed. You . . . lose sight of the difference between your language and someone else's language."[36] While recognizing scholarly traditions of citation and respect of intellectual property, Ambrose's defenders attempted to place his indiscretions in proportion. "It takes only one 'off' day—out of years of poring over notes—to forget a pair of quotes and damage a reputation," observed historian Kolleen Guy.[37] For Professor Thomas Preston of Washington State University at Pullman, Ambrose's minor faults in his latest books were not a compelling reason for removing the other books of a "first-rate scholar." Citing the need to use the very "best books for the class," Preston declared that he intended to continue using Ambrose's early work on Eisenhower and Nixon, because they are "some of the finest history books you can read on these topics."[38]

Other prominent pacesetters of the craft of history rejected such arguments. Jackson Lears of Rutgers noted caustically that if Ambrose were still a "tenured professor, his university career would have been ended by this."[39] James McPherson of Princeton condemned Ambrose's lapses as "a step or two beyond careless." He claimed that "if a professor found the degree of similarity in phrasing and wording [in a student's work] that had been found in Steve Ambrose's case, some kind of sanction or disciplining would be in order."[40]

Much like the Oates debacle, the debate over Ambrose's appropriations ignited controversies ranging far beyond the technical, legal, and moral questions of unattributed citations. Accusations of literary theft served as background for lambasting Ambrose's alleged trivialization and unrelenting commercialization of the field of history, as well as an examination of the politics and ideological underpinnings of his books. Stephen Oates had suffered accusations of writing boilerplate history; Ambrose, by contrast, appeared to be the CEO of a vast history factory in which a host of assembly-line workers put together a historical product comprising mass-produced platitudes, refurbished parts from the works of others, and recycled material from Ambrose's own previous studies. Unlike his institutionally bound colleagues, Ambrose employed a bevy of assistants—including his children—to churn out a breathtaking number of books. Such mechanical reproduction of historical studies had, according to critics, dispensed with the traditional, complex intellectual labor of reconstructing the past. Ambrose had transformed a laboriously crafted intellectual artifact into a lightweight leisure product, the equivalent of a drugstore novel.

Ambrose's critics condemned him largely on the basis of the sheer quantity of his output. No one person, they claimed, could produce nine full-length books in nine years, as well as six essay collections, five edited volumes, countless op-ed pieces, reviews, forewords, and even the occasional scholarly article, while adhering to a demanding lecture schedule. When scholars adopt the ethos of the assembly line, a journalist observed, "there's a danger that the books, like the cars, will all start looking alike," with the occasional "borrowing [of] parts from similar models."[41]

Indeed, Ambrose Enterprises had many of the trappings of the high-powered corporate world, including hostile takeovers and corporate payoffs. Joseph Balkoski, one of the victims of Ambrose's citation practices, declined a lengthy court battle with Ambrose Enterprises, agreeing instead to an out-of-court settlement. Rather than take on a powerful conglomerate, Balkoski accepted Ambrose's offer to write the foreword to the 1999 softcover edition of *Beyond the Beachhead* as compensation for Ambrose's questionable appropriation of Balkoski's texts. As for *The Wild Blue*, which focuses on the military career of George

McGovern, it was once the intellectual property of someone else. Author Michael Takiff had an "oral contract" with George Mc-Govern to write his wartime memoirs. Following a takeover offer by Ambrose, McGovern voiced second thoughts. Realizing that he "was out" of the picture, a reluctant Takiff accepted a buyout of thirty thousand dollars.[42]

Ambrose's tendency to pontificate on a host of subjects beyond his field of expertise alienated him as well. Writing in the *Wall Street Journal*, shortly after September 11, Ambrose effortlessly time-travelled between September 11 and Pearl Harbor. "The attack on the Pentagon and the World Trade Center had the same marvelous effect" as Pearl Harbor's closing of ranks among a divisive American people. Indeed, Ambrose commented, World War II combat offered many important lessons for contemporary American society, which he readily expounded to his audience despite his lack of expertise in military combat, urban planning, counterterrorism, or the eschatology of radical Islam.

> One of the first things you learn in the army is that, when you and your fellow soldiers are within range of enemy artillery, rifle fire, or bombs, don't bunch up. . . . So we must go over, in largest part, to the defensive. That means, first of all, don't bunch up. . . . In this age of electronic revolution . . . it is no longer necessary to pack so many people and offices into such small space as lower Manhattan. They can be scattered in neighboring regions and states, where they can work just as efficiently and in far more security.[43]

An assault on Ambrose's politics was another spinoff from the plagiarism scandal. Ostensibly a political liberal, Ambrose stood accused of championing a very conservative agenda. His books, a caustic critic noted, were all about "what white men did right . . .

an attempt to protect the embattled white male in a critical multicultural society." Ambrose "tends to imbue the soldiers and explorers in his books with a certain Ambrosial quality, painting them as heroes without subjecting them to rigorous historical analysis."[44]

To be sure, the World War II generation, the subject of Ambrose's veneration, were brave and often indeed heroic. But in Ambrose's uncomplicated manner of presentation they were, according to critic Nicholas Confessore, "empty vessels . . . pressed into service as symbols." Ignoring the vast sociological literature on how and why soldiers fight and sacrifice, Ambrose preferred the inaccurate yet lucrative picture of a monolithic Greatest Generation, a comfortable antithesis to the indulgent, if not downright decadent, nature of contemporary society and politics.[45] "It is difficult to meditate on the nature of sacrifice, or examine the corrupting power of war," a caustic Michael Manville observed, "if the beneficiary of the sacrifice is portrayed as indisputably just and utterly incorruptible."[46]

Critics also questioned Ambrose's affinity with and understanding of the common soldier. Ambrose's chief claim to fame was his ability to reveal the human face of World War II. In the pre-entrepreneurial stages of his career, when Ambrose was still a salaried academic, he wrote well-received yet somewhat conventional studies of great men and great deeds. His leap to fame began with his discovery of ordinary soldiers and their unsung heroism. However, this ostensible champion of the enlisted man demonstrated little patience for his rank-and-file readers, who accused the eminent historian of snubs, incivility, and selective pillaging of their memoirs.

The very notion of "citizen soldiers"—supposedly the unique

feature of the American fighting force—was another of Ambrose's extreme and facile exaggerations. "In the mass wars of the twentieth century," Thomas Nutter has noted, "all armies were composed of citizen soldiers," who were mostly concerned with primary group loyalties rather than abstract ideological causes. The notion that "warfare in the twentieth century was a morality play, extending down to the level of the individual soldier," was an example of Ambrose's pandering to the collective but selective memory of his reading public, rather than an accurate description of group dynamics during the course of World War II.[47]

But perhaps Ambrose's most criticized fault was his gross exaggeration of the American contribution to victory over Nazi Germany. Critics argued that the uninformed reader of Ambrose's tomes would inevitably reach the conclusion that the United States had single-handedly achieved victory over Nazi Germany. America's allies were invisible in Ambrose's reconstructions of the past. With little or no apparent help, the United States of Ambrose had defeated a menacing enemy on its own and had made the world safe for democracy. The contributions of both Great Britain and the Soviet Union to the defeat of Nazi Germany have no place in Ambrose's glorification of America's wars. Much to the chagrin of professional historians, Ambrose had practically transformed Normandy into the pivotal battle of the war.

PLAGIARISM AS TEXT

In the final analysis, both Oates and Ambrose stand accused of transgressions far more compelling than plagiarism. Guided by the logic of mass markets, Oates and Ambrose had commodified an inherently noncommercial, intellectual artifact. Both were accused of transforming the writing of history from an intellectual enterprise into a form of infotainment. Both historians were criticized for having cynically exploited a public longing for an idealized era of heroes, free from moral dilemmas. Ambrose indeed agreed that the task of the historian "is not to pass judgment but to explain, illustrate, inform and entertain."[48]

Hence, the recycling of the prose of others was not the main issue, but merely a sideshow of a commodification of the historical enterprise. Upon leaving the academic domain, historians such as Ambrose and Oates did not author books, the columnist Wendy Kaminer observes, but assembled them out of parts produced by "an army of researchers and other, less prominent historians."[49] In transforming history from a complex intellectual puzzle to a standardized product for mass consumption, repetition, simplification, and mechanical reproduction were inevitable. Thus, critics appear much more concerned with the fact that consumers of such mass-produced commodities bypass the intellectual complexities of reconstructing the past, celebrating instead the emotional aura and romantic impulse of pulp pseudohistory. A mechanically reproduced history had lost its "ethereal and sublime" qualities and had become a "fetish."

The works of Ambrose, Oates, and other popularizers of history achieved breathtaking success, partly because they were recognizable and easily digestible. Stardom is achieved when there is nothing unfamiliar about the product, argued Kaminer. "Originality is not much valued in our consumer culture, which is fueled by the urge to conform," rather than to provoke or disturb well-worn conventions.[50] The standardization of the historical imagination, replacing complexity and dilemma with facile hero-worshiping, was the cardinal sin of which both Oates and Ambrose were judged guilty.

As far as the original accusation of plagiarism is concerned, the indiscretions of such academic and literary writers have been interpreted in different ways. In his summary of the Ambrose affair David Plotz observed that "plagiarists steal for reasons both profound and mundane."[51] Yet the routine explanations of the plagiarist as the victim of self-inflicted wounds brought on by haste, sheer carelessness, or an exhausted imagination have lost much of their luster. Others have sought more complex explanations in the role of the unconscious. "You would have to be some kind of fool to plagiarize somebody and then put a footnote on it and tell them where it came from," Ambrose stated before an amused crowd of sympathizers.[52] Advocates of the psychological explanation disagree. The self-incriminating footnote appended to the unattributed text—supposedly evidence that the lack of attribution or quotation marks were harmless or inadvertent—suggests the converse. Such glaring clues, conspicuously thrown before sleuths, both amateur and professional, suggest a guilt-ridden person who perhaps unconsciously hopes to be caught; it is a literary death wish of sorts.

The purloining of literary goods, Thomas Mallon and others have argued, is a form of kleptomania. Just as the classic kleptomaniac shoplifts compulsively and not for personal gain, so the plagiarist compulsively removes sentences for pathological reasons rather than naked personal gain. "Both in his evident wish to be detected and in the circumstances that what is stolen may not be needed," the plagiarist appears to be a case for the analyst rather than the moralist.[53]

For whatever motive, however, plagiarism promises to become

even more conspicuous and contentious. The breathtaking scope of and access to material over the Internet have damaged irreparably notions of intellectual propriety and property. In a world of electronic copy-and-paste, copyright laws have not been able to protect traditional notions of textual ownership.

Yet it was precisely at the moment of tectonic shifts in notions of intellectual property that the guild of historians chose to reconfirm conventional definitions of plagiarism. Looking back at the Oates scandal, journalists Peter Morgan and Glenn Reynolds offered a skeptical glance at the type of evidence advanced to impugn Oates. "The two presidents said little to one another as the carriage bumped over the cobblestones of Pennsylvania Avenue, part of a gala parade." This sentence written by Oates bore "a fantastically strong" resemblance to the earlier text of Benjamin Thomas: "As the open carriage jounced over the cobblestones of Pennsylvania Avenue, Lincoln looked into the faces of the crowd that jammed the sidewalks." To be sure, Morgan and Reynolds observed "the overlap in language is there," and there was a distinct overlap in ideas as well. "But the idea," they observed, "is trivial: a carriage ride." Technically, these similarities in ideas and language constituted plagiarism. But by failing to distinguish between the substantive and the trivial, the plagiarism debates offer little hope for clarification and the acceptance of clear-cut mores in a digital milieu.[54]

TWO

The Noble Lie

"Arming America" and the Right to Bear Arms

A voice in your ear whispers, "You know that Kenyan in the slouch hat really did say that awfully funny thing you think he almost said. Just write it down. No one will ever know. And look, just across the frontier there is that gorgeous flower—the one missing novelistic detail that will bring the whole story alive. Pop across and pick it. No one will notice."

Timothy Garton Ash, "Truth Is Another Country"

A proofreader rebels. While combing through the galleys of a history book entitled *History of the Siege of Lisbon*, a proofreader subverts the narrative by inserting a single word: *not*. Instead of the official version of the founding of the Portuguese homeland, which states that the crusaders *will* aid the Portuguese in expelling the Moors from Lisbon in 1147, the proofreader inverts the foundational myth of his nation. The altered text now reads that the crusaders will *not* come to the aid of the Portuguese. José Saramago, the author of this magisterial tale, argues that the proofreader's ostensibly revisionist version of the past is by no means false. The proofreader's rebellion leads to the subversion of the official version of a historical event, reveals its lacunae, and in the process unearths a whole series of sources on Portugal's multicultural past that have been effaced by the official, Euro-centric foundational myth.

Thus, Saramago argues, changing the past is a legitimate act of imagination. History is a malleable enterprise mostly because the borders separating the domains of fact and fiction are fuzzy, arbitrary, and political. Beneath the official record lie other, different versions of the past that are revealed only by acts of intellectual subversion. The past is not an entity unto itself; it exists as a reflection and refraction of the present. Therefore, to offer different, modified, or imaginative versions of the past is imperative because it enables the construction of a critical and constructive present.[1]

"ARMING AMERICA"

Michael Bellesiles is surely a real-life variation of Saramago's proofreader. By sleight of hand, Bellesiles removed firearms from early American history, creating a new version of the past and a contemporary political furor. In his book *Arming America*, Bellesiles challenged the paradigm of "historical roots" as an explanation for contemporary America's fatal attraction to firearms. In fact, he argued, "an examination of the social practices and cultural customs prevalent in early America suggests that we have it all backward. . . . The nation's past has been meticulously reconstructed to promote the necessity of a heavily armed American public."[2] The unbridled proliferation of firearms and the attendant violent nature of contemporary American society had been grafted onto the nation's past.

Bellesiles claimed that America's obsession with firearms had little to do with its foundational myths—such as its lawless frontier environment, the self-reliance of its pioneers, or even the proverbial and pervasive fear of a tyrannical centralized government. Contrary to received wisdom, he asserted, an abundance of firearms was not an American heritage. The vast majority of Americans of the revolutionary period and the early republic were neither enamored nor familiar with guns. For the most part they expressed plain indifference toward a form of technology that had little significance for their daily lives. The rise of a gun culture, Bellesiles argued, was the result of a heavy-handed campaign of the federal government that sought a cheap alternative to a standing army, and the subsequent rise of a mass-produced weapons industry. The widespread dissemination of firearms was a relatively recent development, starting around the Civil War and promoted by a burgeoning capitalist culture. Bellesiles claimed that prior to the 1850s guns were conspicuously absent from the American scene. In Bellesiles's early America, citizens cared little for firearms. Their attitude toward such lethal weapons ranged from disinterest to outright hostility.

While ostensibly intended as a scholarly clarification of the historical record, Bellesiles's study had immediate political ramifications, as it effectively challenged the historical validation of the right to bear arms. By contending that the proverbial, well-armed, and self-regulated citizenry of the nation's formative years was a figment of a partisan representation of the American past, Bellesiles challenged the powerful myth that the original intent of the Second Amendment was to grant an individual the right to bear arms. Given the material lack of firearms and the absence of a gun culture, he argued, it was highly unlikely that the framers of the Constitution had enshrined a nonissue with no apparent relevance to the lives of ordinary Americans. "The notion that a well-armed public buttressed the American dream would have appeared harebrained to most Americans before the Civil War."[3] The supposedly pervasive obsession with and reliance upon firearms during the formative years of the American entity was, then, an invented tradition.

In support of his novel interpretation, Bellesiles mustered a breathtaking variety of sources and arguments. To begin, he suggested that prior to the mid-nineteenth century weapons were prohibitively expensive, unwieldy, and inefficient. Lacking both gunsmiths and weapons manufacturers of their own, Americans seeking to procure firearms were forced to rely on limited and costly imports. The high price of weapons was not, however, the only reason for a manifest disinterest in firearms. Unwieldy rifles, whatever their price, made little sense in a pragmatic, utilitarian culture such as the United States. Given rifles' notorious lack of accuracy, as well as their laborious mechanisms and loading procedures, the average American found them to be of little value for either sustenance or self-protection.

In fact, Bellesiles claimed, average Americans expressed indifference to the very idea of personal ownership of firearms, even for hunting. "Hunting with a gun is and always has been a time-consuming and inefficient way of putting food on the table," he argued. "To head into the woods for two days in order to drag the carcass of a deer back to his family—assuming he was lucky enough to find one, not to mention kill it—would have struck any American of the Colonial period as supreme lunacy." He claimed that antebellum Americans were mostly "disdainful of the man who felt the need to use a gun."[4]

In support of these claims, Bellesiles quoted travel accounts in which, he pointed out, firearms appeared to be conspicuously absent. A provocative evaluation of early American military history provided additional evidence of a society with little working knowledge of firearms. The myth of a well-armed citizen army of sharpshooters was not, he argued, based on fact. The great battles against the British were not fought by gun-toting citizen militias but by a professional army comprised mostly of foreign mercenaries. To Americans, bayonets, machetes, and mechanical projectiles were the weapons of choice. To the degree that great battles were indeed won by firepower—such as the 1815 Battle of New Orleans—cannons, rather than inaccurate, inefficient, and scarce muskets, had won the day.[5]

Bellesiles was particularly critical of the myth of a well-armed and well-trained citizen militia. During the early republic, he claimed, a ragtag militia persistently showed up for muster armed with canes and walking sticks rather than rifles. These often grotesque enterprises were the epitome of ineptitude and held in low esteem by the population. According to Bellesiles, the 1792 Militia Act implied that Congress was responsible for supplying guns to members of the various state militias; they did not possess their own. In fact, "no gun ever belonged unqualifiedly to an individual," Bellesiles argued. "Guns could not be seized in a debt case, could not be sold if that sale left a militia member without a firearm, had to be listed in every probate inventory . . . and could be seized whenever needed by the state for alternative purposes. Guns might be privately owned, but they were state-controlled."[6]

As for the Second Amendment, Bellesiles argued that it was a reflection of a rhetorical concession to states' rights rather than a meaningful statement on individual liberties. Fearful of a strong national government bolstered by a standing professional army, antifederalists lobbied for, and eventually achieved, an amendment ratifying the right of individual states to maintain a "well-regulated militia" based on the right of "the people"—presumably members of the citizen militias—to bear arms. Given the ragtag nature of militias as well as the lack of privately owned weapons, the Second Amendment was at most an early exercise in political spin rather than a reflection of a gun-besotted reality. In a gun-free America such statements had few obvious ramifications as far as individuals were concerned.

Bellesiles also claimed to draw startling evidence from probate records. Having pored over 11,170 probate records from the period 1765–90 and spanning over twelve hundred different counties, Bellesiles's computations indicated that only about 14 percent of American households during this period possessed firearms, over half of which were either broken or defective. Bellesiles estimated that gun ownership rose at a snail's pace prior to the Civil War: in 1819–21, it was a mere 17 percent; by the eve of the Civil War, in 1858–59, it reached a record high of 32.5 percent.

Bellesiles bolstered his probate finds with statistical data. Before 1850, he argued on the basis of a statistical investigation, guns contributed only marginally to the homicide rate. The symbiotic relationship between guns and homicide was nonexistent even in the supposedly wild and unregulated regions of the Southwest and the frontier. Homicide rates in general and gun-related violence in particular rose with mid-nineteenth-century industrialization, modern warfare, and an ensuing glorification of personal firearms.

These provocative conclusions, based on quantitative evidence, appeared to seal his case. Even though he dedicated no more than a few pages of his exhaustive study to probate records and other statistical data, most reviewers regarded these records as conclusive. Practically all of the glowing reviews of *Arming America* highlighted his painstaking analysis of probate records as irrefutable evidence in support of his controversial theory.[7] By Bellesiles's own account such quantitative evidence was of far greater importance than other impressionistic sources. "Without . . . quantification, we are left to repeat the unverifiable assertions of other historians, or to descend into a pointless game of dueling quotations—matching one literary allusion against another."[8]

As the recipient of Columbia University's 2001 Bancroft Prize for the most distinguished book of American history, Bellesiles swiftly became an academic star. Hailed as one of the most important studies of American history and culture, *Arming America* unleashed crosscurrents of admiration and criticism, both within academia and beyond. Despite its exhaustive length, copious footnotes, and often pedantic style, *Arming America* achieved instantaneous public acclaim, further fueling the debate over the right to bear arms.

Liberal scholars, mostly supporters of gun control, embraced the study with alacrity. Edmund Morgan argued that the book dispelled for once and for all the "bogus historicity on the realities of gun ownership" and had demolished "the credibility of the fanatics who endow the Founding Fathers with posthumous membership in what has become a cult of the gun."[9] Writing in the *New York Times*, Garry Wills hailed *Arming America* for dispersing "the darkness that covered the gun's early history in America." According to Wills, Bellesiles provided "overwhelming evidence that our view of the gun is as deep a superstition as any that affected Native Americans in the 17th century."[10]

Even though Bellesiles claimed somewhat disingenuously that his book had no contemporary policy implications, his relentless dismissal of the overbearing presence of, and fascination with, guns in America offered a vivid moral for contemporary readers: Guns and violence were neither inevitable nor immutable features of American culture. The myth of a gun culture dating back to colonial times was both inaccurate and an impediment to controlling the lethal spread of firearms in contemporary American society. Moreover, his revisionist account appeared to demolish the case of those who claimed that the original intent of the Constitution was to enshrine the right of individuals to bear arms. "Gun possession was not a right but a duty imposed on certain citizens—generally white, Protestant, male property owners." If, as Jack Rakove of Stanford explained, "gun ownership was far less widespread than previously assumed, that firearms had little value for either self-protection or the slaughter of succulent mammals, and that the militia was typically a moribund joke in time of peace and of little military value in time of war," the entire debate concerning original intent and meaning of the Second Amendment demanded revision.[11]

Prior to *Arming America*, Rakove observed, the "Second Amendment controversy has been primarily a debate about the meaning of words." Bellesiles, by contrast, focused on "behavior—the ownership of firearms, their use in daily life, and perhaps most important in this context, the function and operations of the militia."[12] If indeed firearms were rare and of little material, military, or symbolic value, much of the charged debate concerning the resonance of the amendment would become somewhat of a moot point. In a gun-free America, the Second Amendment was recast as empty rhetoric. *Arming America* defied the contention that the right to bear arms had a compelling historical and legal basis. "The image of the armed settler appears a grand mythology intended to formulate a portrait of Americans as many would like to see them: people not to be trifled with, not willing to put up with ill treatment, and very violent."[13]

The reaction of the gun lobby was swift and aggressive. Bellesiles claimed that his critics attacked him personally, with little or no meaningful critique of his work. The chosen strategy of his adversaries, Bellesiles observed, was unrelenting harassment and widespread defamation. He reported a wide range of abuse, from death threats to run-of-the-mill hate mail, most of which was disseminated through cyberspace.

> Over the ensuing months in e-mails, faxes, and on the web, I was castigated as "a paid agent of ZOG" (the Zionist Occupational [sic] Government, not King Zog of Albania), a "tool of the liberals (or state socialists, as they really are) seeking to steal my guns," and a "faggot feminazi." For fourteen months I have received hateful, threatening, and expletive-laced telephone calls, mail, and e-mail, and faxes. Dedicated individuals flooded my e-mail with hundreds of copies of the same message. Others sent repeated viruses from anonymous web addresses that drove me from public e-mail and "hacked" my web site, altering and deleting material.[14]

Such personal abuse, however, turned out to be the least of Bellesiles's worries. Within months of publication, he suffered the ultimate humiliation of being censured by a well-informed army of amateur historians and antiquarians. Employing the Internet as a tool for circumventing the traditional gatekeepers of scholarly journals, these lay critics produced a powerful web of doubt.[15] Barred from publishing their views in the scholarly journals, these outsiders produced Web sites and sensationalist press releases seeking to expose Bellesiles's faults and failures.

The main focus of these early critics was Bellesiles's cavalier dismissal of the effectiveness of primitive firearms. Gun enthusiasts expressed surprise at Bellesiles's sweeping and often ignorant technical statements. "Most scholars agree that the longbow was in fact far superior to the firearms of the sixteenth century, as well as those of the seventeenth and eighteenth century," Bellesiles argued, adding that "as numerous military historians have noted, firearms did not dominate Western Warfare until the nineteenth century."[16] Such broad generalizations, presented without footnotes, left skeptical observers wondering who were the mysterious "numerous military historians" and where were the legions of scholars.[17] Moreover, critics noted, employing a longbow required "virtually lifelong training" and produced infinitely less accurate results than the average rifle. Bellesiles's assertion of an effective range of two to three hundred yards for longbow fire was dismissed as ridiculous. A beginning archer, using the most modern equipment, an observer noted on an Organization of American Historians discussion list, "would have trouble hitting a stationary target at 10 yards," while a professional, using the most modern equipment might be able to achieve a range of 25 yards.[18]

Participants in the ever growing Internet discussion groups questioned as well the alleged uselessness of muskets and primitive rifles as weapons of war. "The famous Kentucky rifle took, on an average, three minutes to load," Bellesiles observed, once again without the benefit of footnote. Citing personal experience with replicas, as well as the published studies of technical experts and military historians, Bellesiles's electronic critics argued that experienced riflemen could fire around four accurate shots a minute.[19] Such sweeping statements of Bellesiles as the ones discussed here, therefore, revealed a consistent pattern of unfounded generalizations permeating *Arming America*, all of which had been uncovered by amateur historians.

Bellesiles's initial rebuttals focused primarily on undermining the scholarly credentials of his critics as well as their method of publication. He claimed that amateurs, unqualified to assess historical complexity and maintain scholarly objectivity, had produced misguided attacks on his scholarship. These politically motivated detractors had manipulated and controlled the discourse of *Arming America* by flooding Internet discussion groups—the most accessible forum of intellectual arbitration—with dissenting opinions. In other words, Bellesiles accused his adversaries of instilling doubt through a skillful use of technology, rather than through the formulation of a cogent argument or intellectual reasoning.

Given the detrimental effect of Internet discussion groups, Bellesiles pleaded for a resurrection of more conventional forums of deliberation. As far as he was concerned, the only legitimate venues for "conversation" regarding his book were "scholarly journals and there it is not really a conversation. It is more a long-term dialogue."[20] Only gatekeepers of professional publications, who controlled professional discourse and maintained its standards, could protect legitimate scholars, such as himself, from the wrath of marauding cyber warriors. "The web is chaotic," he argued. "There are no rules. There are no demarcators of who is and who is not an expert." The Internet, he stated, undermines scholarship and "can trick, fool, mislead the public widely and wildly."[21]

Bellesiles's plea for professionalism and scholarly exchange through conventional channels backfired, however. When heightened public interest in his work attracted the scrutiny of professional historians, Bellesiles's peers raked him over the coals for his selective analysis of qualitative evidence, his amateurish analysis of statistical data, and his apparent tendency to embellish evidence in the service of ulterior political motives.

First to fall were his excursions into literary sources and travel accounts, in particular the controversial "assertion that travelers in Jacksonian and antebellum America 'somehow . . . just did not see the guns that were supposedly all around them.' " Historian Daniel Justin Herman countered that even a cursory "survey of any number of bibliographies of early western travels and/or sporting literature would have revealed dozens of travel narratives that record guns and hunting on the frontier and occasionally in the vicinity of major cities. One thinks here of a line from Simon and Garfunkel, 'still a man hears what he wants to hear and disregards the rest.' "[22]

Inevitably, Bellesiles's analysis of probate records grabbed center stage. James Lindgren, a professor of law at Northwestern University, and his student Justin Heather produced a troubling picture of Bellesiles's methods and results. In "Counting Guns in America," they argued that about a hundred wills from Providence, Rhode Island, cited by Bellesiles did not exist; that he constantly presented the wills of women—where guns were unlikely to be mentioned—as the wills of men; that he tended to list weapons as old and broken even though most of the records contained no such information; that he offered no cell counts from the counties he examined; and that he did not reveal his method of extrapolating a national average from his sample.

Initially circulating their paper over the Internet, Lindgren and Heather dismissed Bellesiles's findings that only 14.7 percent of his 11,470 probate records for the period spanning 1765 to 1790 listed guns. Bellesiles's conclusion appeared to be "mathematically impossible," given the fact that, in their own analysis of three of the four regions that he had examined, they found gun ownership to be about 63 percent in white-male estates, of which only 9 percent were listed as broken or in poor condition. Guns appeared more frequently in probate inventories than Bibles, swords, tomahawks, or any other "edged or bladed weapons."[23] In fact, critics observed, gun ownership was probably higher than even the Lindgren-Heather account because family members presumably removed prized items such as guns "prior to inventories." Moreover, "most men who died . . . were well beyond their hunting primes," and had probably "passed on guns to sons and grandsons prior to their deaths."[24]

Yet, even if Bellesiles's figures were accurate, a skeptical Jackson Lears observed, did this mean that guns were not valued? Chiding Bellesiles for his incoherent definition of a "gun culture," Lears argued that a lack of weapons did not necessarily entail the absence of a gun culture. Bellesiles had defined a gun culture as "a shared and widespread culture idolizing firearms . . . a fascination distinct from and unlike the popular attitude towards guns in all other cultures with which the United States shared basic values."[25] This definition, a guarded critic observed, was not a historical observation but a "derivative from the present. It is clearly advanced with a teleology to it, in terms of what we know (or think we know) to come after."[26]

Such charges of sloppy research and poor definitions changed into hardened suspicions of wrongdoing when Bellesiles failed to identify the archival depositories of his probate records. In response to insistent queries concerning the whereabouts of his sources, Bellesiles led scholars on wild goose chases through a maze of archival centers, some of which he had not visited, while others did not contain the records that Bellesiles claimed to have used. The most incriminating discovery occurred when scholars attempting to trace Bellesiles's probate records from San Francisco County discovered that all the documents he claimed to cite had been destroyed in the great earthquake and fire of 1906. Bellesiles subsequently claimed to have viewed the San Francisco records in other sites—none of which held records of the documents he claimed to have used.

Bellesiles's response to these accusations ranged from the vitriolic to the sophomoric. He dismissed criticism of his probate record analysis as "the Jihad of technical nitpickers."[27] As for the calls to share his probate records by means of a Web site, Bellesiles claimed that his notes, containing thousands of tabulations, had been written up on yellow legal pads that had been destroyed in a May 2000 flooding of his office at Emory University. Perhaps forgetting this assertion, however, Bellesiles did revise his original figures on gun ownership, suggesting that they should have been slightly higher, "more in the neighborhood of 22–24 percent."[28] Bellesiles admitted, as well, that he had misread the Militia Act of 1792, one of the most crucial documents supporting his claim of a gun-shy militia. The 1792 version of this act did not, as Bellesiles originally had claimed, state that the government would provide the militia with arms and ammunition. By his own admission, he had conflated this text with other versions of the Militia Act.[29]

Despite his confusing defense brief, Bellesiles was not without supporters. Whatever its faults, supporters noted that *Arming America* had succeeded in challenging axiomatic assumptions on the role of guns in early America. *Arming America* was perhaps faulty in certain critical respects, but such errors—nine paragraphs out of a six hundred pages of text—amounted to a "tempest in a teapot." The "non-quantitative data in *Arming America* stood on its own"; even "without the probate data the thesis was strong."[30] As for Bellesiles's qualitative sources—literature, travel accounts, legal debates—supporters accused the book's detractors of disingenuously presenting differences in interpretation as evidence of fraud. *Arming America* was, these supporters claimed, a "groundbreaking study" for having opened "up a subject in a manner in a way or from an angle that hasn't been done before."[31] No book, whatever its quality, could stand up to the scrutiny to which *Arming America* had been subjected. The controversy, Bellesiles's supporters suggested, had nothing to do with scholarly error; it was, rather, a frightening example of the type of treatment meted out to those who dared to challenge the politically powerful.

Reactions among professional historians were at first hesitant, protective, and even defensive. When urged to review its decision to bestow the Bancroft Prize on *Arming America*, a spokesperson for the prize committee replied that "the committee stands by its decision." Edmund Morgan and Garry Wills, two of the river gods who had lavished praise on the book, declined offers to reassess their reviews. The OAH executive board steered a steady course away from any meaningful examination of the queries raised by critics of *Arming America*, preferring instead to address the less controversial issue of personal attacks on Bellesiles. While acknowledging that it "is appropriate to subject all schol-

arly work to criticism and to evaluate that work's arguments and
its sources, the Executive Board of the Organization of American
Historians considers personal attacks upon or harassment of an
author, as we have seen directed at Michael A. Bellesiles following publication of *Arming America: The Origins of a National Gun
Culture*, to be inappropriate and damaging to a tradition of free
exchange of ideas and the advancement of our knowledge of the
past."[32]

The Newberry Library in Chicago, which had granted Bellesiles a large NEH-funded grant even though its selection committee was aware of the growing clouds of doubt hovering over
Arming America, produced a torturous explanation of its position,
only to be humiliated by a demand from the NEH to remove its
sponsorship from the Bellesiles award. The NEH accused the
Newberry Library of neglecting to take seriously "the many sub-
stantial questions that had been raised about the accuracy of Mr.
Bellesiles's scholarship. These questions were widespread before
the award committee made its decision; indeed some of them
were discussed in the national press, in the letters of support for
Professor Bellesiles, and on a web discussion group on which the
Newberry was regularly posting notices before the award was
made." The Newberry Library, thus, had "failed to meet the high
scholarly and ethical standards necessary for any award bearing
the NEH name."[33]

Arming America's death knell was sounded as early as January
2002, upon publication of an issue of the *William and Mary Quarterly* dedicated to the book. The various scholarly articles in this
journal produced a cumulative negative evaluation of Bellesiles's
scholarship and integrity. Gloria Main, an expert on early American quantitative sources, fired the opening shot. She dismissed

Bellesiles's claim that probate inventories "scrupulously recorded every item in an estate . . . including those that had already been passed on as bequests before death" as "nonsense."

> As for the absence of guns from bequests in wills noted by Bellesiles, this is a true but meaningless observation. Most men's wills that I have read from early New England and Maryland forbear itemizing any bequests beyond describing specific parcels of land, probably because they had to pay someone by the page to prepare the will for them. Very few wills mention horses or cows, for instance, yet these animals could be quite as valuable as a good gun. No one would claim that the absence of horses and cows from bequests meant the testator did not own them. Why then should the failure to stipulate a gun mean there was no gun to give? Nor was there anything in the law that required inventories to list personal possessions that had been given away by the deceased prior to his last illness so long as his estate covered his debts.[34]

Main pointed out that Bellesiles's naïve partisans had failed to address the fact that all previous scholarship on gun owner- ship and probate records—including her own—offered well- documented evidence on widespread gun ownership. How was it, she mused somewhat testily, that "no editor or referee ever acted to set him straight?" Barely stopping short of accusing Bellesiles of outright dishonesty, Main observed acidly that the ten years re- portedly spent on researching the book was "far too short a time for one person to have read all the other sources cited in the vo- luminous notes in addition to the probate records stored in each of forty courthouses scattered across the United States from Boston to Los Angeles."[35]

The military historian Ira Gruber was equally skeptical of

Bellesiles's use of military history to bolster his thesis, claiming that his dismissal of muskets as an ineffective weapon in the arsenal of militias "must make very selective use of current scholarship." As for Bellesiles's characterization of militias as an early version of the Keystone Kops, Gruber stated that his "treatment of the militia is much like that of guns: he regularly uses evidence in a partial or imprecise way." Gruber was particularly perplexed by Bellesiles's description of the relatively peaceful life in the New World.

> To argue that peace was "the norm" in the colonial period and that "the years from 1815 to 1846 were notably peaceful ones for the United States" (pp. 71–72, 296) requires so many qualifications or evasions as to raise doubts about the generalizations. . . . He also ignores many examples of deadly white on white violence (particularly in the South during the Revolution) and sees no inconsistency between the ferocity of the Black Hawk and Seminole Wars and the peacefulness of American life between the War of 1812 and the Mexican War (pp. 293–96). . . . His efforts to minimize the importance of guns, militia, and war in early America and to portray the Civil War as the catalyst for a national gun culture is founded on a consistently biased reading of sources and on careless uses of evidence and context.[36]

Randolph Roth, an expert on violence and homicide in early America, expressed similar incredulity: Bellesiles's "errors on homicide are similar to his errors on gun ownership. He cannot appreciate how violent frontier societies were or how violent seventeenth-century European colonies were because he confuses the low number of homicides reported in surviving court records with low homicide rates." In actual fact, Roth stated, early

America was significantly more homicidal than twentieth-century America.[37]

When called upon to respond to the criticism in the *William and Mary Quarterly*, Bellesiles attempted to minimize his differences with his critics, preferring instead to ponder the ambiguity of the historical record and to recall the indignities of personal attacks. As a point of departure he attempted to reframe the significance of his book by explaining that "*Arming America* is about *The Origins of a National Gun Culture*; it is concerned with culture, not the number of guns in America. I did try to include as many statistics as I could toward that end and for the future use of other historians . . . but my focus was" the more traditional grist of cultural history. Having established this line of defense, Bellesiles, like Oates, invoked the defense that only a small segment of his book could be described as flawed. Why he had condensed years of painstaking research and archival work on probate records into such limited space remained a mystery.[38]

While willing to concede inaccuracies in his statistical data— at the most they "only suggest a pattern, not a conclusion"— Bellesiles avoided confronting his suspect responses to various criticisms. Irrespective of strong evidence, Bellesiles continued to claim the destruction of his records in the Emory flood.[39] He offered no reference to the phantom archives housing nonexistent material, nor did he defend his selective reading of travel accounts. "We sometimes seem to read the evidence differently," appeared to be Bellesiles's main line of defense.[40]

The final act in this drama unfolded in July 2002, when the independent committee set up at Emory University delivered its report. The committee members—Stanley N. Katz of Princeton, Hanna H. Gray of the University of Chicago, and Laurel

Thatcher of Harvard—were unwaveringly severe in their assessment of Bellesiles's integrity. They corroborated most of the criticism of Bellesiles's study of probate records. His numbers, they concurred, were a meaningless collection of sporadic, unverifiable records, and, as numerous critics had pointed out, were "mathematically improbable or impossible."[41]

Bellesiles's response dwelled on the microscopic scrutiny of his work, claiming that never before had a historical study been subjected to such an intense and overtly hostile examination. Historical inquiry, particularly of a period with fragmented archival records, was inevitably inexact. Historians challenged received knowledge, provoked discourse, and offered new angles for assessing familiar material. Contrary to popular perceptions, an irrefutable representation of events past was not part of the historian's mandate. Inaccuracy was inevitable.[42]

Bellesiles claimed that he had confronted not the normal academic process for rectifying error and clarifying the historical record but virtually a kangaroo court. A few minor and unintentional misdemeanors were hardly a reason for capital punishment. "The report casts aspersion on my integrity as a scholar based on three paragraphs and a table in a six-hundred-page book. It seems to me that raising uncertainties that question the credibility of an entire book without considering the book as a whole is just plain unfair."[43] As for his inability to match his records with the pertinent archives, Bellesiles trotted out the destruction caused by the Emory flood.

On October 25, 2002, Emory University announced that "Dr. Michael Bellesiles has resigned from his position as Professor of History at Emory University, effective December 31, 2002."[44] On December 13, 2002, Columbia University's trustees announced its decision to rescind Bellesiles's Bancroft Prize. The official announcement cited "scholarly misconduct," and the contravening of "the norms of historical scholarship" as the basis for this unprecedented decision.[45] In early January 2003, Knopf announced that the press had decided to stop selling *Arming America* and to terminate the contract with Bellesiles. The author of the controversial study "reportedly had offered to revise the book; the revisions were considered inadequate." According to a Knopf spokesperson, *Arming America* had already sold eight thousand in hardback and sixteen thousand in paperback.[46]

THE NOBLE LIE

His claims of a witch hunt notwithstanding, Bellesiles was ultimately the victim of self-destruction. Most of his technical explanations for the many lacunae discovered in his book turned out to be imaginative fantasies rather than truthful recollections of honest error or random misfortune. His woeful story of probate notes destroyed in an accidental flood appeared to be nothing more than "pulped fiction."[47] Contrary to his explanation, Bellesiles had not been abroad when the flood caused some minor damage to some of the offices on his floor; nor had he ever reported water damage in his office. An experiment conducted by one of his critics and validated by experts appeared to prove that the yellow legal pads were resilient to water damage.

Bellesiles's downfall was caused by a consistent pattern of lying and inconsistencies that had little to do with the text, such as the collapse of his self-representation as the victim of cyberspace framing. Insinuations that his nemesis, James Lindgren, had fabricated e-mails in order to defame him were swiftly refuted, leav-

ing Bellesiles once again seeking a way out of a web of inaccuracies that he himself had created. Moreover, Emory University officials dismissed Bellesiles's claim that hackers had broken into his
Web site and had altered some of the probate records he had
placed there for public scrutiny. Finally, Bellesiles's claim that he
had been driven off e-mail by electronic stalkers did not accord
with reality; as late as December 2000, he was still using his
Emory e-mail address.[48]

How and why did his much flawed version of the American
past achieve such august claims of scholarship? Bellesiles inadvertently offered an insightful explanation: "The power of image
and myth repeatedly overwhelms reality" in historical studies, in
general, and the right to bear arms, in particular, he wrote.[49]
Thus, the mostly liberal leadership of the American historical
community apparently embraced *Arming America* because "it appeared to confirm what they long have wanted to believe: that the
Second Amendment protects only a collective right to bear arms,
that individual gun rights were deemed unimportant at the time
of writing and ratification of the Constitution."[50] Bellesiles was
guilty of embracing a "noble lie."

No less important was the apparent "trust in numbers" espoused by a scholarly community largely ignorant of statistics.
Bellesiles's principal supporters continuously argued that his statistical evidence defied refutation. Literary sources were open to
interpretation; quantitative evidence was not. Thus, even though
the number of pages dedicated to probate records was relatively
modest, these troublesome statistics were by all accounts the most
compelling part of the book. As James Lindgren and Justin
Heather observed, "The probate data are the only data purporting to show systematic changes in gun ownership over long peri-

ods of time. . . . Further, the probate data are by far the most important evidence purporting to show that guns in private hands were mostly in poor working condition."[51] By Bellesiles's own account, only quantification could dispel the haze often associated with clashing textual interpretations.[52]

This trust in numbers was all the more curious given the fact that the findings of all quantitative historians who had published and specialized in the analysis of probate records were ignored by those who lauded the book for its use of objective data. Bellesiles, a mystified Randolph Roth observed somewhat belatedly, "is the only researcher who has produced such low estimates of gun ownership,"[53] yet somehow his figures were uncritically embraced. Moreover, Roth observed that *Arming America*'s other statistical data were equally contentious if not an outright fabrication. Bellesiles's claims for an exceedingly low homicide rate prior to the 1850s was, he wrote, false or misleading. For reasons that had nothing to do with scholarship, Bellesiles's statistical claims were embraced with alacrity. Conversely, the wealth of studies directly contradicting Bellesiles's sketchy, suspect, and unreliable mustering of numbers were marginalized by silence.[54] A whole array of cultural historians, most of whom had forged their careers by avoiding quantitative measurements, embraced uncritically data they could not understand and would not criticize.

The focus on quantitative data distracted attention from the underlying logical flaw in Bellesiles's book: that lack of guns signified popular disinterest. In fact, critics claimed, "the obsessive debate on how widespread" guns were prior to their mass production "was at best a subordinate one."[55] Numbers were not an indication of the cultural resonance of firearms. Nor did the actual number of arms per citizen have any bearing on the meaning of the Second Amendment. The ideological underpinnings of the right to bear arms "are surely more important than the 'reality' accompanying them," observed constitutional scholar Sanford Levinson.[56]

Bellesiles's work achieved notoriety because of the blurring of borders between traditional historical scholarship, with its emphasis on the uniqueness of events past, and historicism, an obsessive search for timeless ideas and a teleological past. Bellesiles's book was a popular and compelling exercise in presentism: the deliberate, willful, and mostly erroneous construction of the past as a device for explaining contemporary reality. According to Ira Gruber, Bellesiles was enamored by the idea of "using the past to reform the present."[57] A critical Jackson Lears observed that *Arming America* offered the "antihistorical" but attractive premise that the past was first and foremost a "compendium of useful lessons." In tailoring the notion of a usable past to popular demand, Bellesiles found no redeeming quality in recognizing "the finality of the past."[58] Thus, another commentator noted, his study was not truly a historical investigation but, rather, "advocacy journalism with lots of footnotes."[59] "Once a field gets sufficiently unmoored from what happened," Lindgren and Heather argued, "the assessment of reality is treated not as a matter of evidence, but rather as one of narrative, taste, and politics."[60]

In the final analysis, Bellesiles was no different from the army of mythographers he had set out to challenge. In his quest for a usable past he had enshrined a narrative no less mythical and hallucinatory than the version he had set out to debunk. "America's gun culture," an emphatic Bellesiles claimed, "is an invented tradition." Yet, in his zeal to undermine the power and resonance of this "invented tradition," Bellesiles had willfully and consciously employed exaggeration, selective quotations, and distortion of evidence to invent a tradition of his own.

THE CYBER DEBATE

As far as Bellesiles was concerned, the Internet was the proverbial golem rising to attack its creator. Bellesiles complained that a marauding group of interlopers had invaded his private space by e-mail; they had driven him into virtual seclusion and had defamed his character by flooding the Internet with a deluge of false accusations. Bellesiles accused his adversaries of hacking his Web site and altering the probate records posted at this location. When confronted by an incriminating exchange of e-mails with James Lindgren, he even went so far as to accuse his main critic of fabricating the exchange. "Anyone can print up anything and say I received this e-mail," Bellesiles wrote in response to queries regarding an e-mail he had allegedly sent to Lindgren. "Shouldn't you go by what I say rather than what someone else asserts?"[61]

This somewhat apocalyptic picture of technology run wild did not stand up to scrutiny. Despite protestations to the contrary, Bellesiles did not abandon his use of e-mail; there was no evidence of covert altering of records on his Web site, and James Lindgren swiftly and convincingly refuted charges of fabricating e-mails. It would appear that Bellesiles's last and futile resort was a desperate appeal to the technophobe. In actual fact, cyberspace produced a sobering mechanism of checks and balances, public scrutiny, broad access, and an important dialogue between the once-protected scholar and a demanding public.

The electronic interrogation of Michael Bellesiles was spearheaded by Clayton Cramer, a software engineer, the bearer of a master's degree in history from Sonoma State University, California, and a self-professed gun aficionado. It is perhaps fitting, then, to conclude this chapter with one final observation from the keyboard of the whistle-blower. "Over the last thirty years, the academic community in general, and historians in particular, have become quite concerned about the need for diversity: sexual diversity; racial diversity; and ethnic diversity," noted Cramer. "Unfortunately, it seems to me that the Bellesiles scandal exposed the lack of *political* diversity within the profession." Most historians, Cramer argued, accepted *Arming America*'s "preposterous claims" because it dovetailed with the prevailing liberal political climate of their guild. *Arming America* "created a system of thought so comfortable for the vast majority of historians, that they didn't even pause to consider the possibility that something wasn't right."[62]

Whether Cramer's comments were correct is almost beside the point. The resonance of his observations—not their veracity—offers vivid illustration of the demise of academic insularity and the dissipation of intellectual borders separating academia from its audience. Bellesiles's professional behavior was scrutinized by a host of experts far removed from early American history; a number of critiques, many of them quite professional, originated outside the groves of academe. A once-invisible lay audience now critically and visibly challenged the professional historian's methodology, ethics, and politics. The interrogation of *Arming America* led to a more general critique of American historians' modes of representation and to a challenge of accepted notions of objectivity and accountability.

Bellesiles's ordeal represented the termination of a form of historical discourse fashioned and shaped to exclude those outside the guild. The collective energy dedicated to exposing Bellesiles's lack of objectivity on gun control deflected attention from the most intriguing revelation of this scandal: the changing status of the interpretive voice in American historiography. *Arming America* offered glimpses of an important empowerment of laypersons and an attendant shift in the politics and culture of American historiography.

As this book goes to print, Michael Bellesiles's recuperation of his scholarly credentials proceeds with alacrity. *Arming America* has been reissued by Soft Skull Press, a New York publishing house specializing in dissident views on American society. The new edition contains appropriate changes in Bellesiles's discussion of probate records. Bellesiles's fast track to absolution is most evident within the community of scholarly journals, where he has already published several book reviews.[63] According to History News Network, Bellesiles also has a contract with Oxford University Press to produce a new book on violence in America.

Bellesiles is now a regular contributor to the History News Service (HNS), a "syndicate of professional historians who seek to improve the public's understanding of current events by setting these events in their historical contexts."[64] Directed by Joyce Appleby of UCLA and her colleague James Banner, Jr., HNS syndicates op-eds written by practicing historians who are chosen by an editorial board comprised of distinguished historians and journalists. Through the good offices of HNS, Bellesiles's opinions on a variety of subjects—ranging from the United States' military strategy of "shock and awe" in the Gulf region, and congressional attempts to regulate area studies, in general, and Middle Eastern studies, in particular—have found their way into the nation's newspapers.[65]

When called upon to defend the inclusion of Bellesiles among its list of contributing historians, HNS codirector James Banner explained:

> Whatever Michael Bellesiles did and was held responsible for doing, he remains a historian. The History News Service is a syndicate of professional historians—not just of academic historians but of all those who can by any decent definition of the term be considered historians. This certainly includes Mr. Bellesiles. . . . If our decision, not one difficult for us to arrive at, is seen by some as aiding in Mr. Bellesiles's rehabilitation as a practicing historian, we see nothing wrong with that. There is no reason why there should be no second acts in America.[66]

THREE

"A Self of Many Possibilities"

Joseph Ellis, the Protean Historian

For me, the teaching side of my life and the writing side of my life are part of the same collective whole.

Joseph J. Ellis

What would you rather see—a Disney crocodile robot or a real crocodile? The Disney version rolls its eyes, moves from side to side, and disappears beneath the surface and rises again. It is designed to command our attention at all times. None of these qualities is necessarily visible at the zoo where the real crocodiles seemed to spend most of their time sleeping. And you may have neither the means nor the inclination to observe a real crocodile in the Nile or the River Gambia.

Sherry Turkle

"Late in his life," the literary scholar Milton Cohen observed, F. Scott Fitzgerald revealed "two juvenile regrets—at not being big enough (or good enough) to play football in college, and at not getting overseas during the war." Fitzgerald compensated for this romantic void by immersing himself in "Princeton football lore and World War I history," creating protagonists of great athletic skills and military prowess, as well as by indulging in "childish waking dreams of imaginary heroism," on the playing fields of Princeton and the battlefields of France.[1]

In June 2001, the renowned historian Joseph Ellis acknowledged that he, too, had imaginatively compensated for the romantic voids of his own sedate and scholarly life. Following a *Boston Globe* exposé, the Pulitzer Prize–winning scholar of the American revolutionary age admitted that his public persona was a shapeshifting man for all seasons. Ellis—a professor of history at Mount Holyoke College and a media-anointed presidential scholar—had fabricated for himself a term of active duty in the Vietnam War. In addition, he had invented a period of activism in the civil rights movement of the 1960s and heroic athletic accomplishments as a high school football star. "Even in the best of lives, mistakes are made," a chastised Ellis remarked in his first public reaction to the revelations.[2]

The *Boston Globe*'s Walter Robinson revealed that Ellis had routinely embellished his lectures and public interviews with evocative descriptions of his service in Vietnam as an officer with the 101st Airborne Division and subsequently as a member of General Westmoreland's staff. His personal wartime experiences, Ellis proclaimed in his lectures on Vietnam and American culture, had led him to become an active member of both the antiwar and the civil rights movements.[3]

But Ellis had not served in Vietnam at all. Robinson—a bona fide Vietnam veteran—reported that Ellis had spent most of the war years "safely ensconced in graduate school at Yale." In 1965–66, when Ellis claimed that he was stationed in Indochina, he was in fact a first-year graduate student. Ellis eventually began his deferred service in 1969. However, his military records indicated that he had served his country as a member of the history faculty at West Point until he was discharged in June 1972. Ellis had boasted of his role in the antiwar and civil rights movements, but the *Globe* found no evidence that he was in "any visible way part of the antiwar movement." In other interviews Ellis delved into his youth, once relating to a reporter how, as a high school running back, he had scored the winning touchdown in the final game of his senior year. Yet, according to the *Globe*, Ellis's high school had lost the final two games of the season; moreover, high school records suggested that he had not been a member of the school's football team.[4]

Ellis's stories of his involvement in Vietnam and other pieces of history had become an integral and vital component of his lectures on contemporary American history. Curiously, he had not posited himself in particularly activist historic roles. His reconstructed past, an observer remarked, "seemed like an attempt to make himself 'present at the creation' of a new era—much in the way that the subjects of his books were front and center at the dawning of theirs."[5] "Being there" apparently added a modicum of authenticity, an element of persuasion that captivated his student audience. He had been "near My Lai," but not a witness to the massacre. Instead of casting himself in heroic battle scenes, he offered maudlin observations, such as his recollections of a burly comrade in Vietnam weeping as he read the poems of Emily Dickinson, with the terrible sounds of warfare rumbling in the distance. Ellis's crowning achievement was, he claimed, his insights on Westmoreland that he had shared with David Halberstam, author of *The Best and the Brightest* (1972). Needless to say, Halberstam did not recall ever meeting Ellis.

Mount Holyoke's initial reaction was to question the motives and integrity of the messenger. The college reportedly attempted to dissuade the *Boston Globe* from publishing the story, based on the "questionable legal basis of investigating statements made in the classroom." Hinting at unspecified ulterior motives, the college president, Joanne Creighton, wondered "what public interest the *Globe* is trying to serve through a story of this nature."[6] Somewhat taken back by criticism from colleagues, students, parents, and alumni, the college eventually promised a full and thorough investigation.

On August 17, and after much painful deliberation, President Creighton issued the college's official response. Rebuking Ellis for "his lie about his military experience," Creighton acknowledged the harm done to the community's students, the primary victims of his misrepresentations. "Misleading students is wrong and nothing can excuse it. Professor Ellis illegitimately appropriated an authority that was not his and abused his students' trust." She acknowledged as well "the disrespect that Professor Ellis's lie has shown to Vietnam veterans," and offered the college's apologies "for any pain his misrepresentation has caused them or their families." Creighton suspended Ellis without pay for one year. In addition, Ellis agreed to step down from his endowed chair "until such time as the Trustees may wish to reinstate him."[7] Ellis also issued an apology through his solicitors for doing "something both stupid and wrong." He accepted with grace his one-year exile, promising that during that period he "intend[ed] to find time for self-reflection and to begin work on a new book."[8]

Public reactions ran the gamut of condemnation for Mount Holyoke's excessive leniency to dismay over the college's overreaction. The nation's media primarily sought context, by placing Ellis alongside a variety of eminent and not-so-eminent Americans who had embellished their pasts for no apparent reason. The list was endless. It included Franklin Delano Roosevelt, who claimed a *Harvard Crimson* scoop he had never written; the Supreme Court nominee Douglas Ginsburg, who claimed to have litigated thirty-four times on behalf of the Supreme Court (thereby exaggerating his Supreme Court caseload by thirty-three); Larry Lawrence, once ambassador to Switzerland who was disinterred in 1997 from Arlington National Cemetery following revelations that he had lied about his World War II service in the Merchant Marine (he had been, in fact, a junior college student during the war); and Los Angeles Superior Court judge Patrick Couwenberg, forced to resign for falsely claiming combat service in Vietnam and a stint with the CIA in Laos. These disclosures avoided sweeping political or ideological generalizations; they tended to privatize the motives of culprits, offering glimpses of the hollow, empty soul of those who lied to compensate for a nagging sense of personal shortcomings.[9]

In contrast, conservative commentators approached the Ellis case as indicative of an all-too-common lack of integrity among politically motivated custodians of the past. Ellis's most immediate companion in crime was the law professor Annette Gordon Reed, a fellow Jefferson scholar, whose much-acclaimed 1997 study of the liaison between Thomas Jefferson and his slave Sally Hemings had allegedly entered "as evidence a nineteenth century letter in which words had been changed in order to reverse its original meaning." The philosopher Martha Nussbaum at the University of Chicago was similarly criticized following her controversial court briefing on the Christian origins of homophobia, in which she had allegedly offered false testimony regarding the benign response of Plato and other classical thinkers to homosexuality. "What is to be expected when the very word truth is fashionably supplied with ironic quotation marks?" queried the Christian monthly *First Things*.[10]

The *National Review*, in contrast, argued that Ellis was singled out for public humiliation because, unlike Gordon-Reed and Nussbaum, he lacked the political credentials of garden-variety tenured radicals, whose attitude toward truth was, at best, casual. The magazine cited as example a 1989 petition signed by over four hundred prominent historians, claiming that when the Constitution was adopted the common law protected a woman's right to abortion. Despite the egregious fraudulence of this historical claim, the *National Review*'s Ramesh Ponnuru complained that neither "the media nor the academy is willing to act . . . at least when the lying in question serves liberals' political objectives."[11]

Predictably, Ellis's academic colleagues discussed whether it was possible to differentiate between Ellis's writing and his teaching. Having deliberately mixed truth and invention in presenting himself to his immediate public, scholars wondered whether his research should be taken on faith, and to what degree his embellishments tarnished the courses he taught. Colleagues at Mount Holyoke, many of whom had been beholden to Ellis in his former capacity as dean of the faculty, were mostly forgiving. "Professors do sometimes alter or embellish their personal histories as a teaching method," professor of politics Joan Cocks observed, offering a tepid and irrelevant example of her own classroom presentation of incidents from her mother's life as the experiences of an aunt. Cocks reminded the public that Ellis had not lied "about the public history of Vietnam but about his private role in it." His lapses were, "at the very worst, in the middle of a continuum with deadly deception at one end and poetic license at the other."[12] Donal O'Shea, Ellis's successor as dean, agreed that Ellis's lapses were no more than an issue of controversial didactics. "There is a classroom persona you have as a teacher that's really not quite you," O'Shea explained. "There's an element of great teaching that's theater. And Professor Ellis was expert at that."[13]

Colleagues on other campuses were sympathetic as well. Richard Jensen of the University of Illinois dismissed the scandal as preposterously blown out of proportion and "curiously postmodern." Ellis's misdeeds focused on "irrelevant colorful claims and background details ('I was nearby') rather than the core historical" disputes surrounding the war itself.[14] "Morally speaking," retired University of Buffalo professor of education and medicine David Nyberg pronounced, Ellis's fiction "was trivial. Pedagogically speaking, it was brilliant; he got his students to think about something serious."[15] In fact, the University of Maine's Howard Segal mused, the Ellis affair offered a prime example of the profession's obsession with irrelevant misdeeds and its pervasive unwillingness to clarify the historian's obligations toward the past. Ellis had indeed committed a grave error, but he had been singled out for political rather than pedagogical reasons. Segal complained that the same system that had rushed to judgment in this minor case of intellectual misdemeanor appeared paralyzed by "political correctness" when confronted with the teachings of pseudoscholars "like Wellesley College's Tony Martin," who taught and published anti-Semitic "nonsense" with impunity.[16]

Such sympathy notwithstanding, the majority of comments emanating from academia were unforgiving. Michael Burlingame, one of the main witnesses for the prosecution in the Stephen Oates affair, offered a typical verdict: "Mount Holyoke's action is a step in the right direction, but a small one. For lying to students over the years he should be dismissed."[17] As far as Emory historian David Garrow was concerned, the distinctions between Ellis the scholar and Ellis the impersonator were irrelevant. Garrow stated that there was no meaningful moral distinction between "lying to your students" and "lying to your readers in print."[18] College professors were role models, teaching by personal example the difference between right and wrong, true and false. "Today's students have come of age in an era of relativism" and deception, while "learning history through fictional films," observed Jim Sleeper of Yale. Professors had a sacred obligation to provide students with the necessary intellectual skills for sifting between fact and factoids, reality and virtuality.[19] Most of Ellis's colleagues agreed that the Mount Holyoke professor had misinterpreted the role of the historian, whose task was "to interpret the past, not to be part of it." Ellis had "denied the real actors in Vietnam a voice in what was their struggle."[20] As such, his transgressions were far from an irrelevant sideshow.

Ironically, some of the eminent academics offering insight on Ellis's teaching and public personae would later endure scandals and public humiliation of their own. Doris Kearns Goodwin, who subsequently had to explain her expropriation of the words of others, declared that the only meaningful subject to debate was Ellis's teaching methods. Goodwin recalled that during her stint as history professor at Harvard, she had enthralled her students by relating her conversations with President Lyndon B. Johnson. Such personal recollections, she explained, transformed the somewhat abstract dynamics of decision making during the Vietnam War into a more believable concept. Goodwin never felt the urge to invent any aspect of the conversations. "There was no need to with Lyndon Johnson," she recalled, "though he himself was probably embellishing."[21] Ann Lane of the University of Virginia—who would later endure her own scandal when accused of plagiarizing sections of her 1971 dissertation—found pedagogical benefits in the Ellis affair. Universities, she complained, tended to define "excellent teaching as mesmerizing lectures," a form of "showmanship" usually practiced by men. The separation of this species of academic entertainment from the less glamorous, traditional tasks of instilling values and knowledge would, she argued, restore confidence in the academic enterprise.[22]

Some of Ellis's most severe critics pointed out that he had, in fact, demonstrated a casual attitude toward the historical record in his written work as well. With an eye fixed firmly on the pervasive voyeuristic obsession with the private lives of the rich and famous, Ellis had written extensively on the alleged intimate relationship between Jefferson and Hemings. Initially, Ellis had offered the ultimate backhand compliment by declaring Jefferson too timid to actually have slept with a woman he truly lusted for or perhaps even loved. "Jefferson preferred to meet his lovers in the rarefied region of his mind rather than the physical world of his bedchamber," Ellis pronounced, with more than a touch of contempt.[23]

In 1998 Ellis coauthored a paternity study of the Jefferson-Hemings liason that led him to declare a change of mind. In a series of dramatic interviews, Ellis claimed that the report, authored with pathologist Eugene Foster, proved beyond doubt that Jefferson had fathered Hemings's last child. Ellis's pronouncements received extensive media coverage in part because they occurred during the impeachment hearings regarding President Clinton's relationship with the White House intern Monica Lewinsky. Apparently seeking to excuse Clinton's sexual lapses, Ellis argued: "It is as if Clinton had called one of the most respected character witnesses in all of U.S. history to testify that the primal urge has a most distinguished pedigree." And yet, as coauthor Foster observed a few months later, their joint study proved nothing of the sort. Foster declared that DNA evidence merely suggested that a Jefferson male had fathered her son. Twenty-five male Jeffersons were living at the time.[24] When faced with the contradictions between his conclusion and that of his coauthor, Ellis disarmingly explained that his convictions were more imaginative than legalistic. History, he explained, "is more like a classroom than a courtroom, a more capacious space where room remains for shaded versions of the truth."[25]

THE PERRY MILLER SYNDROME

Why had Ellis chosen to embellish the past? To what degree did his lapse reflect his own inner world or broader social and intellectual trends? To be sure, Ellis had no apparent professional reason for reinventing his past; his position had been assured with a 1997 National Book Award for *American Sphinx*, his study of Thomas Jefferson. He had also received the 2001 Pulitzer Prize for *Founding Brothers*, an elegant study of America's revolutionary generation. Ellis's eloquent writing, and not his extracurricular deeds—imaginary or otherwise—had transformed him from a conventional history professor to a major media figure, called upon by television networks and the printed media to voice an opinion on a host of issues.

At face value, there appeared to be no conscious intellectual subversion in Ellis's acts of imagination. "I am not a novelist," he explained. "I am also not a person who believes that there is no fundamental distinction between fiction and nonfiction." He asserted that "the difference between the historian and the novelist is that the historian's imagination must be tethered to the evidence." Moreover, Ellis consistently condemned the splicing of fact and fiction in historical writing. "In the end," he declared, "there's an ironclad rule in history and biography that's been true for at least three hundred years: you cannot make it up."[26]

Ellis's scathing 1999 review of *Dutch*, Edmund Morris's biography of Ronald Reagan, illustrated an intolerance for imaginative reconstructions of the past. Morris's official biography of Ronald Reagan consciously blurred the line between fact and fiction. With Forrest Gump–like flourish, Morris's authorial persona popped up at every major point in the life of the former president, even appearing at historical events prior to Morris's birth.

"I marveled at the unique combination of Morris's writerly skills and the extraordinary good fortune he enjoyed" in following Reagan from his youth and throughout his tumultuous career, observed a sarcastic and visibly annoyed Ellis.[27] Yet, he continued, Morris's book was not history; it was not even a novel. At very best it was a shallow and manipulative docudrama, "a prose version of Oliver Stone's 'JFK' which splices together historically accurate evidence from oral interviews and legitimate archival sources with" pure and utter fabrication. Ellis lashed out at Morris for his excessive poetic license and malicious mixing of "verisimilitude and the truth." The text, he argued, deliberately and outrageously "disguises Morris's blending of fact and fiction, real and fabricated dialogue. . . . In the blurred post-modern genre within which Morris is working, the gap between history and fiction" was irreparably effaced.[28]

Yet Ellis failed to practice what he preached. He, too, showed up at various places he had never been, describing to his students events he had never seen. His imaginary experiences at the side of General Westmoreland, his encounters with racist law-enforcement officers during the Summer of Freedom, and other events were, in fact, more perniciously constructed than the fiction making he denounced. Edmund Morris's playful cameo appearances were transparently fictitious, a rhetorical device employed for dramatic purposes. Ellis was engaged in willful deception.

Such deception, Yale scholar Mark Oppenheimer speculated, was the result of the historian's all-too-human obsession with greatness and relevance. To Oppenheimer it seemed that Ellis was determined to follow in the footsteps of the likes of Perry Miller, the greatest scholar of early America, "who created his own legend, famous in the profession, of a young expatriate, sitting on the banks of the Congo" River and deciding that upon repatriation he would become the great American historian, the maker of a past that would shape the present.

> In 1956, more than 30 years after dropping out of college to see the world, Miller wrote words that should haunt Joseph Ellis today: "I came [to Africa] seeking 'adventure,' jealous of older contemporaries to whom that boon had been offered by the First World War." Deep in Africa, Miller thought of Gibbon, author of The Decline and Fall of the Roman Empire, and resolved to do for the United States what Gibbon had done for Rome, become its chronicler. If he could become the best writer of American history, he could become part of American history, much as the frontier historian Frederick Jackson Turner had shaped the West by shaping its mythical image.[29]

Motivated by the same urge to be relevant, Oppenheimer argued, Ellis chose "the dead white males who mattered most"—an early version of Stephen Ambrose's "Greatest Generation"—in order to make his mark on American thought. The Perry Miller myth demanded that the marriage between historian and historical subject should come to pass during a formative odyssey or in the wake of a traumatic, momentous personal experience. Yet, lacking Miller's adventurous spirit, Ellis experienced his rite of passage in spirit only. One can only speculate that Ellis believed that the quality of his writing, his ability to move his readers, would compensate for the eventual discovery that his travels were of the armchair variety.

Ellis seemed to yearn for the golden age when "thinkers could be doers," an age in which principles were born out of experience and active engagement. "Here he was studying 'engaged' intellectuals such as Jefferson, Adams, Franklin, and Madison," observed the historian and Vietnam veteran Peter Rollins, "yet he was essentially a bookish person who spent his military tour of duty (honorably) as a teacher of history at West Point. It must have been frustrating to see those young men and women march off to Vietnam while he remained behind speculating about Thomas Jefferson's ideas, Jefferson's enigmatic personality—and years later, Jefferson's (supposed) illicit sex life."[30] It is under these circumstances that Ellis joined in his imagination the legions of Americans who had participated in the Vietnam odyssey and/or joined the struggle for civil rights—who, in short, had made history.

Liberal Americans like Ellis, observed Geoffrey Wheatcroft from the ironic distance of the *Guardian*, had reason to agonize over Vietnam. They "saw no reason to fight in a war which they didn't support, which seems fair enough. But they are haunted by the knowledge that others did fight in it, poor whites and blacks chosen by a peculiarly unfair system of selective service." In his rewriting of his past, Wheatcroft speculated, Ellis overcompensated by inventing "a doubly admirable past for himself, as a man who first fought for the home of the brave and then didn't study war no more."[31] The war in particular and the sixties in general, with their great moral divide, were "essentially our passage to adulthood," Rutgers historian David Oshinsky was quoted in the *London Times*. "Some people actually went to Mississippi, and some people went to Mississippi in their heads."[32] Hence, said an editorial in the *New York Times*, "one might almost suppose that he was not so much reinventing his past, as confirming his present, projecting his current degree of success backward in time, living up to a version of himself."[33]

PROTEUS UNLEASHED

Biography, Andrew Burstein has noted, "is the most narcissistic form of nonfiction. On some level, even the best writer exchanges his or her life for that of the biographic subject."[34] Joseph Ellis's ability to reconcile his aversion to imaginary history with his own indiscretions may lie in his portrayal of Thomas Jefferson, who was, by all accounts, his alter ego.

In explaining the background to his *American Sphinx*, Ellis described the mystical relationship he shared with Jefferson. The Jefferson-Ellis connection was consummated by a chance encounter on a cold evening in November 1993. In a large brick church in Worcester, Massachusetts, a fascinated Ellis witnessed a magical bonding between the second president of the United States and an enthusiastic audience captivated by Jefferson's rambling discourse on such far-ranging topics as "the American revolution, his love of French wine and French ideas, his accomplishments and frustrations as a political leader and president, his obsession with education, his elegiac correspondence with John Adams, his bottomless hope in American Democracy."[35]

That evening Jefferson appeared in the person of Clayton Jenkinson, an English professor and popular "scholar-impersonator," who appeared regularly on college campuses, before state legislators, and at other auspicious gatherings—such as a gala celebration hosted by President William Jefferson Clinton—"where he won the hearts of the White House staff by saying that Jefferson would have dismissed the entire Whitewater investigation as 'absolutely nobody's business.' "[36]

An admiring Ellis noted the audience's willingness to suspend disbelief and accept, for a miraculous moment, that the man onstage was Jefferson incarnate. Although he was impressed with Jenkinson's performance, it was the audience's "extravagant enthusiasm" for the Jeffersonian persona that impressed Ellis the most. Jefferson, he noted, "beckoned to our modern sense of multiple identities" because he "was a fascinating bundle of selves." As a "shapeshifter," and the bearer of multiple identities, Jefferson met the psychological needs of modern American society. He appealed to contemporary sensibilities because he was a "willful eclectic," a precursor of "postmodern man," a composite of fact, fiction, and poetry that produced "overlapping and interacting personae."[37]

Even as he dismissed Edmund Morris's postmodernist blend of fact and fiction, Ellis expressed an affinity with Jefferson's deceptive performances. Jefferson, he explained, was a "promiscuous" individual, by which he meant that he was a person "comprised of diverse and unrelated parts." In fact, Ellis urged his readers to move beyond their fixation on politics and Jefferson's "reverential posture," to focus instead on his "interior agility"—Jefferson's addiction to embellishments, denial, or shapeshifting—when confronted with "inconvenient realities."[38] Ellis's Jefferson was a protean figure: confronted by inquisitive and critical interlopers.

The image of Thomas Jefferson as protean man was by no means an Ellis original. As early as 1973, renowned psychoanalyst Erik Erikson had offered a representation of Jefferson as the latter-day Proteus, "a man of many disguises; a man of chameleon-like adaptation to passing scenes; a man of essential thoughts."[39] In that same year, Merrill Peterson had adopted the Jefferson-Proteus metaphor as well. Ellis's variation on this theme was to efface all godlike qualities from the latter-day Proteus. Jefferson's acts of deception were, he explained, all too human. His shapeshifting was first and foremost a manifestation of self-delusion rather than political maneuvering. Ellis's Jefferson created "an interior world constructed out of his own ideals into which he retreated whenever those ideals collided with reality." Jefferson's most significantly protean quality was "his extraordinary capacity for denial . . . his uncanny manipulation of different voices and personae" and "his capacity to play hide-and-seek within himself."[40] Ellis insisted that Jefferson was unaware of his lies; his conflicting internal voices did not hear one another. This complex manner of keeping secrets from himself as well as others was not, Ellis argued, the type of duplicitous behavior one expects from politicians. Such complexity, he argued, occurred "only [in] the pure at heart."[41]

In applying these standards to his own case, Ellis explained that the president's protean qualities were especially suitable for contemporary American life. Thus, Ellis expressed admiration for what the psychologist Robert Jay Lifton has called "the protean self," the ability to live with numerous interchangeable identities as a strategy for dealing with contemporary complexities. Quoting a review of Lifton's book *The Protean Self* (1993), Ellis observed that "in a world of jarring, unpredictable change, a world lacking clear borders between illusion and reality, with no shared sense of truth or morality, a premium was put on the ability to keep on the move inside yourself."[42]

Indeed, Ellis's writing provides ample evidence that he saw himself and Jefferson as two near-identical versions of the "protean man." Ellis indirectly explained his transgressions by drawing analogies—physical, philosophical, and psychological—between the self-deluded protean president and himself. "When you think about Jefferson, what man comes to your mind?" interviewer David Gergen asked Ellis, hoping perhaps to hear about the second president's worldview or deeds. Instead, Ellis chose to initiate his discussion with a description of the president's physical attributes, making note of the fact that in height, and in other physical features, Ellis and Jefferson were strikingly alike.[43] Elsewhere, Ellis made the same point. He alerted readers, "I was a native Virginian who, like Jefferson, had graduated from the College of William and Mary. I even had reddish blond hair like Jefferson."[44] And beyond these superficial physical and biographical similarities lay a more intricate symbiotic relationship. He and Jefferson, Ellis declared, were also "kindred spirits." Psychologically and intellectually they had much in common.

As part of his identification with Jefferson, Ellis apparently felt compelled to re-create himself as a renaissance man and a man of action: not only an astute observer but also a soldier and civil rights activist; not only a scholar, but also a star athlete. Ellis adopted Jefferson's compartmentalized psyche, comprised of "a series of overlapping . . . personae that talked to us but not to each other." Jefferson, he observed, could walk past his "slave quarters at Monticello thinking grand thoughts about human freedom and never seem to notice the disjunction"; by the same token, Ellis could pontificate on the importance of factually based history even as he practiced the opposite.

Ellis's fascinating *American Sphinx* presented a Jefferson—and presumably an Ellis—who strove to please by revealing, and sometimes inventing, a personality or political belief in order to captivate his audience. His inner world was a study of seemingly incompatible tensions. As a private person and a public figure, Ellis wrote, Jefferson was given to flights of creative imagination. He "constructed interior worlds of great imaginative appeal," even though these self-representations often clashed with reality. Ellis's Jefferson was able to square the inherent contradictions between such inconsistencies with his "internal ability to generate" and live comfortably with multiple versions of the truth. And yet, Ellis-Jefferson was "not a hypocrite. . . . He had almost separate chambers in his psyche, where he could put things and seal them, where you didn't have to—he didn't have to—confront them." All he desired was "to always come out nicely, and therefore, he would tell you what you wanted to hear."[45]

Ellis's study of his alter ego was no simple recitation of hagiographic accounts of a great man and his great ideas. There was an element of self-loathing in this portrayal. *American Sphinx*, Benjamin Schwarz noted, was at best "a portrait of an intelligent, graceful but conventional mind."[46] Quoting poet and Mount Holyoke colleague Mary Jo Salter, Ellis had noted that we "love the fact that our favorite politician was a writer and a farmer and a scientist and an aesthete and a violinist"—in sum, a man of many selves.[47] Yet, in the same breath, Ellis observed that this celebrated polymath was in fact a derivative scholar with a provincial and even pedestrian mind: nothing, in sum, close to the hagiographic renditions passed on to a public craving for larger-than-life role models from the distant past. Behind the erudite facade, Ellis discerned a self-righteous, superficial individual, addicted to "platitudinous cant," and given to "hysterical and apocalyptic" outbursts when confronted with difficult decisions that he could not wish away.[48]

In the final analysis, Ellis wrote, Jefferson "combined great depth with great shallowness, massive learning with extraordinary naiveté, piercing insights into others with daunting powers of self-deception."[49] Psychologically, he lived in a state of denial, "a man who was self-deceived, and whose denial mechanisms worked in such a way that he could sincerely say somewhat different things to different people."[50] Yet, as Emily Eakin observed, it was Ellis, not Jefferson, who displayed the ultimate "talent for self-deception."[51]

"THE REAL THING"

To dismiss the Ellis case as a simple example of psychological delusion or bad personal judgment is to ignore the broader didactic and intellectual significance of his transgressions. Ellis's embellishments reflected issues far greater than a personality complex or a personal obsession with the Vietnam War or the 1960s. The most obvious, yet somewhat simplistic, explanation for his conduct was that Ellis was a pretender seeking to enhance personal claims by creating and relating active participation in a defining moment in the nation's past. In this he was not alone. A number of politicians, professors, and other public figures also invented personal experiences in Vietnam, sometimes with tragic consequences.

Edmund Morris, the author of *Dutch*, offered a more compelling cultural explanation for Ellis's behavior. He described it as a reaction to changing strategies of communication in a society where reality and fiction seemed to intertwine. Morris described Ellis's imagined past not as fabrication but as "creative license," an acceptable tool for communicating with his students, whom he described somewhat dismissively as a generation "rendered comatose by MTV. . . . How better to awaken their interest than to say—as the old have been saying to the young since time immemorial—'I know what it was like, I was young then, I felt those passions.' And then by degrees (as the technique begins to work) to add incautiously, 'I was there . . . over there! I flew, I fought!' "[52]

Ellis may have been responding to the enticing siren song of "experiential" history, the learning of the past through "a sensuous form"—experiential archives such as Holocaust museums; historical theme parks; historical films laced with real or pseudo-real footage; and of course the direct encounter with the protagonist or impersonator, who claims an authentic connection to the past. Historical memory in modern American culture, Alison Landsberg explains, is composed of "prosthetic memories," or "memories that circulate publicly, that are not organically based, but are nonetheless experienced with one's body" or mind "by means of a wide range of cultural technologies" and narrative strategies.[53] This sensuous, virtual engagement with the past, Robert Burgoyne argues, has collapsed the distinction between memory and history.

> Memory in the traditional sense, describes an individual's relation to the past, a bodily experience. . . . History, on the other hand, is traditionally conceived as impersonal, the realm of public events that have occurred outside of the archive of personal experience. But in contemporary media culture, the most significant "historical" events are often transformed into "experiences" . . . with the media continually and effortlessly re-presenting the past; history, once thought of as an impersonal phenomenon, has been replaced by "experiential" collective memory.[54]

By offering his students a "physical, literal relationship to actual historical figures"—in this case himself—Ellis encouraged them to learn about the past by experiencing history in a "personal bodily way." Adopting techniques much like those used in movies such as *Zelig* and *Forrest Gump*, Ellis "remastered" the past by grafting his presence into historical episodes. Students responded favorably: "The course was something so central to him because he did serve there, while his experience with Jefferson and Adams is otherworldly, so distant in comparison," one student noted, adding that Ellis's personal experiences in the battlefields of Vietnam and the segregationist South "allowed me to imagine myself in the circumstances he faced."[55] Ellis was immersed, then, in the pervasive public obsession with the "real thing."

The seductiveness of an imaginary persona who appears more authentic than the "real thing" is, of course, neither distinctively contemporary nor distinctively postmodern. Henry James's 1893 short story "The Real Thing," about discontent with a reality that appears less appealing and believable than a contrived facsimile, suggests that there is a certain timelessness to the attractions of verisimilitude. James's story portrays an artist's quest for suitable models for illustrations in a dime novel. When called upon to produce drawings of the English upper class, James's artist decides to employ a couple of "real" members of the aristocracy who happen to be down on their luck. These ostensibly perfect models turn out to be less believable than his usual models, a pair of versatile lower-class actors who portray a multitude of stereotypical and believable characteristics at will. In order to produce persuasive representations, the artist has no recourse for authenticity. Instead he needs people who can convincingly perform the formulaic part. Appearances, the artist realizes, are much more convincing than "the real thing."

Our contemporary culture emphasizes this attraction. Ellis's students, like most of us, obligingly embraced—in fact demanded—a Vietnam veteran, real or imaginary. In an age jaded by reality-like fiction, the comments of a detached scholar, removed from the events by both time and personal circumstances, lacked the immediacy sought by a reality-craving public. "We desperately want to know the truth and to be absolutely certain about it. We want an eyewitness."[56] Simultaneously and somewhat paradoxically, we are attracted to the fake because, as sociologist Sherry Turkle reminds us, "the fake seems more compelling than the real."[57]

If Ellis's autobiographical fictions seemed plausible to himself and others, it is because "so much else in our culture . . . [has] made simulations seem real." The mass media's insistence on high drama, the role-playing associated with communication in cyberspace, and the postmodern affinity with permeable and multiple truths raise the question of an audience's ability and willingness to separate representation from reality, fact from fraud. Such tendencies are compounded by academic fashions. "Down from the academy has trickled the poison of postmodernism," a caustic George Will observed, in which "facts hardly matter, only interpretations are real." Postmodern history, he continued, "invests the historian with the heroism of an artist, creating reality rather than fulfilling the mundane role of describer and interpreter of reality." While basically agreeing with these comments, Joyce Appleby offered an important corrective. The confusion of fact and fiction, interpretation and reality, has not trickled down from the academy; rather, broader cultural trends have affected the academy. History, in particular, and the academy, in general, had been infected by a pervasive "cultural milieu . . . imbued with factoids, infomercials and so on."[58]

THE "PUBLICITY INTELLECTUAL"

Ellis's case is a particularly vivid example of the tenuous status of the media intellectual, a variation of the traditional public intellectual. Unlike the majority of his university colleagues, Ellis is a public figure: a best-selling writer and TV personality. By virtue of his professional duality—media celebrity and serious scholar—he has allowed himself to comment on issues beyond his field of expertise, often with dubious consequences. He is a "publicity intellectual."[59]

In contrast to the mythic generation of American public intellectuals in the 1940s and 1950s, David Samuels has observed, today's breed of media-savvy publicity intellectuals "exercise their talents not in the writing of poetry, fiction, history, or essays, but in the fabrication" of intellectually pretentious tomes for high-profile media outlets. While traditional public intellectuals were persons whose profundity and erudite "ideas gained them some measure of public significance, the order now is abruptly reversed." The media intellectual achieves celebrity by simplifying ideas and reducing complex issues to a sound bite.[60] Contrary to the conventional public intellectual—a social critic and demystifier—the media intellectual is a provider of easily digestible, intellectually distracting infotainment.

This new species of public intellectuals, Jean Bethke Elshtain observes, are more public and less intellectual.[61] They willingly indulge in fanciful ruminations, because, as Richard Posner has observed, there is no meaningful price "for getting it wrong"; tenure removes accountability. As providers of cerebral "punditry for the people," the media intellectuals privilege voyeurism over insight and offer confessionals rather than social critique. The fruits of celebrity and the pleasures of media exposure have, according to Posner, undermined the rigor and acuity of the current generation of publicity intellectuals, whose main assets appear to be radiophonic voices, photogenic qualities, and a predilection for pontificating on any and every subject.[62]

Among the many varieties of publicity intellectual, the media historian has the task of presenting to the public dissertations on great men and great ideas. The subjects of such historians are giants who make them feel effete and insignificant by comparison. To compensate for such inadequacies, some historians cut their heroes down to size. Others, Mark Oppenheimer has observed, puff themselves up by telling feckless stories in which truth is only of secondary importance.

Like other celebrities, intellectuals who frequent the media are flirting with personal disaster. Fame entails the construction of a media persona in which imagination and creativity play a significant part. Contrary to the reclusive intellectual—a marginalized person in contemporary, anti-intellectual American society—the publicity intellectual thrives on adulation. Ellis sought adulation by claiming to actually have made history, rather than merely interpreting it.[63]

Being an intellectual and a historian, observed Peter Rollins, is to "study and . . . think," and to "share ideas orally and in print." Intellectuals do not have to be public figures and they do not have to be the scorers of winning touchdowns or warriors." By contrast, David Garrow observes, the power of media exposure drives the public intellectual "who ought to know better than to go with the most dramatic or memorable version of an historical story"—personal and public—rather than with the most plausible account or even the plain truth.[64] A historian who tries to play the roles of both scholar and publicity intellectual may find that the two collide disastrously.

SERGEANT ELLIS

The Joseph Ellis scandal is now a fading memory. By March 2002, Ellis was back on the media wagon, reviewing books for prestigious publications.[65] Mount Holyoke announced Ellis's return to the classroom for the fall semester in 2002, one year after a self-imposed leave of absence.

An American citizen by the name of Joseph Ellis did, however, serve in Vietnam. Army Sergeant Harry Joseph III Ellis served in the 173rd Airborne Brigade until March 14, 1968. He was stationed in Kontum, Binh Dinh province, South Vietnam. Born on

January 6, 1947, in Atco, New Jersey, Ellis attended Camden Catholic High School, where he was a member of the baseball team. Sergeant Ellis is inscribed on panel 44E, row 45, of the Vietnam Veterans Memorial Wall in Washington, D.C.[66] He died by friendly fire.

PART II

Scandals in Anthropology

FOUR

The Ghost of Caliban

Derek Freeman and "the Fateful Hoaxing of
Margaret Mead"

It is hard to reach the truth in these islands.
Robert Louis Stevenson, Samoa (1892)

In 1983, Derek Freeman, a New Zealand anthropologist, became
an instant media star, with appearances on the front page of most
major metropolitan newspapers and magazines—including cover
stories in *Time*, *Life*, and the *New York Times*—and commercial
TV. Freeman achieved celebrity with his sensationalist debunking
of Margaret Mead, the anthropologist, social reformer, and symbol of the revolution in sexual mores, gender relations, and child-
nurturing practices in midcentury America. In his somewhat be-
lated critique of *Coming of Age in Samoa*, Mead's famous 1928
study of adolescence in a premodern, non-Western society, Freeman claimed that Mead's portrayal of a trouble-free, sexually permissive coming-of-age in a South Sea paradise was ideologically

biased and poorly researched, a hoax foisted upon a young inexperienced woman by mischievous adolescent informants. Moreover, Freeman portrayed Mead as a compliant victim of this hoax; he said that it suited her worldview and politics.

MARGARET MEAD'S SAMOA

Freeman began his indictment of Margaret Mead's anthropological iniquities with the year 1925, when the twenty-three-year-old Mead arrived in Samoa, where she intended to study the role of biological and cultural determinants of human behavior. Guided by her mentor, Franz Boas, Mead planned to challenge the "adolescent stress hypothesis," the assumption that the stormy, rebellious period of adolescence was an inevitable stage of biological development and had little, if anything, to do with social conditioning or cultural influences. Given her Boasian wariness of biological determinism, Mead saw the Samoans as the perfect subjects for assessing the relative merits of nature and nurture. Samoan culture was significantly different from the American milieu in which the biologically deterministic theories of adolescence in particular and human behavior in general had been developed. Moreover, the village she had selected for study appeared to be still unspoiled by the complexities of modernism. In a "primitive" and culturally uncontaminated Samoa, Mead would not have to untangle the intricate variables and uncertainties confronting researchers in modern Western surroundings.

Mead's fieldwork was based on the "deceptively simple methodological approach called the 'negative instance' or the 'anthropological veto'—that is, the attempt to find a single negative case that could disprove an axiom" or paradigm, "such as the universality and biological basis of adolescent stress," and refute genetically deterministic theories of human behavior in general.[1] Following her nine-month sojourn in Samoa, Mead declared that she indeed had found it. She reported that adolescence in Samoa was an idyllic, stress-free period, characterized by minimal responsibilities, casual sexual experimentation, and harmonious family and community relations, an experience that stood in stark contrast to its Western counterpart. She argued that, unlike the turbulent period of adolescence in America, which experts tended to assign to transitional hormonal change, adolescence among Samoans was free of stress and storm.

Mead claimed that the only viable explanation for such markedly different behavioral patterns was "social environment." Contrasting experiences of adolescence, she argued, were the result of different cultural circumstances: a relaxed attitude toward sex, the comforting presence of a nonstressful and extended family environment, and the noncompetitive nature of Samoan society.

> The Samoan background, which makes growing up so easy, so simple a matter, is the general casualness of the whole society. For Samoa is a place where no one plays for very high stakes. . . . Disagreements between parent and child are settled by the child's moving across the street, between a man and his village by the man's removal to the next village, between a husband and his wife's seducer by a few fine mats. . . . In personal relations caring is slight. Love and hate, jealousy and revenge, sorrow and bereavement are all matters of weeks. From the first months of its life, when the child is handed carelessly from one woman's hand to another's, the lesson is learnt of not caring for one person greatly, not setting high hopes on any one relationship.[2]

Mead offered provocative glimpses of the casual "familiarity with sex" and its fostering of "a scheme of personal relations in which there are no neurotic pictures, no frigidity, no impotence," or any of the other sexual dysfunctions prevalent in the West. She also produced titillating descriptions of the "very brittle monogamy" of adult Samoans, "often trespassed" with casual instances of adultery that "hardly threaten the continuity of established relations." In matters of sex, Mead's girl informants were "perplexed by no conflicts, troubled by no philosophical queries, beset by no remote ambitions. To live as a girl with many lovers as long as possible and then to marry in one's own village, near one's own relatives, and to have many children," was a uniformly accepted cultural pattern and one of the main reasons for the sedate ways of Samoan culture.[3]

Samoan adolescence and family life, as portrayed in Mead's *Coming of Age in Samoa*, contrasted sharply with the American experience. Growing up in American society, a sharply critical Mead observed, created a "battlefield mentality where each group is fully armored in a conviction of the righteousness of its cause." The "tiny ingrown biological" American family, with its crippling monopolization and regularization of emotions and its unwavering contrasting of "its closed circle of affection" to a hostile world, fostered among its adolescents a whole series of emotional afflictions, psychological maladjustments, and sexually obsessive behavior patterns that were nonexistent in the emotionally libertarian Samoan culture.[4]

Mead's ostensibly professional observations achieved unusually widespread public exposure. With its provocative conclusions, *Coming of Age* swiftly achieved the status of a foundational text for studying a range of social transitions in midcentury

America, such as the rise of feminism, changes in sexual mores, and the revolution in child-rearing practices. Most important of all, *Coming of Age* was highly influential in instilling notions of cultural relativism, weakening the hold of racist concepts, and piercing the parochialism of the American mind. The book "contained within itself" what Nancy Scheper-Hughes has described as the "very *American* notion that one can tinker with and change one's society, one's social, economic, and political destiny. It 'fit' the American ideal of the *self-made* man or woman."[5]

The enthusiastic reception of *Coming of Age* transformed the young Mead into an authority within her discipline. Although occasionally confronted with critiques of the methodological apparatus of her work, she was untouchable. Whatever professional misgivings existed were swept aside by public acclaim. Mead's work was the ultimate example of what Peter Worsley has called "the classic anthropological 'project': the demonstration that anthropology is not a purely scholastic discipline fixated on the study of exotic cultures and customs 'out there,' " with little relevance beyond the pale of a community of experts. Instead, Mead skillfully provoked meaningful self-reflection within American society, as well the realization that the "culture of the United States was only one among very many cultural forms" and not "necessarily the culmination of human evolution."[6]

Derek Freeman was a founding member of a small but persistent cohort of the unimpressed. Beginning in 1963, when Mead visited Australia, and until her death in 1978, Freeman confronted Mead with exhaustive inquiries and challenges concerning the data and methodological underpinnings of *Coming of Age*. Freeman claimed that his interrogations were neither personal nor political. As a novice, he had arrived in Samoa in 1940 "very much a cultural determinist" in the Margaret Mead tradition. His first major academic article declared that the "aims and desires which determine behavior are all derived from the social environment." Freeman recounted that only after several years of living in Samoa—during which he had acquired a fluent command of the language and culture, when he was writing his dissertation, "The Social Structure of a Samoan Village Community"—he "became aware of the extent of the discordance between Mead's account (in which I had hitherto unquestioningly believed) and the realities that I was regularly witnessing."[7]

When Mead paid a visit to the Australian National University in 1963, Freeman spoke to her of his misgivings, informing her of his intentions to publish his findings. Although the two anthropologists corresponded sporadically until Mead's death, Freeman reserved publication of his findings, doubts, and accusations, claiming "other anthropological interests and academic responsibilities."[8]

In 1983, Freeman made his concerns public in a scathing critique published by Harvard University Press. Freeman's book was a far cry from the genteel exchange of views he had held with Mead since their first encounter. His ostensibly scientific refutation questioned Mead's personal and professional integrity and her commitment to objective scientific inquiry. She had, according to a Freeman partisan, confused her "role as a scientist with her roles of prophet and propagandist for her vision of utopia."[9]

To begin with, Freeman accused Mead of practicing a shallow form of anthropological inquiry. Mead, he observed, had spent no more than nine months in Samoa, living in the sheltered household of an American naval official. She never mastered the language; her contact with her informants was selective and mostly held through translators and intermediaries. Regarding Mead's assertion in *Coming of Age* that "biological variables are of no significance in the etiology of adolescent behavior," Freeman wrote that it was "preposterous" and "contrary to nature, reason, or common sense." Her "unfactual" and patently false dismissal of the biological roots of human behavior was primarily a political project, bereft of any meaningful scientific validation.[10]

Mead, he claimed, had arrived in Samoa with her conclusions already formed. Her main objective in Samoa was to provide ethnographic evidence to support the theories of her mentor, Franz Boas, on the cultural origins of human behavior. According to Freeman, Boas had staked his reputation on proving that human behavior was not rooted in biology but rather was determined by culture. In sharp contrast to the dogmatic and politically pernicious eugenic paradigm of biological determinism, Franz Boas impressed upon his students the argument that "the social stimulus is infinitely more potent than the biological mechanism." Yet Boas's motives were not purely scientific. In the early twentieth century, "the eugenics movement had effloresced into a pseudo-scientific cult, and Boas had come to see both eugenics and the racial interpretation of history as irremediably dangerous." Boas's solution, according to Freeman, was the cultivation of an extreme doctrine of "absolute cultural determinism" that totally excluded biological variables.[11]

Mead's study of adolescence in Samoa provided ample evidence for Boas's views on cultural determinism. Yet, according to Freeman, Mead's texts were distortions—willful or otherwise—of the meager data she had collected. The fact that her conclusions were poorly researched was of little importance to Boas, Freeman argued, because they supported his stance. On numerous occasions, and in different published venues, Boas publicly and conspicuously lavished praise on Mead's "painstaking investigation."[12]

Freeman was particularly indignant with Mead's portrayal of Samoa as an idyllic paradise, especially for its youth, who benefited emotionally from a permissive atmosphere of sexual experimentation. He declared that Mead's findings had little to do with reality. The Samoan society of his own, ostensibly objective research was as violent, sexually repressive, and highly competitive as any Western society. Freeman's Samoa suffered from a whole range of pathological behaviors, including high rates of rape, suicide, and murder. As far as Freeman was concerned, the Samoans were an unusually bellicose people. Delving back into the accounts of nineteenth-century missionaries and explorers, Freeman presented a Samoan culture addicted to warfare and quite casual about the use of the most extreme measures of violence.

As for the source of Mead's portrayal of a sexually permissive Samoan adolescence, Freeman cited the testimony of Fa'apua'a Fa'amū, who claimed to have been one of Mead's primary informants. In dramatic fashion, the by-then elderly Samoan woman swore that her tales of sexual license as revealed before the young Mead had been merely an adolescent prank. The young girls' bragging of sexual permissiveness had been nothing more than "recreational lying" foisted upon a gullible white girl.[13] Freeman claimed that Samoan attitudes toward sex were, to the contrary, quite puritanical and were driven by a widespread obsession with chastity among potential brides. Freeman presented a Samoan society in which the virginity of an adolescent girl, "whatever her rank," was jealously guarded by family members, "especially at night." Moreover, he observed that among Mead's twenty-five girl informants, more than half "were virgins on

Mead's own evidence." Freeman offered high court records from American Samoa as proof that "in the prudish Christian society of Samoa in the 1920s, sexual intercourse between unmarried persons was held to be both a sin and a crime."[14] Freeman also dismissed Mead's assertion that "adultery was not regarded as very serious" as "seriously in error." Once again, he offered legal evidence from the 1920s of fines leveled against offenders—both men and women—as well as recollections of extralegal punishments, such as expulsion and the confiscation of property.[15]

Freeman further denied Mead's portrayal of Samoan family structures as loose, almost informal, with large extended families, many alternative authority figures, informal adoption of children, and a general indulgence of adolescence and childhood foibles. Reported patterns of child swapping and weak parent-infant bonds were, he claimed, the results of Mead's disregard for fundamental biological facts, such as the innate and universal maternal instinct. Mead, he argued, was an enthusiastic and blind follower of behaviorist J. B. Watson, who condemned the Western mode of the mother-infant bond for fostering a destructive dependency and insularity that left the child unable to cope with "real" human relations. Watson had convinced Mead that an optimally adjusted child grew up in a society with loose bonds between offspring and mother, which, according to Watson, would transform the period of adolescence into "just a stretch of fertile years."[16] Contrary to Mead's depiction of the well-adjusted Samoan child, free of emotional bonds to biological parents, Freeman discovered strong infant-mother relations that were no different from those in Western cultures. In an incident that he was fond of repeating, Freeman and his wife conducted a "simple experiment of having the women of an extended family walk away from an infant one at a time. The agitated reaction of the infant to being separated from its mother (and her alone) demonstrated that attachment in Samoa, as elsewhere, is with but rare exceptions monotropic."[17] After Freeman "taxed" Mead about this matter, "Dr. Mead confessed in a letter dated New York, 2 December, that 'unfortunately' in Samoa she 'did not study infancy or early childhood,' " and that her assertions were, at best, unverified impressions.[18] This instance, he explained, was typical of Mead's frivolous and imaginary accounts of Samoan culture.

Freeman claimed authority for his interpretation by virtue of the many years he had spent in Samoa, during which he had been adopted by a local family and had been elected to the council of elders. His superior knowledge of Samoan culture, his command of the local language, and the fact that he was a male researcher in a male-oriented society stood in stark contrast to Mead's secluded and brief sojourn and her exclusive reliance on adolescent female informants, he asserted. In addition, he claimed that Mead's interest in Samoan culture was marginal. Her main purpose was to find—and, if necessary, invent—a basis for recommending the restructuring of American society and its child-rearing practices.

Freeman argued that the gap separating his objective and scientifically valid portrayal of Samoan society from Mead's flight of fancy originated in Mead's politically driven and scientifically invalid rejection of the biological origins of human behavior. As a cultural determinist, Mead ruled out "any consideration of the relevance of biological variables" for explaining "highly complex and quite imperfectly understood anthropological phenomena." Her motives, however noble, were unscientific, a reflection of ideological concerns that had little place in a discipline dedicated to truth seeking.[19]

Freeman hastened to add that he was far from being a counterrevolutionary biological determinist. To him, the only meaningful scientific course for analyzing human behavior lay in a fusion of biological and cultural explanations.

> The doctrine of cultural determinism was formulated in the second decade of the twentieth century in deliberate reaction to the equally unscientific doctrine of extreme biological determinism. We must thus identify biological determinism as the thesis to which cultural determinism was the antithesis. The time is now conspicuously due, in both anthropology and biology, for a synthesis in which there will be, in the study of human behavior, recognition of the radical importance of both the genetic and exogenetic and their interaction, both in the past history of the human species and in our problematic future.[20]

FREEMAN'S CRITICS

Predictably, Freeman's representations of Mead's lapses were subject to a swift and harsh counterattack. Mead's defenders denounced Freeman's exposition as a pure and simple "vendetta against a woman whose immense authority had kept his own research in obscurity for so long." His tactics were particularly annoying to Mead's supporters because he had waited until "Mead could no longer defend herself" before unleashing his "yellow anthropology." He was accused of manipulating the thirst for fallen gods in order to "catapult himself" into celebrity. His fame was not due to any original contribution to the field but rather was the result of sensationalistic criticism of a colleague. "I think it is a sad day for anthropology and science in general," the Mead partisan Lowell Holmes observed, "when an individual who studies another's work states in a nationally published interview . . . that as a result of his efforts he expects Margaret Mead's reputation to 'do a 32' (32 feet per second being the rate at which fallen bodies accelerate toward earth)."[21]

Freeman's call for a fusionist approach to the study of human behavior, based on coherent interfaces between biology and culture, was dismissed as mere regurgitation of the work of others. Moreover, Freeman's depiction of Mead as the ultimate example of a cultural determinist was, according to critics, either willful distortion or the fruit of pure ignorance.

Critics argued that his distortions began with his misrepresentation of the legacy of Franz Boas. Freeman offered a simplistic portrayal of Boas as an embattled ideologist "faced with the unrelenting attacks of biological determinists, who retreated from open-mindedness to an unscientific dogmatism crowned in 1928" by the work of his protégé in Samoa. This simplistic version of Mead's mentor, a critical Richard Handler observed, imperiously glossed over Boas's significant contributions to biological anthropology. Freeman had cavalierly effaced the extensive research that Boas devoted to "isolating hereditary from environmental influences, and the reconciliation with biology effected by some Boasians in the 1930s."[22]

As for his reading of *Coming of Age*, Freeman was accused of taking the sexual aspects of the book out of context. Freeman, Holmes noted, had focused single-mindedly on sex, as if this were the sole preoccupation of Mead's book, whereas *Coming of Age* was a rich and multifaceted study replete with "a full account of child rearing and discipline, of typical activities and interests of Samoan children of all ages, of family structure and the interaction of its members, of courtship and marriage and of what is expected of young people by the age-mates, families, community and church."[23] Freeman ignored such apparently mundane matters, Holmes complained, in order to focus on sex—the one subject guaranteed to attract the attention of the mass media.

Freeman was also accused of ignoring much of Mead's scientific writing on Samoa. *Coming of Age*, Mead defenders explained, was a book aimed at the general public rather than the scientific community. Had Freeman bothered to read her scientific papers on Samoa, as well as her notes and private correspondence—"available for almost a year before the book's publication"—he would have discovered that "Mead never denied that there is a biological, especially a hormonal, basis to adolescence." She merely rejected the notion that "adolescence is simply a period of physiological puberty."[24]

Even Mead's most ardent supporters acknowledged that Mead had exaggerated and oversimplified the idyllic life of Samoa. Yet, they argued, a careful reading of the book revealed a complex depiction of Samoan society replete with tensions, psychological stress, and clashing cultural imperatives. Had Freeman been somewhat less obsessed with Mead and her sexual mores, and somewhat more engaged with her work, he would have discovered that *Coming of Age* was indeed "two books in one." At one level, indeed, it was a book of broad generalizations and a certain amount of exaggeration aimed at capturing the attention of a middlebrow audience. Mead belonged to a generation of scholars who believed that it was the duty of intellectuals and scientists to make specialized knowledge accessible to laypersons. Under these circumstances exaggeration and embellishments were inevitable hazards. But *Coming of Age* was also a book replete with insight and complexity. Throughout the book, Mead qualified her generalizations and oversimplifications with sensitive observations on the frustrations of growing up in a society that offered little personal freedom beyond youthful sexual experimentation. Even in her conclusions, in which she derived lessons from Samoa for contemporary American society, a sympathetic Richard Feinberg discovered level-headed assessments of paradise and its discontents. Mead argued that "among Samoans stress is mitigated at the expense of individuality, while emotional equilibrium and sexual adjustment are maintained at the expense of creativity and romantic love. And this, contrary to the popular view, she viewed as too high a price to pay."[25]

If Mead seemed more concerned with contemporary American society than with her Samoan informants, her defenders argued, that was simply the climate in which anthropology in the United States was practiced at the time. Anthropology was a vehicle for reflection and self-examination. In the spirit of her times, she approached her craft as a tool for "defamiliarizing home, a heuristic enabling readers to gain distance on the cultural truths they hold as natural."[26] Thus, to judge her work in accordance with the standards and objectives of latter-day anthropology—with its single-minded goal of discovering the proverbial other—was at best anachronistic.

According to Freeman's critics, his insistence that his fieldwork of the early 1940s and mid-1960s refuted the observations of Mead's 1920s study was misleading. Moreover, differences between their findings could be explained by significant social and geographical differences in their areas of study. Freeman had worked in Western (British) Samoa, whereas Mead had been stationed in American Samoa. Mead's island, Ta'u, was over two hundred miles away from Upolu, where Freeman conducted his research. Ta'u was remote, sparsely populated, and rugged; Upolu was densely settled, accessible, and more subject to outside influences.

Freeman was also accused of practicing the very type of politically driven anthropology he had ascribed to Mead and her mentor. He was labeled a sexist for his dismissal of Mead's informants as frivolous and unreliable young girls, as well as for his portrayal of Mead as an immature girl psychologically dependent on her mentor. In contrast, the Berkeley anthropologist Bonnie Nardi portrayed Mead as a sexually assertive, independently minded, and towering intellectual figure, whose trip to Samoa represented a rebellion against the gendered mores of her times and a defiance of two significant representatives of male authority in her life— her father and Franz Boas—who had both disapproved of her Samoan trip. As for the criticism of Mead's reliance on female informants, Nardi argued that Freeman's informants—all of them male—were equally restricted. The assumption that his male informants were somehow more reliable than Mead's "frivolous" girls was more a reflection of Freeman's personal bias than of some objective insight.[27]

Freeman was criticized as well for his harsh and mostly insulting description of his adopted society. Other Pacific ethnographers never validated his depiction of Samoan society as disrupted by ruthless competition, oppressed by strong authoritarian currents, and riddled with psychopathology. In contrast to Mead's easygoing, promiscuous Samoa, Freeman offered an alarming portrait of a male-oriented culture addicted to "rape" and other demeaning sexual customs, with little supporting evidence offered.

Freeman's objective, critics argued, was not merely personal fame and fortune. His discontents were also political and ideological. Freeman barely controlled his personal antipathy toward Mead—the "totemic mother"—and her cultlike status among cultural anthropologists and American liberals. Her mesmerized followers, he argued, had transformed her pop anthropology into a "sacred text" and her shallow cultural determinism into the "hallowed dogma" of the decadent age of liberation in American society.[28] "In Freeman's fable," a critical Virginia Yans-McLaughlin wrote, "Mead's Samoa, the lush land of plenty and sexual liberty, represents liberalism and its failure. Conversely, Freeman's harsher, more violent Samoa . . . warns for reconsideration of the biological and economic limits of human societies, of the futility in trying to transform them, of the necessity to return to more conservative family, religious, and sexual controls."[29]

The reaction to Freeman's study, then, was more a reflection of a changing culture than an acknowledgment of Freeman's superior research. Much like Mead's, Freeman's book was only marginally concerned with engaging an academic issue. His ultimate concerns were "the social descendants of the readership of *Coming of Age*," who were beset with doubts and discontents concerning the political message of Mead's study.[30] Skepticism about the type of cultural determinism that permeated Mead's study was born out of the "pessimistic spirit of the 1980s" and the attraction of sociobiological theories concerning the innate "determinants of sex roles, temperament, intelligence, and achievements."[31] Discontent with the values associated with Mead's text provided the context for a political debunking of her work.

Driven by his antipathy toward Mead's "hallowed dogma," Freeman attributed frivolous motives to all of Mead's Samoan observations and research strategies. Thus, he described Mead's decision to live with an American family rather than among her informants as a sign of personal and scientific immaturity. He apparently failed to note Mead's own reasons for this decision. Living apart from her informants, Mead explained in the acknowledgments section of *Coming of Age*, allowed her to study dispassionately "all of the individuals in the village and yet remain aloof from native feuds and demarcations."[32] Seeking distance from informants was considered an appropriate practice in the anthropology in the 1920s.

Freeman's detractors denied that their critique was the result of an instinctive defense of a "mother goddess." Indeed, prior to Freeman's critique of Mead, other anthropologists had questioned her scientific integrity without the furor of Freeman's publications. Freeman's first book was published contemporaneously (in 1983) with Richard Goodman's *Mead's Coming of Age in Samoa: A Dissenting View*. In 1996, Martin Orans published *Not Even Wrong*, in which he lashed out at Mead's Samoan research as so oversimplified that it was "not even wrong"; it was, moreover, "seriously flawed" and littered "with internal contradictions and grandiose claims to knowledge that she could not possibly have had."[33]

Goodman's solid yet polite critique was all but ignored, and the work of Orans barely rippled the academic waters. Derek Freeman explained why. Orans and Goodman, he claimed, had erred in their decision to avoid any personal "appraisal" of Mead herself.[34] Freeman, by contrast, peppered his scientific analysis with personal attacks, innuendo, and links between Mead's intellectual persona and questionable aspects of her personal life. Apparently dissatisfied that his methodological critique of *Coming of Age* would achieve the necessary resonance, Freeman laced his exposé with revelations concerning Mead's marital infidelity and her alleged lesbian relationship with Ruth Benedict.

Critics lashed out at Freeman and his Harvard publishers for luring the attention of the media with sex, violence, aggression, and the ever-popular sight of lapsed gods and fallen idols.[35] Such misgivings notwithstanding, Freeman's tactics were superbly successful. Exaggeration, innuendo, and the personalization of an academic dispute riveted broad public attention, bypassed mechanisms for debate within the discipline, and led to Freeman being showered with accolades that eluded more conventional colleagues.

An intriguing element of the criticism was the portrayal of Freeman as an obscure and parochial New Zealander, a marginal figure from the academic backwaters of Australia. Such marginality paradoxically made Freeman exotic and interesting and bolstered interest in his position. The battle for Mead's unquestioning authority was a lost cause. By the 1980s, a multicentered and sharply split anthropological guild had little energy for defending its founding fathers and mothers.

The controversy was uneasily resolved by agreeing upon the "Rashomon effect," the acceptance of multiple, clashing, yet equally valid interpretations of an event.[36] This somewhat unsatisfactory compromise suggested that Freeman and Mead had captured different and seemingly irreconcilable aspects of Samoan society without realizing its capacity for complexity and contradiction. Even Martin Orans, one of Mead's harshest critics, noted that Freeman was "certainly aware of aspects of Samoan ethos and practice" that supported at least some of Mead's assertions, and he was "certainly aware that even neighboring villages may differ in precept and practice."[37] Advocates of the Rashomon effect concluded that Mead and Freeman had each captured a Samoan truth but not *the* Samoan truth, which was complex, diffuse, and subject to continuous revision.

Thus, on the issue of sexuality, Freeman's study offered the version of public morality endorsed by mature, male leaders of Samoan society, while Mead had "access to the 'backstage' performance—the views" and perhaps even the behavioral norms of adolescents and girls. The Samoan obsession with virginity, as portrayed by Freeman, was, then, "important at the level of ideology"; reality was somewhat more complex, less monolithic, and significantly more permissive.[38] Truth was a by-product of positionality, chronology, and geography. Neither Mead nor Freeman offered timeless truths. Both had constructed selective portrayals of two very different angles of Samoan society.[39]

While ostensibly presented as a compromise based on empirical research, the Rashomon interpretation acknowledged the lack of authority in a multicentered academic world. According to George Marcus, a founding father of postmodern cultural anthropology, competing interpretations of Samoan culture were not a sign of epistemological crisis but rather the very essence of anthropological knowledge. The "real myth" was the expectation of a single truth, the very notion that there can be only "one an-

thropologist to one tribe." Thus, he noted somewhat conde-
scendingly, Freeman's sweeping revisionism, with its intolerance
of alternatives, was quaintly "old-fashioned."[40]

Mead and Freeman shared common assumptions often ignored during the controversy. Both anthropologists assumed that
they could decipher primitive cultures without acknowledging
the destabilizing influence of outside forces, in particular, the
forces of colonization and "its thinly veiled successor, called economic dependence." Rather than meticulously describing Samoa,
both Freeman and Mead had created the image of a distant culture demanded by their own particular social and political milieu.
Both were involved in the "invention of culture," the reframing,
translation, and ultimate distortion of distant mores into the familiar terminology of the metropolis.[41] Both Mead's construction
of the gentle savage and Freeman's portrait of the pathologically
violent Samoan had far-reaching political consequences. "Despite
the sharp contrasts in their presentations," Eleanor Leacock has
observed, "both provided images that could easily be incorporated into ideologies used by the West to rationalize" its claim to
superiority and cultural hegemony.[42]

Moreover, by the very act of their visible reporting on Samoan
culture, both Mead and Freeman had altered life in Samoa beyond recognition. Both sought to convey Samoa as a remnant of
a pristine culture, relatively unspoiled by the forces of Western
civilization. Both chose to understate their role as authoritative,
imperious interpreters of the primitive other. Whatever their
differences, both scholars detrimentally affected the Samoans'
self-image and the framing of their culture in the public eye.

Whether Samoa was a promiscuous and primitive Eden, or
conversely, "a violent, competitive, extremely puritanical, delin-

quent, rape and suicide prone, Jehovah dominated" society was, as far as Mead and Freeman were concerned, beside the point.[43] Their concerns lay elsewhere. In their haste to promote pet theories, personal politics, and scholastic reputations, Mead, Freeman, and their respective partisans implicitly acknowledged that Samoa per se was of little interest to them beyond its role as a control group in an inquiry centered somewhere else.

CALIBAN'S ISLAND

As Frank Miele has observed, the Mead-Freeman controversy was an illustration of the unhappy fate of anthropology "marooned on Caliban's Island."[44] Miele was referring to *The Tempest*, William Shakespeare's tale of Prospero, Duke of Milan, forced into exile on an island inhabited by spirits and by Caliban, the man-beast. Prospero, who rules over the island, describes Caliban "as a born devil, on whose nature, nurture can never stick." Unable to accept Prospero's verdict, yet unwilling to reject it, anthropology remains haunted by a paralyzing nature-nurture identity crisis.

The impasse of the nature-nurture controversy is only partially a scientific issue. Many of the highly charged briefs of both genetic determinists and culturalists are political texts and ideological manifestos, in which science plays only a supporting role. The transformation of the nature-nurture controversy into a middlebrow tempest is the result of the posturing of eminent and often brilliant scientists who should have known better. Some advocates of both positions are celebrities, recognized by the general public for their polemics and entertaining performances rather than their scientific acumen.

Stanford University's Paul Ehrlich, one of the most celebrated critics of genetic determinism, is a case in point. Ehrlich initially gained public recognition with his provocative book *The Population Bomb* (1968), in which he predicted a Malthusian collapse of the human population in the 1980s.[45] Since the 1970s Ehrlich has revised but never abandoned his doomsday predictions, merely pushing back the timetable for catastrophe.[46]

Ehrlich—whose sensational prophecies have transformed him into a media star—has offered equally entertaining observations on the nature-nurture controversy. According to Ehrlich, genetic evolution has had little effect on human behavior. Our shared genetic heritage, he explains, has not produced a shared human nature. While acknowledging the role of genes in constructing the human brain, Ehrlich maintains that the very flexible human organism has produced an infinitely flexible variety of "natures," which are primarily the product of environmental conditions. Human beings may indeed be "biologically singular," but they are also "culturally plural." Such thoughtful observations are, however, entwined with irrelevant dissertations on World War II in the Pacific theater, a mystifying pronouncement on the evolving "nature" of postwar Japanese society, and a soaring speculation on the origins of capitalism, all of which are tied to his belief that the human genome has a modest role in dictating behavior.[47] As for the "the flood of literature" among evolutionary anthropologists and other adherents of behavioral genetics who claim that human nature is programmed by natural selection, Ehrlich dismisses these claims as "just-so stories," sociobiological folklore masquerading as a scientific explanation on the origins of human behavior.[48]

A similar situation exists on the other side of the scientific tracks. There, Stephen Pinker of MIT, the author of several popular books on human cognition and evolutionary psychology, produces, like a number of other researchers, tangential connections between his views on human nature and just about everything else. Unwilling to limit himself to a scientific refutation of the "modern denial of human nature," Pinker attributes all the malaise of contemporary society to the machinations of blank-slaters, those who believe that the human species acquires all its knowledge socially. As far as Pinker is concerned, blank-slaters are not merely scientifically wrong. Their preaching of alternative, pseudoscientific theories is responsible for most of the political atrocities and cultural travesties of modern times, including totalitarianism, poor child-rearing, the scourge of relativism, postmodernism, and, of course, modern art.[49]

Pinker's attacks on his adversaries suggest a significant reason for the irreconcilable differences of culturalists and biologically inclined interpretations: the rift is more political than scientific. Between the lines of their scientific expositions, evolutionary scientists and other members of the nature camp preach a doctrine of limits and boundaries. Evolutionary sciences appear to celebrate rather than merely describe the primal role of "family ties, the limited scope of communal sharing, and the universality of . . . ethnocentrism," to mention but a few of the most common themes. The nature camp "has shown human nature to be fixed, human beings to be flawed and human politics constrained by the inadequacies of the human psyche." Most proevolutionary texts, Kenan Malik explains, celebrate a limitation of "political horizons" and a recourse "to science to explain why we cannot do certain things rather than to politics to see how we can."[50]

By contrast, culturalists approach the notion of limitations "as artifact," the product of political cant rather than human nature. They dismiss the notion of human beings as preprogrammed "gene machines"—a mechanical species impervious to modification via nurture—not because it is scientifically unsound, but because it fosters a deadening conservative political agenda; it legitimizes inequality and promotes a resignation to the injustices of this world. In the liberal mind, human beings possess consciousness and agency, and are endowed with the mental faculties to transcend the limitations of nature. Public acceptance of Richard Dawkins's "selfish genes" and "blind watchmakers" encourages disenchantment with altruistic premises of social organization. According to culturalists, the concept of organisms mechanically pursuing their own selfish interests, completely indifferent— "blind"—to any greater cause than self-reproduction, encourages the politically pernicious view that alternative social arrangements that pursue anything but personal gain and isolation are destined to fail.

The politically charged nature of the debate allows little ground for compromise. As a scientific controversy, the nature-nurture debate is impoverished by the monolithic stance of both positions; in political discourse, such isolationism is almost inevitable. In strictly scientific terms, Kenan Malik argues, there appears to be ample evidence that while humans are shaped by both nature and nurture, "we are also defined by our ability to transcend both" and by a unique "ability to overcome the constraints imposed both by our genetic and our cultural heritage." Such an explanation may make scientific sense, but is politically unacceptable.[51] Even though "both parties to the debate, or at any rate their more clearheaded representatives, are completely committed to the view that humans develop as a consequence of countless interactions between their biological endowment and their environment," John Dupre notes sadly, each side compulsively "portrays the other as benightedly monistic."[52]

For all of the above, and for reasons that are only remotely related to scientific rigor, anthropologists of all persuasions have demonstrated a reluctance to join forces in demystifying the mythical Caliban. The rift separating concepts of human beings as independent moral agents or as creatures at the mercy of biological forces is too politically charged to invite compromise, scientific or otherwise.

FIVE

Violent People and Gentle Savages

The Yanomami Controversy

In the summer of 2000, a sensational e-mail hurtled through cyberspace, igniting in the process one of the most acrimonious controversies of academic wrongdoing in recent years. In their electronic communication, Cornell professor of anthropology Terry Turner and his University of Hawaii colleague, Leslie Sponsel, advised the chief officers of the American Anthropological Association of a pending book documenting "sheer criminality and corruption . . . unparalleled in the history of anthropology." Written by journalist Patrick Tierney, the book accused senior American academics working in the rain forests of South America of being the protagonists of a "nightmarish story—a real anthropological heart of darkness beyond the imagining of even a Josef [sic] Conrad (though not perhaps a Josef Mengele)."[1] Within days, this missive had spread in a viruslike fashion throughout the electronic networks of American academia, also weaving its way into the mainstream media. Well before its publication date, the mostly unseen contents of the Tierney galleys were the subject of acrimonious public debate and anxious soul-searching among anthropologists.

Tierney's book, *Darkness in El Dorado: How Scientists and Journalists Devastated the Amazon,* accused the recently deceased geneticist James Neel of aiding and abetting the spread of a deadly measles epidemic among the Yanomami, an indigenous people inhabiting the Amazon River basin spanning Brazil and Venezuela. Tierney accused Neel of engaging in epidemiological experimentation rather than attempting to contain the disease. Tierney' s prepublication manuscript—as seen by Turner, Sponsel, and other privileged insiders—argued that Neel had deliberately inoculated the Yanomami with a faulty vaccine as part of a U.S. government genetics research project. Rather than contain the disease, Tierney argued, the vaccine (known as Edmonston B) had actually infected its recipients, thereby causing the death of hundreds, perhaps thousands, of Yanomami. Neel's conduct, the argument continued, was a natural outgrowth of a "big science" beholden to the priorities of the military-industrial complex and ridden with an imperialist attitude toward the proverbial "other."

In the final version of the book, Tierney deleted accusations of a direct link between the Neel inoculation campaign and the death of the Yanomami. Nevertheless, he maintained that the administration of the obsolete Edmonston B vaccine—whose side effects were aggressive measles-like symptoms—dovetailed neatly with Neel's eugenic project. "Precisely because it was primitive," the Edmonston B vaccine "provided a model much closer to real measles than other, safer vaccines in the attempt to resolve the great genetic question of selective adaptation."[2]

Tierney went on to accuse Neel and his protégé—Napoleon Chagnon of the University of California at Santa Barbara—of a host of lesser sins. To assist the Atomic Energy Commission's comparative study of mutation rates between radiation-contaminated and unexposed populations, the two allegedly had collected blood samples from unsuspecting Yanomami, under false pretenses and without adequate consent. Moreover, both Neel and Chagnon were accused of collusion with fortune-seeking politicians and mining entrepreneurs; they appeared willing to sell their souls and jeopardize the well-being of the Yanomami by siding with government and commercial invaders who promised them unrestricted access to their native subjects.

Tierney singled Chagnon out for particularly savage criticism, claiming that Chagnon, more than any other Western interloper, had hastened the decline and destruction of the Yanomami. He accused Chagnon of cynically and methodically fomenting violent, warlike behavior among the Yanomami. For both ideological and pecuniary reasons, Chagnon had single-handedly disseminated the image of the Yanomami as "the fierce people" in order to boost the appeal of his book *Yanomamo: The Fierce People*. The book became a classic, selling more than one million copies. Chagnon's construction of a violent Yanomami, Tierney claimed, legitimized the often intrusive and always destructive actions of private individuals and host governments in the land of Yanomami. While acknowledging that the Yanomami did indeed exhibit bellicose behavior, Tierney claimed that recourses to violence were the result of Chagnon's intervention in, and transformation of, native society.

Chagnon, Tierney claimed, had allegedly filmed staged fights and encouraged intervillage rivalries in order to support his findings on the essentialist presence of violence in human behavior. Driven by a research agenda that clashed with Yanomami taboos and customs, Chagnon resorted to aggressively and divisively distributing gifts. He became "a one-man treasure fleet" of axes, machetes, and other steel products, offering them gratuitously to his "Stone Age" informants. According to Tierney, this gift giving precipitated warfare between villages seeking part of Chagnon's riches and those intent on monopolizing his treasure cove. "Within three months of Chagnon's arrival on the scene, three different wars had broken out, all between groups who had been at peace for some time and all of whom wanted a claim on Chagnon's goods." Chagnon, he claimed, had "introduced guns, germs and steel across a wide spread of Yanomamiland—and on a scale never seen before."[3] Such "checkbook anthropology," Tierney argued, upset the delicate balance of Yanomami society and self-interestedly fomented the type of behavior that allowed Chagnon to present his anthropological subjects as "fierce people."

Tierney's study also exposed the abuses of trust by a host of other Western interlopers. He claimed that the French anthropologist Jacques Lizot, one of the many anthropologists who had built their reputations among the Yanomami, had organized a harem of young boys to satisfy his insatiable sexual appetite. Western journalists emerged as callous, self-centered observers, willing to sacrifice the lives of the local Indians to produce sensationalist footage for a jaded audience back home. Tierney offered an unsettling description of a *NOVA* production as the equivalent of a snuff film. During the course of filming a documentary feature, the film crew documented with painful detail the last agonizing days of a young woman and her baby without offering her any form of help. Instead of transporting the woman and her offspring to a nearby medical center, the film crew preferred to film

a voyeuristic and pornographic rendition of the death of an authentic "Amazonian Madonna."

Beyond Tierney's exposure of individual indiscretions and incidents lay a powerful denunciation of the depraved and corrupt
nature of modern American science as represented by Neel and
Chagnon. Tierney reminded his readers that Neel was not a mad
scientist but a disciplined member of a complex and ambitious
project. Neel had been part of the Manhattan Project's genetic research team, which studied the impact of radiation on humans. In
this capacity he had led the team that studied radiation effects at
Hiroshima and Nagasaki and on the Marshall Islands, a postwar
test site for atomic weapons. Neel's study group allegedly carried
out secret radiation experiments in the United States, including
"injecting people with radioactive plutonium without their
knowledge or permission, in some cases leading to their death or
disfigurement (Neel himself appears not to have given any of
these experimental injections)."[4] Tierney speculated that Neel's
Yanomami expedition was a continuation of the Atomic Energy
Commission's secret program of experiments on human subjects,
seeking to study their reaction to pathological phenomena, natural or otherwise. Neel's Yanomami enterprise was not, then, an
isolated episode, but instead a reflection of the callous and racist
underpinnings of Western science.

Tierney argued that Neel's scientific doctrine, in particular the
positive evolutionary role he assigned to violence and aggression,
was a forceful illustration of the intellectual resonance of neo-
Darwinism in Cold War American academia. Neel had claimed,
and had attempted to prove, that the inherently aggressive
Yanomami headmen were both biologically superior and highly
polygamous. Given their physical prowess, they impregnated a

disproportionate number of fertile women, thereby passing on a large percentage of superior genes to subsequent generations. Enraptured by his own beliefs, Tierney insinuated, Neel may have neglected, aggravated, or at least welcomed the spread of the measles epidemic in order to test his theory of the biological superiority of aggressive headmen in primitive societies. If, indeed, the genetically superior members of the Yanomami had "differential levels of immunity and thus higher rates of survival to imported disease," such devastating pandemics "might actually be shown to increase the relative proportion of genetically superior individuals," thereby vindicating in the process Neel's "eugenic program."[5]

In Napoleon Chagnon—"the best-known anthropologist since Margaret Mead"—Tierney portrayed a belligerent executor of Neel's eugenic philosophy, an unadulterated partisan of Cold War Western science.[6] In his fieldwork Chagnon had allegedly transgressed every conceivable ethical standard. Driven by a combination of greed, pride, and ideology, Chagnon had pursued evidence for his sociobiological evolutionary theories at the expense of his "fierce people." Touting the Yanomami as the last untouched primitive society, Chagnon was committed to proving that warfare and inequality were the most significant factors leading to humankind's spectacular evolutionary separation from other primates. "Violence is a potent force in human society," he wrote, "and may be the principal driving force behind the evolution of culture."[7]

Tierney claimed that under the guidance of an approving Neel, Chagnon provided empirical evidence supporting the claim that the most violent of the Yanomami—the men who kill more, "reproduce more, and have more female partners"—are the dominant members of their societies. Chagnon argued that, contrary to conventional wisdom on primordial egalitarianism, all societies, including the most primitive, were characterized by a disparate distribution of strategic resources. Violence—by threat or by action, organized or individual—was the strategy of choice for accumulating such resources. Armed with evidence gleaned from the Yanomami, Chagnon chastised his anthropological colleagues for erroneously characterizing preagricultural societies as egalitarian. He acknowledged that there was no meaningful inequality in material assets in primitive society, but this did not mean that such societies enjoyed an egalitarian distribution of crucial resources. In Stone Age societies, such as the Yanomami, inequalities did not involve the "means and ends of production"—which were abundant and therefore without symbolic prestige—but rather "the means and ends of reproduction." Success in such societies was manifested first and foremost by an enlargement of one's kinship network through reproduction. The most successful members of primitive societies—invariably the most violent—practiced polygamy, thereby increasing their hold on the most crucial resource of their culture: the gene pool of future generations.[8]

As for anthropologists who disputed his claims, a critical Chagnon observed that "industrialized citizens" who just happen "to bear the status 'anthropologist' " were consciously oblivious to this crucial manifestation of inequality, and tended instead to project their own concerns and values on primitive societies.[9] Hence, they constructed egalitarian social arrangements where they did not exist. Naïve anthropologists from industrialized societies are obsessed "with sticks, stones, and the means of production—with material resources." By contrast, actors "in tribal societies are concerned about sex, quality of mates and the means of reproduction." Chagnon's theories suggest, then, that modern societies were not an abrupt departure from the unadulterated and innocent ways of the noble savage. Instead, the inherent inequalities of primitive societies, as well as their imbedded genetic propensity for violence, supposedly offered proof that ruthless competition and social inequality "cannot be legislated away by idealistic do-gooders"; these forces, a bemused Clifford Geertz observed in his commentary on the scandal, were the ostensible driving forces of civilization.[10]

In order to validate his Darwinian theories on the headman's control of the means of reproduction, Chagnon had to construct genealogical charts. This task represented a major obstacle because of the Yanomami prohibition on the public uttering of the names of kin and an attendant taboo on naming the dead. Chagnon, Tierney argued, bribed informants and induced divisions and mutual suspicions in order to trick the Yanomami into supplying him with the necessary information. Moreover, he resorted to distributing steel gifts—machetes, axes, and fish hooks—among these "Stone Age persons," with disastrous consequences. Fearing that the available evidence did not provide the necessary props for his theories, Chagnon allegedly employed fabrications. Thus, Tierney argued that Chagnon had fabricated *The Axe Fight*, perhaps the most renowned ethnographic documentary film ever produced. Created in collaboration with the late film ethnographer Tim Asch, the movie depicts the violent confrontation between two groups of Yanomami, sparked by an insult hurled by a visiting clan at one of the host's women. Tierney claimed that Asch had informed his close associates that the entire scene was staged for the benefit of supporting Chagnon's image of a fierce and warlike people, who, at the drop of the proverbial hat, would lash out with few inhibitions. These re-creations of violent confrontations left residues of bitterness that led to real violence long after the camera crew had moved on.[11]

Armed with realistic film footage and other scientific appara-tus to prove his case, Tierney argued that Chagnon's theories on human aggressiveness, as well his embracing of war as a primary attribute of human evolutionary adaptiveness, provided an im-portant intellectual prop for the so-called realist school in Amer-ican foreign policy. Research provided by Neel, Chagnon, and others defied assertions that "changes in norms, ideas, and cul-ture, have the power to tame the historically war-prone nature of international anarchy."[12] With eyes fixed firmly on the present imperfect rather the past primitive, Chagnon explained that "since many of life's resources are finite, conflicts of interest . . . are inevitable."[13] Violence was, indeed, a genetic trait, but its fre-quent manifestation made evolutionary sense. Had violence merely expressed some blind release of emotion, rather than serving evolutionary adaptiveness, this trait would have gone the way of the human tailbone.

To critics, the assertion that "aggression plays a positive role in human evolution" represented a revival of Victorian notions of "progress through violent struggle." In one way or another, scien-tists such as Neel and Chagnon appeared to argue that violence, and warfare in particular, "improved the species by elimination of the unfit and by selective breeding for intelligence and courage; it pro-moted the habits of cooperation which made possible civilized life; and it forced the evolution of larger and more complex societies."[14] Placed within the context of the Cold War, Tierney implied that a dominant current in evolutionary genetics, sociobiology, and anthropology—as represented, in particular, by Chagnon—served the cause of an intrusive American expansionism. An interpretation of war as an inevitability of human interaction—an unavoidable outcome of a genetically programmed proclivity for violence—supported the priorities of the national-security state, with its massive investment in defense, aggressive management of international relations, and self-centered monopolization of crucial resources. Such anthropological interpretations of innate human aggression, Leslie Sponsel observed, dismissed the role of ideas and culture in shaping human behavior and provided a reductive "apology for war—it is universal, ergo just human nature, ergo inevitable, unalterable, and unavoidable."[15] Accepting warfare as a positive evolutionary form that is immune to nurture precluded investment in peace and conflict resolution, and, conversely, encouraged massive defense spending, gunboat diplomacy, and a Darwinian approach to international relations. Claims such as these, rather than the particular wrongdoings of specific individuals, represented the ultimate target of *Darkness in El Dorado*. Moreover, an acceptance of violence and its manifestation in warfare stood in contradistinction to the beliefs of cultural anthropologists, who still endorsed Ruth Benedict's astute assertion that "if we justify war, it is because all peoples always justify the traits of which they find themselves possessed, not because war will bear an objective examination of its merits."[16]

In subsequent months most of Tierney's serious allegations concerning James Neel were swiftly and methodically refuted. At times, Tierney's representations of Neel bordered on libel. By Tierney's own admission, Neel could not have spread the lethal virus because, contrary to Tierney's original claims, no inoculation—including the much-maligned Edmonston B strain—could induce disease. Moreover, the American Anthropological Association's El Dorado Task Force—the producers of an authoritative, albeit contested, report on *Darkness in El Dorado* and the Yanomami's anthropologists—provided ample evidence that Neel and his team had employed extraordinary means to combat the spread of the disease.

The archival record suggested that Neel had sought advice from the Centers for Disease Control, had employed the Edmonston B vaccine because it was the optimal available strain at the time, and had administered doses of gamma globulin in order to minimize adverse effects of the vaccine. Moreover, Neel's travel log in Yanomami territory suggests that he had altered his itinerary in order to reach isolated villages and administer inoculations before the spread of the epidemic into hitherto pristine areas. Even though the task force recognized an ulterior "research dimension to the vaccination campaign," its members concluded that the vaccination effort "was not planned as an experiment, and that Neel was genuinely concerned for the health of the Yanomami." The task force found that he had acted in good faith and beyond the call of duty. "While the death rate among the Yanomami in the 1968 epidemic is a great tragedy," the task force found that "unquestionably the vaccination program of the Neel expedition saved many lives."[17] The task force findings on this crucial issue were corroborated by Susan Lindee of the University of Pennsylvania, the author of a critical biography of Neel as the ultimate Cold War scientist. Lindee stated that Neel's field notes directly contradicted the *Darkness in El Dorado* narrative. Neel had conducted his inoculation campaign as a humanitarian campaign and not as an experiment.[18]

At the very most, Neel appeared guilty of practicing a "colonial" style of anthropological research, a model of inquiry "carried out without attention to the wishes, desires, or feelings of the study population, with research questions and design being shaped entirely by the concerns of the researchers." While acknowledging that such imperious science did not necessarily endanger the target population—Neel after all had been exonerated and even praised for his humanitarian efforts—the AAA task force concluded that he had neglected the development of a mutually beneficial research program based on the informed consent and active collaboration of his subjects.[19]

Neel's defenders also refuted allegations about his endorsement of eugenics. Neel, they claimed, had espoused a theory of sexual selection based on "cognitive abilities"—intelligence—more than physical strength, a propensity for violence, resistance to disease, or any other biological attribute. He had argued that the headmen among the Yanomami and other native American populations "achieve their position largely on the basis of 'mental agility,' " by which he meant intelligence. Given the polygamous nature of such societies, Neel partisan John Tooby explained, the cognitively superior headmen were more likely to have more children than other men, thereby suggesting "a strong selection pressure for cognitive abilities" rather than solely for physical prowess or a low threshold for violence. While Neel did indeed state that "physical strength is an asset" for a headman, he claimed that mental agility is even more important: the headman "will not be stupid."[20] In fact, Tooby argued, Neel suggested "that sexual selection for superior cognitive abilities (not disease resistance) might have driven human evolution for the past several million years, explaining the explosive growth in human cranial capacity during this period."[21]

"It is hard to see how any experiment involving Yanomami susceptibility to measles or measles vaccine . . . would test any part of Neel's theory about the evolution of human intelligence," Tooby concluded. Contrary to competing contemporary theories on selective genetic resistance to disease, Neel believed that social factors—in particular unmonitored contact with infected persons—"outweighed genetic factors in measles epidemics." Despite Tierney's adamant statements to the contrary, Neel's papers revealed no inherent connection between his views on the evolution of "mental agility" and disease resistance.[22]

Tooby offered several correctives to what he considered distortions of Chagnon's record. To begin with, he characterized Tierney's portrayal of Chagnon's views on human nature as a caricature. Chagnon, he claimed, never suggested that human beings are fatally and unavoidably programmed for violence. In reality, Chagnon recognized "that people throughout history have based their political relationships with other groups on predatory versus religious or altruistic measures," concluding that " 'we have the evolved capacity to adopt to either strategy,' depending on what our culture rewards."[23] As for Tierney's accusations that Chagnon had disrupted Yanomami social relations and contaminated his "fierce people" with goods, disease, and the corrupt ways of the West, Tooby said that Tierney had presented the Yanomami "as if they were isolated in a petri dish, except when Chagnon visited and sneezed." Ignoring the long roll call of intruders in Yanomamiland—"gold miners (over 40,000), highway workers, government officials, tin miners, loggers, ranchers, rubber tappers, drug smugglers, soldiers, moralists like Tierney, and on and on"—Tierney "strangely insists that disease, like war, somehow specifically dogs Chagnon's movements."[24]

Tooby and others refuted the charge that Chagnon had fabricated evidence of Yanomami violence such as the famed documentary *The Axe Fight*. Peter Biella, an anthropology filmmaker who had worked with Tim Asch and who was the producer of the "Yanomamo Interactive," a CD-ROM containing *The Axe Fight*, dismissed the charges of fabrication as preposterous. Moreover, he accused Tierney of willfully misinterpreting *The Axe Fight*, which, he claimed, had little to do with violence. "The film's structure . . . bends over backwards to qualify and reject stereotypic impressions of irrepressible Yanomamo violence. . . . The film is about ways that violence is muted, restrained and non-fatal. Essentially it argues that without police, Yanomamo manage to make their system of dispute settlement work pretty well, with nobody in this case getting very hurt."[25]

Such defensive maneuvering notwithstanding, Napoleon Chagnon emerged significantly tarnished from the debate. Even though the AAA task force declined to pass judgment on Chagnon's promotion of violence and his disruption of customs through gift giving, the report concluded that "his representations of Yanomami ways of life were damaging to them and that he made insufficient effort to undo the damage." The task force condemned Chagnon for his casual and sometimes dangerous manipulation of informants, as well as his "playing off of enemies against one another . . . in a context where conflict is dangerous and easily precipitated."[26] Moreover, task force members agreed that Chagnon's ties with a suspect Venezuelan foundation "that sponsored his research represented an unethical prioritizing of his own research concerns over the well-being of the Yanomami."[27]

Finally, the task force methodically challenged Chagnon's most famous contention of Yanomami aggressiveness. The authors of the report accepted that, far from being a predatory and fierce people, the Yanomami were the "helpless victims of aggressive expansion by Whites into their territories." Consequently, the AAA task force offered prominent space to critics claiming that Chagnon's "characterization was incorrect ethnographically, that it reflected specifically North American concerns about the place of violence in human nature at the height of the Vietnam war, or that it reflected preoccupations with violence and aggression emanating from Chagnon's own personality and background."[28] In perhaps its most damaging assertion, the task force claimed a strong connection between Chagnon's 1988 *Science* article on Yanomami violence and a disastrous Brazilian government reduction of Yanomami territory into "Bantustan-like island reserves."[29]

In the *Science* article, Chagnon had offered statistical evidence to support his hypothesis that Yanomami were indeed a fierce, almost animal, people. Citing studies "during the past 23 years," Chagnon argued that 44 percent of Yanomami males "estimated to be over 25 years or older have participated in the killing of someone, that approximately 30 percent of adult males deaths are due to violence, and that nearly 70 percent of all adults over an estimated 40 years of age have lost a close genetic relative due to violence." Chagnon's objective was to prove that such predatory behavior was a powerful evolutionary strategy and not a gratuitous animal urge. The primary purpose of violence and warfare was the appropriation of finite and scarce "material and reproductive resources." However, Chagnon's article was promoted widely in Brazil and Uruguay as evidence of the need for governments to control, curtail, and protect the Yanomami from others and from themselves alike.[30]

The task force accepted *Darkness in El Dorado*'s critique of

Chagnon's theory of genetic preponderance for individual violence and organized warfare, and in fact offered space for the less exotic explanations of rival anthropologists, among them Brian Ferguson of Rutgers. Contrary to Chagnon's assertion that fighting in general and disputes over women in particular constituted the "normal way of doing things" among Yanomami men, Ferguson described such practices as the ultimate result of the devastation of the Yanomami by disease. Epidemics, he claimed, had led to the disruption of families and a subsequent, desperate attempt to reconstitute decimated reproductive units by kidnapping women from rival clans.[31] Other critics hypothesized that the Yanomami engaged in warfare not because of a primal urge but because of such social and economic factors as chronic food shortages caused by overhunting and ecological blight. Others claimed that the type of warfare that Chagnon had assigned to the original Stone Age culture of the Yanomami was, in actual fact, a postcontact phenomenon brought on by the destruction of traditional ways by missionaries, Western fortune seekers, and anthropologists. Chagnon, who claimed to have been "studying primitive culture at its purest, turns out to have been recording his own direct effects on it."[32]

Chagnon's intellectual adversaries did not dispute the existence of precontact warfare as a way of life. They merely claimed that neither Chagnon nor anyone else had produced evidence to support claims of contemporary Yanomami culture as a reflection of the way humans lived "at the dawn of agriculture." The theory that warlike and ferocious precontact societies were primordially warlike and ferocious was, they argued, scientifically indefensible. "Had not the Yanomami always made war, even pre-contact?"

Brian Ferguson wondered. Perhaps, he acknowledged, but "I can't find pre-contact."[33]

As for his central assertions on the evolutionary role of violence, Chagnon found himself confronted with strong conflicting evidence. Chagnon had claimed that men who killed had twice as many wives and three times as many offspring than their more sedate kinsmen. Critics observed, however, that Chagnon had omitted a crucial factor. Many of the more violence-prone members of Yanomami clans lost their lives in warfare or were driven into exile characterized by low reproductive rates. These individuals did not appear in Chagnon's selective and scientifically unsound count, they claimed. Tierney, in fact, argued that Chagnon's infatuation with the sociobiological impulse—his theory that the most violent males gained the most women, thereby passing on a genetically imprinted fierceness to future generations—was first and foremost a reflection of Chagnon's own "libidinous impulses." Lacing his book with tales of Chagnon's alarming personal conduct—his obsession with attack dogs, his drunken brawls, his participation in native rites involving psychotropic drugs—Tierney implied that Chagnon projected his own predilection for violence on the Yanomami.

THE MEANING OF THE CRITICISM

Irrespective of such revelations, an uncomfortable tone permeated the task force report as well as other pro-Tierney publications. The AAA task force acknowledged that the evidence leveled against Chagnon in *Darkness in El Dorado* was a compilation of secondhand knowledge. Nothing in the content of the book warranted a sudden awakening of the AAA and the attendant public fury. Other researchers had criticized Chagnon's theses and anthropological practices for years. Moreover, the only original allegations in *Darkness in El Dorado*—those concerning the measles epidemic—appeared to be unfounded, the result of a faulty understanding of scientific data and a rigidly antiscientific ideology. Tierney's exposé was, the task force concluded, seriously flawed: ill-informed, deliberately sensationalist, and offering an unconvincing conspiracy thesis of Western "science as an evil knowledge system linked to nuclear weapons and corporate capital."[34] The startling charges of genocide leveled against Neel were discredited, and instead of mass murder, Neel appeared to have been "convicted of a parking violation," at worst.[35]

Tierney's forays into genetics and epidemiology were indeed often amateurish, always clumsy, and potentially libelous. Charges of individual malfeasance were mostly rhetorical devices aimed at drawing attention to Tierney's subtext of the evils of Western science. Nevertheless, the sheer scale of the charges produced a visible and public interrogation of the role of science and technology in the service of the military-industrial complex. Whether the charges were true appeared to be almost beside the point.

Despite or perhaps because of its inherent flaws, *Darkness in El Dorado* radically revised the anthropological agenda in the United States. In marked contradistinction to previous aborted efforts, Tierney had riveted attention on the plight of the Yanomami and the misdeeds of major figures within the profession. His most important contribution resided not in the occasional revelation but in the self-examining mood he had induced among American anthropologists. *Darkness in El Dorado*, the AAA task force members concurred, "opened a space for reflection and stocktaking about what we do and our relationships with those among whom we are privileged to study."[36] Thus task force contributor Joe Watkins reminded his colleagues that, irrespective of good intentions and unobtrusive objectives, the very presence of an anthropologist invariably upsets and irreparably alters indigenous cultures. The interpretations of authoritative metropolitan anthropologists, he wrote, "are often accepted over those of untrained populations, including, in most instances, those of local and descendent communities."[37]

Not all anthropologists recognized the virtues of such soul-searching. Prominent members of the profession condemned the AAA for its very involvement in the inquiry. They reminded their colleagues that a 1995 AAA resolution had prohibited adjudication of unethical behavior because of the divisive political nature of most such affairs. In the El Dorado scandal, they alleged, the AAA was "swept away by a riptide of political righteousness" and had caved in to a vulgar, sensation-mongering tide, thereby exacerbating the discipline's schisms and fault lines. The AAA's involvement in what appeared to be scandal mongering and a poorly executed piece of political journalism did little to resolve the internal conflict between "scientifically oriented data-driven research and interpretative approaches" in contemporary American anthropology.[38]

Critics of AAA involvement in the *Darkness in El Dorado* controversy were particularly incensed by the task force's radical interpretation of "informed consent" in anthropological studies. The AAA report appeared "to demand that anthropologists surrender to their subjects the task of defining the topics to be investigated. 'Informed consent' is not sufficient, says the report.

Theoretically significant topics 'may have to be set aside' if they are not of equal interest to research subjects."[39]

According to David Stoll—a controversial anthropologist in his own right, following his involvement in the Rigoberta Menchú scandal discussed in the next chapter—Tierney's indiscriminate attack on science threatened to aggravate pandemics among indigenous persons. Controlling disease among the Yanomami, he explained, was not merely a matter of timely and thorough vaccination. "Exactly why such groups are vulnerable is not a simple matter; and protecting them from ravages such as drug-resistant tuberculosis requires medical research of the kind that, thanks to the kind of headlines generated by Tierney's book, is easily interpreted as genocidal conspiracy. Careless journalism that increases suspicion of vaccination campaigns could take many more lives than the kind of errors that Tierney reports." Was the much-touted notion of "informed consent" the best possible strategy if, for instance, the provision of Western medicine—by force, duplicity, or any other means—would help "unwilling subjects . . . to survive threats they barely comprehend?" Stoll mused.[40]

MEDIA AND MESSAGES

Given its regurgitated and sometimes false revelations, *Darkness in El Dorado*'s catalytic effect and the sense of crisis it ignited demand an explanation. Allegations of professional misconduct among American scientists studying the Yanomami had, indeed, surfaced prior to this controversy. As early as 1982, Florinda Donner's sensational *Shabono* related a larger-than-life tale of her going "native among the Yanomami," including drug-induced sexual contacts with a shaman, participating, or a least bearing witness to, endocannibalism, infanticide, and fierce bouts of gratuitous warfare. An angry article in *American Anthropologist* revealed that Donner had plagiarized portions of her book and probably invented the rest. Her deeds stoked an ongoing, internal dispute concerning the growing current of "fictocriticism" or "fact/fiction" anthropology, where imagination and reality were mixed in order to achieve a complex "decoding" of both anthropologists and their informants. Even though the merging of fact and fiction in ethnography threatened to tear the community of cultural anthropologists apart, it had limited resonance beyond professional journals and conferences. Neither the morals and mores of professional anthropologists nor the fate of exoticized "primitives"—obviously affected adversely by such representations—appeared to spread controversy or arouse indignation outside the academy.[41]

Previous attempts to defame Napoleon Chagnon had achieved equally modest results. The 1995 annual meeting of the AAA centered on a confrontation between Chagnon and the authors of two forthcoming books criticizing the means and morals of the anthropological project among the Yanomami. Neither the very charged debate with Chagnon nor the prepublication copies of the manuscripts sent out to major anthropologists working in Amazonia aroused much attention beyond the AAA meeting. In fact, the books were easily dismissed as the machinations of Salesian missionaries seeking exoneration for the own misdeeds or the knee-jerk reactions of misguided environmentalists.[42]

Presumably cognizant of the fact that previous interrogations of the motives of American scientists, of Chagnon in particular, had achieved dismal results, Tierney chose a different manner of presentation and dissemination. As a journalist, Tierney was well aware of what it took to sell a story. Hence he chose dramatization and exaggeration in order to propel his accusations from the protected precincts of professional deliberations to the front pages of newspapers and magazines. Portraying the tragedy of the Yanomami merely as a result of good intentions led astray would lack the sensationalism necessary to capture media attention. Even when apprised of the fact that Neel had not induced the measles epidemic or inoculated selectively with a faulty vaccine, Tierney failed to remove the accusation from his text entirely. He continued to insist that Neel "may" have used the wrong vaccine and to imply that the Edmonston B may have aggravated, and perhaps even directly caused, the epidemic that Neel was ostensibly trying to contain. Maintaining the "prop" of the suspicious vaccine and the murky motives of Neel was crucial, Brazilian anthropologist Alcida Rita Ramos argues. Without this hint of unadulterated evil, "*Darkness in El Dorado* loses much of its edge and becomes just one more narrative of unethical scientific behavior." Insinuations of "medical experiments involving a highly respected scientists and a highly exoticized people saved this book from the near oblivion" of previous accounts.[43]

Well before the actual publication of the book, Tierney's claims captured the attention of the mainstream media, where synopses of the still-unread book appeared "behind screaming headlines": "Macho Anthropology" *(Salon);* "Anthropology Enters the Age of Cannibalism" *(The New York Times);* "Mad Dog Anthropologists" *(The Nation);* "The Wages of Anthropological Incorrectness" *(The National Review);* "Is Anthropology Evil?" *(Slate);* "Yanomami: What Have We Done to Them?" *(Time);*

" 'Scientist' Killed Amazon Indians to Test Race Theory" *(The Guardian)*; to mention but a few.[44]

Yet Tierney's ultimate stroke of genius was technological rather than literary. He had skillfully used the technological attributes of the Internet to enhance the resonance of his study. Before the publication of a synopsis of the book in the *New Yorker* in November 2000, the publishers remained publicly silent but actively encouraged debate via cyberspace. The ostensibly private e-mail sent by Turner and Sponsel to the presiding officers of the AAA became the proverbial "e-mail heard 'round the world.' " Within a matter of days, their message had ricocheted through cyberspace, with most anthropologists receiving it at least a dozen times from different electronic sources. Subsequent e-mail contributions to the controversy were mass circulated in a similar fashion.

The warring sides relied on volume and speed, rather than persuasion and deliberation, for winning the public opinion war in both academia and the public sphere. The medium—in this case the use of cyberspace—was the message. Exchanges via the Internet were democratic, immediate, and accessible. They were also frequently inflammatory, lacking reflection, and patently inaccurate. The searing partisan cyber wars erupted long before the book itself was released, a fact that did little to stop the flood of opinionated electronic exchanges concerning every conceivable angle of a yet still nonexistent product. "Once upon a time, the book's publication would have been the starting point for a deliberate discussion refereed by academic journals and scholarly panels," a somewhat shocked reporter noted. "But the Yanomami affair demonstrates that, for better or for worse, those gatekeepers cannot keep up with more nimble combatants on the Internet."[45]

Even Tierney acknowledged that his strategy of electronic teasers had perhaps spun out of control and expressed surprise over the "tawdry quality" of Internet exchanges. Tierney claimed to be disappointed that the "ephemeral chatter" cluttering cyberspace had transformed his book from a critique of Western science into a melodramatic account of personal greed and hubris. Neel and Chagnon were supposed to have been mere examples of a pernicious structural flaw in the practices of science, but somehow they had become the center of a personalized debate.

The *Darkness in El Dorado* cyber debates irreparably destabilized the parochial and often condescending American anthropological discourse, a self-serving enterprise that only rarely entertained the opinions of international scholars. Electronic mailing lists and bulletin boards were inundated with the comments of experts from outside the United States, some of whom had previously published criticisms of Chagnon only to be damned by the faint praise or condescending dismissal usually reserved for the outsider. Critics could not help noticing that in contrast to the unsuccessful efforts of Latin American anthropologists to "alert North American social scientists to the harmful effects of careless ethnographic renderings of Yanomami life," a sensationalist book—riddled with inaccuracies and embellishments, yet published by a renowned press—had elicited an immediate response from the AAA governing body.[46] Thus, the anthropologist Fernando Coronil observed, *Darkness in El Dorado* made "evident that in matters of knowledge, as in real estate, location is decisive."[47]

The AAA task force acknowledged that the few substantive allegations raised by Tierney's book had been expressed previously by Brazilian and Venezuelan colleagues—whose reservations, however, had been ignored by metropolitan scholars. Such selective vision led the chastened members of the task force to reflect that "we must attend carefully to the responses of colleagues internationally, who have asked why American anthropologists are moved to action by an attack from outside the profession, but not by collegial inquiry and concerns of our fellow anthropologists in other countries."[48]

MODERNISM AND THE YANOMAMI

The Yanomami scandal exposed several different controversies permeating American anthropology and American academia in general. Comparisons of Neel's and Chagnon's practices with Nazi atrocities highlighted the fundamental rift between exponents of the modernist project of objective science—seeking to uncover the governing laws of *Homo sapiens* by employing dispassionate inquiry—and its critics, who condemned modernism, in science, culture, and politics, as the root cause of human depravity. Holocaust analogies in the Turner-Sponsel e-mail and other critical documents were not the result of rhetorical flourish but actually the crux of the debate. "Every ingredient of the Holocaust," Zygmunt Bauman wrote in his seminal analysis of the Nazi murder machine, "was normal . . . in the sense that of being fully in keeping with everything we know about our civilization, its guiding spirits, its priorities, its immanent vision of the world."[49]

Echoes of this loss of faith in modernism informed Tierney's critique. In placing the blame for the Yanomami tragedy on the shoulders of scientists, Tierney deliberately conflated the gains of modernism with the iniquities of capitalism, rejecting in the process the pursuit of an objective and rational understanding of the natural and social world. His protestations to the contrary, Tierney implied that this modernist project was, at best, a dangerous fantasy that caused significantly more harm than good. Science was the ultimate manifestation of an impersonal, perhaps even evil, knowledge system indelibly linked to the arch villains of antimodernists: the military-industrial complex.

As far as anthropology was concerned, *Darkness in El Dorado* defined the front lines of the controversy between partisans of a mostly sociobiological strain of "science" and cultural anthropologists, each side claiming the discovery of latent political bias and intellectual dishonesty among its rivals.[50] The nature-nurture divide exposed by the Yanomami affair left observers marveling at the enduring marriage of convenience between two incompatible intellectual traditions. In fact, in some domains, such as Stanford University, the union was dissolved. Stanford's anthropological community split into a Department of Anthropological Sciences and a Department of Cultural Anthropology, a gesture that reflected a change far more profound than mere technical or administrative reorganization. "The split is really between those who use and stand behind scientific methods in field and lab work, and those who think science is just another way of knowing," Stanford's Bill Durham commented. "It just so happens that anthropologists often divide on this issue between physical and cultural anthropologists, but not always. There are plenty of cultural anthropologists who conduct rigorous quantitative research. But many others are steeped in" texts and abstract theorizing.[51] In fact, Napoleon Chagnon's *Yanomamö: The Fierce People* was published in a series entitled Case Studies in Cultural Anthropology.

The sheer acrimony of internal conflict within anthropology, the sociologist Ullica Segerstrale observed, was not, however, a

typical case of miscommunication caused in the heat of battle between clashing paradigms. Instead, it appeared that participants
on both sides "actively seek to miscommunicate."[52] The controversy over sociobiology, its application in anthropology, and its
manifest results among the Yanomami was not simply a conflict
between positivistic-leaning "planters who want to produce useful knowledge" and critical weeders seeking to remove morally
contaminated knowledge by its roots.[53] Had this been the case,
some sort of middle ground might have been found. Instead, the
struggle appeared to be between two radically divergent schools:
the collectors of data and the abstract theorists. Compromise,
consilience, or fusion of theories was, under these circumstances,
impossible.

Thus, the Yanomami scandal addressed the fate of indigenous
persons only in passing. The debate was first and foremost a
showdown between competing schools of authority and control
in contemporary American knowledge production. As for the
Yanomami themselves, Susan Lindee observed, they had been
overwhelmed by the burden of different roles that that they were
expected to perform for the benefit of others.

> They have been asked to be Stone Age people who could re-
> veal how human evolution occurred and therefore how soci-
> ety should be organized. They have been asked to be the se-
> ductive messengers of the potential of liberal humanism.
> They have also been asked to demonstrate the terrible impact
> of industrialized steel goods and technocratic rationality. Yet,
> who should bear the burden of such chaotic industrialized
> longings?[54]

And yet the tragedy in El Dorado should not be placed solely
at the doorstep of a patronizing geneticist, an overambitious an-

thropologist, or any other member of the American scientific community. The Yanomami disaster was the product of the type of neglect usually assigned to marginal groups in advanced societies. Long before Chagnon began his somewhat dubious interventions among his "fierce people," the Yanomami had suffered disease and destruction at the hands of civilizing missionaries, rapacious prospectors, and callous governments.

It would appear that Napoleon Chagnon was indeed an astute observer. The Yanomami wars were based, as he claimed, on the rites of reproduction—not those of the native inhabitants of the Amazon, but of a far fiercer people: warring scholars. Hostile battles for scarce resources—research grants, recognition, and publications—reflected a Darwinian struggle for the multiplication and reproduction of graduate progeny, who, in turn, would reproduce for future generations the intellectual positions of their headmen-mentors by means of seminal articles and other intellectual reproductive devices. The fact that such battles had consequences for a distant people's lives was overshadowed, inevitably, invariably, and tragically, by the concerns of belligerent scholars.

SIX

The Willful Suspension of Disbelief

Rigoberta Menchú and the Making of the Maya Holocaust

In a war between unequals, especially when the more powerful side is rampantly duplicitous, we expect the truth will be on the side of the innocent. . . . Testimony is the people's history, but it is only powerful if it is true.

New York Times editorial, December 17, 1999

Testimony has been and continues to be the principal avenue by which semiliterate and illiterate people can communicate with those who wish to understand their struggles. . . . Testimony is itself inherently political, and Stoll attacks the very essence of *I, Rigoberta Menchú* which is the right of the Maya in general and Maya women in particular to political consciousness, self-representation, and political action.

Victoria Sanford, "Between Rigoberta Menchú and La Violencia"

In 1992, a contemplative Western world marked the Columbian quincentenary of the much-maligned "discovery" of the New World. Rather than inspire a celebration of the spirit of Western progress, the anniversary generated somber reflections on the dark side of Western expansionism and its devastating effects on the indigenous peoples of the Americas. In this general atmosphere of atonement and self-reflection, the 1992 Nobel Peace Prize was awarded to Rigoberta Menchú, an indigenous Guatemalan civil rights activist. The award acknowledged the historic injustices inflicted upon indigenous peoples throughout the Americas, and offered at least symbolic penance for sufferings past and present.

Menchú had become a symbol of the Guatemalan tragedy in the wake of her published biography, *I, Rigoberta Menchú: An Indian Woman in Guatemala*, the extraordinary testimony of the social and political awakening of an illiterate Maya peasant and her eyewitness report of the Maya genocide in Guatemala. Published in English in 1984, at the height of the Maya holocaust, her book rallied worldwide support for the plight of her people, eventually forcing a reluctant Guatemalan government to initiate peace negotiations with its internal rivals.

Her account brought to light one of the most horrific chapters of political violence in Latin America, impugning in the process American involvement in and acquiescence to the genocidal policies of Guatemala's military. Guatemala had been in the grip of civic and political strife ever since a CIA-inspired military coup toppled the country's elected government in 1954. The civil war between American-backed security forces and Cuban-backed Marxist-Leninist guerrillas remained confined to urban centers until the late 1970s, when it spread, with disastrous consequences, to the country's rural areas. Using tactics of pacification learned from the Vietnam War, Guatemalan counterinsurgency forces relocated villages, destroyed crops, and employed indiscriminate terror to sever ties—real or suspected—between peasants and guerrillas. By the time the peace accord had been signed in 1996, about 150,000 Maya had been killed, most of whom were victims of army brutality.

Menchú's recollections of the systematic destruction of her family, village, and people, as recounted to the French-based Venezuelan anthropologist and political activist Elisabeth Burgos-Debray, offered graphic and moving accounts of the destruction of the K'iche'-Maya way of life, the natives' struggles against callous Ladino landowners, and the brutal massacres instigated by U.S.-backed Guatemalan security forces. Menchú's most effective weapon, and the main reason for the success of her book, was her ability to describe the atrocities involving herself and her family.

Born in the village of Chimel, in the Guatemalan highlands, Menchú was part of the K'iche' tribe, one of twenty-three different Maya groups in Guatemala. Her autobiography relates the daily misery and exploitation suffered by a devout Catholic, poverty-stricken Indian-peasant family with nine children. In order to survive and to remove themselves from the vicious circle of exploitation and poverty, the family joined forces with a left-wing guerrilla movement, only to be murdered or driven into exile by government forces. Menchú's skill in universalizing her personal ordeal accounted in no small measure for the autobiography's literary and commercial success. Menchú's story wove together bleak tales of immiseration and killing with fascinating descriptions of indigenous life—the making of food, religion and folkways, the role of family in Maya society, gender relations, and vivid depictions of the surrounding flora and fauna of the Altiplano as seen through the eyes of the land's dispossessed. Her story riveted worldwide attention on the plight of indigenous inhabitants in a country normally far removed from the gaze of the Western media. The book became a best seller and found its way into college curricula across the United States.

I, Rigoberta Menchú was particularly well received at Stanford University, where, in the wake of a faculty and student program to increase cultural diversity in the 1980s, the university instituted a radical revision of its freshman Western Civilization requirement. This traditional Western-culture "great books" course had offered a corpus of readings aimed at providing students with a comprehensive understanding of the (European) roots of their culture. A powerful cohort of faculty critics argued that this anachronistic approach to culture featured the proverbial, exclusive, and intellectually stifling list of Dead White Males—ranging from the Greek philosophers through the artists and thinkers of Renaissance Italy to, in the spring quarter, the writings of Marx, Darwin, Goethe, and Mill. Opponents of this format of teaching Western culture claimed that it failed to address the multiplicity of cultures on the Stanford campus, with its many students of Asian, Latin American, and African descent. Moreover, none of the great books in the curriculum were written by women. As for the Anglo-American component of Stanford's student body, they were for the most part from Western states— reputedly as culturally distant from Goethe as they were from Mars.[1]

In 1988, following a heated debate, Stanford replaced its "Occidental civilizing mission" with a broad and inclusive freshman course titled "Cultures, Ideas, and Values" (CIV) that included such multicultural reading material as *The Autobiography of Frederick Douglass*, Frantz Fanon's *Wretched of the Earth*, and *I, Rigoberta Menchú*. As CIV's architect, Mary Louise Pratt, explained, the change was not merely an exchange of one list of books for another. CIV represented a profound intellectual shift. The course sought to destabilize Eurocentrist "interpretive monopolies" and to interrogate cherished Western concepts of "truth, goodness, and beauty." CIV decentered the traditional "cultural and geographic panorama" offered in classic Western-civilization introductory courses by rearranging the study of European classics and texts from other cultures from their compartmentalized and hierarchically shelved niches, placing them instead "in dialogue with each other (Augustine's *Confessions* with a Navajo life story; Shakespeare's *Tempest* with Aimé Césaire's 1968 rewrite, *A Tempest;* Caribbean vodun with Greek ecstatic cults, for example)." The CIV format of cultural juxtaposition reputedly generated a critical rethinking of cardinal intellectual issues, such as "the 'representation' of subalterns in academic inquiry," an attendant "decolonization of knowledge," and the fostering of "non-hegemonic" political, cultural, and social perspectives among America's best and brightest undergraduates.[2]

Opponents of the Stanford sea change lashed out at the displacement of great classics by books of inferior quality, all in the name of an alleged diversity-run-wild. In an utterance that perhaps he came to regret, Saul Bellow expressed concern over the CIV's valorizing of mediocre third world literature, declaring that "when the Zulus have a Tolstoy, we will read him." George Will expressed incredulity at the fact that Shakespeare's *Tempest* had somehow lost its sublime and universal qualities and had been transformed into a crypto-racist text. A *Wall Street Journal* editorial, titled "The Stanford Mind," cited Alan Bloom's dismissal of Frantz Fanon—a pivotal author in the new curriculum—as "a demonstrably inferior and derivative thinker to whom no one would pay attention if he were not currently the ideologue of popular movements and if as a black Algerian he did not fit the Stanford job description."[3]

Dinesh D'Souza, the indefatigable watchdog of right-wing causes on campus, declared that the new canon diminished, trivialized, and relegated cherished Western treasures to a plane populated by "various systems of thought . . . considered on a roughly equal" basis.[4] He reserved particular scorn for Menchú's testimony as the ultimate sign of the stranglehold of an anti-American academic left. As a pivotal part of the "Europe and Americas" track of CIV, Menchú's book contributed to what D'Souza described as the superimposing of a single-minded race and gender template on the impressionable minds of undergraduates. D'Souza protested that the Stanford curriculum presented the Euro-American encounter solely and exclusively as a narrative of oppression perpetrated by a cynical Western civilization on people of color. One of the major devices for disseminating this view at Stanford was, he claimed, *I, Rigoberta Menchú*, adopted because it was "a mouthpiece for a sophisticated left-wing critique of Western society." As a woman, a person of color, a victim of imperialism, and the subaltern of a dominant Latino culture, Menchú was a perfect "quadruple victim," D'Souza declared.[5] Menchú's political consciousness, he complained, included the multiple sins of "politically correct causes such as feminism, homosexual rights, socialism, and Marxism." Moreover, *I, Rigoberta Menchú* promoted a shallow and melodramatic approach to history as a cartoonlike battle between the forces of good and evil.

Even the decidedly milder C. Vann Woodward had his gen-
teelly phrased misgivings. While acknowledging that D'Souza's
inflammatory description of the book was misguided, misleading,
and inaccurate, he had his own criticisms. "The unasked question
is how to justify the attention demanded for this interview taped
in Paris in one week and adapted by the writer to read like an autobiography. Ms. Menchú was then twenty-three, an illiterate
peasant woman from Guatemala. Her story is indeed a moving
one of brutal oppression and horrors," Vann Woodward acknowledged, "but I am left with some unresolved doubts about
the place given it in the new multicultural canon."[6]

THE PARADIGM OF "LAST RESORT"

Menchú's most severe test was not, however, at the hands of
D'Souza or other pundits whose motives were transparently
polemic and partisan. A more uncomfortable trial erupted around
Christmas 1998, when the Stanford-educated anthropologist
David Stoll published the results of his inquiry into the life story
of Menchú, *Rigoberta Menchú and the Story of All Poor Guatemalans*. Stoll's study discredited many key portions of Menchú's autobiography, claiming that crucial incidents in her account relied
on "experiences she had never had herself" and that others were
embellished. Contrary to Menchú's assertion that she "never went
to school," was illiterate, and could speak no Spanish until shortly
before she dictated the text, Stoll revealed that she was, in actual
fact, proficient in Spanish and the beneficiary of eight years of education at two private schools. By Latin American standards, she
was well educated.

Stoll also questioned many of the gory details, such as

Menchú's harrowing eyewitness accounts of her brothers' deaths, one by starvation and the other by immolation. Nicolas, a young brother who, Menchú claimed, had died of malnutrition during the family's forced relocation to a coffee plantation, turned out to "be alive and well, the owner of a well-kept homestead," when tracked down—at Stoll's behest—by a *New York Times* reporter.[7] Moreover, Stoll argued that Menchú could not have witnessed the particularly horrific death of another brother, Petrocinio, who was allegedly burned alive by military forces in the town of Chajul. By Menchú's own account she was elsewhere at the time. In addition, eyewitnesses informed Stoll that such a form of execution had never transpired, although they acknowledged that the army had indeed killed her brother.

Stoll also challenged Menchú's representation of her father as an impoverished villager whose land was confiscated by predatory Ladino landlords backed by a ruthless military establishment. Stoll argued that Menchú's father, Vincente Menchú, was a fairly well-off individual, whose violent confrontation over his lands was part of a bitter family feud with his in-laws. The dispute was not, as Menchú had claimed, the reason for her father's social awakening and political mobilization, nor was it indicative of the type of repressive violence faced by Guatemala's indigenous population. As for the circumstances surrounding the death of her father and other members of the revolutionary movement who had been holed up in the Spanish embassy, Stoll dismissed Menchú's story that they had died after Guatemalan security forces deliberately set fire to the building. Instead, he claimed that Menchú and his entourage were victims of self-immolation. "In short," observed Jan Rus, "Rigoberta's testimony of deprivation, racial discrimination, and repression, eventually leading to redemption through the act of taking up arms against her own people's oppressors, appeared to have been at least partly fictionalized."[8]

If anything, Stoll argued, the tragic fate of Guatemala's Maya was an example of the fractious nature of Maya society, in which internecine family feuds, intervillage conflicts, and other local divisions wreaked havoc on the peasant population. The fragile and contentious nature of Maya peasant society was exploited by both the American-backed army and the Cuban-supported guerrilla movements in their quest for allies and proxies in Guatemala's civil war. The victims were the indigenous inhabitants of the region.

At no point, however, did Stoll challenge the fundamental truth or the essential elements of the collective tragedy depicted in the book. He accepted as irrefutable that Menchú, her family, and her people were the victims of political violence and that the Guatemalan army was responsible for unconscionable human rights violations, including the deaths of many members of Menchú's family. "There is no doubt about the most important points: that a dictatorship massacred thousands of indigenous peasants, that victims included half of Menchú's family, that she fled to Mexico to save her life, and that she joined a revolutionary movement to liberate her country," he stated.[9] Fully aware of accusations that he had hurt the cause of human rights by deflecting attention from indisputable facts to irrelevant details, Stoll explained that his aim was not to refute irrefutable evidence. Instead, he sought to rectify ideologically motivated distortions and fabrications of Menchú's personal story, which served ulterior motives and weakened, rather than strengthened, her representation of the Maya tragedy.

Menchú, according to Stoll, had romanticized the guerrilla

movement in Guatemala, and in the process had transformed the complex internal struggle in Guatemala into a recognizable but false narrative of a war between Indians backed by a popular guerrilla movement and rapacious landowners supported by state security forces. While acknowledging that the security forces were responsible for most of the carnage among the Maya, Stoll argued that the urban-based guerrilla movement was guilty of shifting the conflict from Guatemala's cities to the countryside. The war in rural Guatemala was not the result of a spontaneous peasant uprising supported by noble guerrillas, but rather a deadly foreign import foisted upon reluctant peasants.

Menchú's narrative had falsely presented the Guatemalan tragedy as the lethal, inevitable outgrowth of a struggle between dispossessed Indians and rapacious Ladino landowners, thereby encouraging "the Guatemalan Left and its foreign supporters to continue viewing the countryside as a contest among social classes, ethnic blocs, and structural forces."[10] Actually, Stoll argued, most of the region's land disputes—supposedly the fuse igniting the peasant uprising—were not between Ladino landholders and Indian peasants, but rather among the Indians themselves, who were beset by rampant population growth, destructive agricultural practices, and ancient familial feuds. The internal rifts and age-old animosities that wreaked havoc among the Indians had no place in Menchú's book. She preferred establishing "a firm identification between peasants and insurgents, firmer than what many peasants felt," thereby turning "a nightmarish experience into a morality play," Stoll observed.[11] This maudlin construction of the Indian plight had, however, little to do with reality.

Stoll's account was by no means a politically innocent retelling of events; nor did his book represent a dispassionate academic corrective to Menchú's ideologically driven narrative. Stoll openly and defiantly espoused a radically different political interpretation. Notably, he rejected the "last-resort paradigm," the assumption that peasants joined forces with the guerrillas because they saw no other way to escape poverty and oppression. Stoll rejected Menchú's underlying assumption that deteriorating economic conditions and growing repression had provided the impetus for an alliance between the guerrilla movements and impoverished indigents. In fact, prior to guerrilla provocations in the region, Stoll claimed that the Maya were even making modest gains.

While Menchú began her story with the political awakening of peasants in response to brutal, unprovoked attacks by the Guatemalan army, Stoll claimed that it was the guerrillas who had instigated violence in the region. Contrary to the implication arising from Menchú's text—that the guerrilla presence was a defensive response to government oppression and violence—Stoll stated that "the guerrillas committed the first political executions of nonindigenous landowners," hoping to attract in this manner the support of the Maya. Only then, Stoll argued, "the army occupied and militarized a region which until then had been policed." Even though "the Guatemalan army ended up doing most of the killing," Stoll claimed that it was the radical left that had made a conscious decision to move the struggle from urban areas to the countryside. In other words, the guerrillas had fired the first shot. Consequently, responsibility for the war lay on their shoulders.[12]

As for the Maya, Stoll claimed that they were mired in their own internal rifts and had little understanding of or patience for the type of political debate that had moved with such suddenness from the metropolis to Guatemala's rural areas. Based on research conducted in another part of Guatemala, Stoll claimed that the Maya of the Altiplano region were caught "between two sides." Forced to choose between them, the peasants inevitably suffered brutality perpetrated by both sides.[13]

By "making armed struggle sound like an inevitable reaction to oppression at the time when Mayans were desperate to escape the violence," Menchú's narrative reframed the insurgents as saviors deeply involved in a localized conflict, whereas, as far as the guerrilla movement was concerned, the Maya were merely expendable proxies in an international liberation struggle of cosmic proportions.[14] In order to gain ground in the larger struggle, Stoll claimed, the leftists callously and stubbornly continued fighting for a lost cause in the Guatemalan countryside, quite willing to sacrifice their Maya pawns for their cause.

In deconstructing Menchú's testimony, Stoll argued that he was also waging an important intellectual battle against a "new standard of truth" that imperiled enlightened Western scholarship. For reasons that had little to do with sound scholarship, "well-intentioned foreigners" and engaged anthropologists were willing to cede authority to a suspect text because it empowered and offered a voice to the subaltern. The main casualties of this well-intentioned but misguided project were veracity and objectivity, the two cornerstones of strict scholarly standards.

Menchú had become the vox populi, Stoll argued, even though her book was a transparent piece of sectarian propaganda. In part, the resonance of her story lay in her artful pandering to the sentimental and patronizing precepts of her audience, such as her self-representation as an unschooled peasant with broken Spanish. Contrary to the Western habit of inflating accomplishments,

Daphne Patai observes, Menchú "does the reverse, as if she were wise to the strange competition going on in the contemporary world over what groups are to be accorded most-oppressed status."[15]

As for permitting the subaltern to speak, Stoll claimed that, in contrast to Menchú's singular voice, his own study offered space to a wide spectrum of victims, in particular those who felt trapped in the middle but were rendered "voiceless" by Western intellectuals who preferred Menchú's more artful narrative of oppression and revolt. Elisabeth Burgos-Debray, who appears to have experienced an epiphany since transcribing and editing *I, Rigoberta Menchú*, acknowledged that Stoll's deconstructive exercise revealed the political biases of his critics and the vulnerability of truth seeking in confusing surroundings.

> The critics have mixed their scholarly calling with their political beliefs, in the process converting oral literature—the most supple of genres and the most subject to personal invention—into an almost religious canon bordering on the absolute. By delegitimizing every attempt at critical skepticism, they have obtained a contrary result; the status of the texts, specifically in the case of Rigoberta Menchú, has actually become fragile, vulnerable to any misstep.[16]

Rigoberta Menchú's text had become in the eyes of her advocates, by their own admission, "sacred" and "untouchable," the work of a "living icon" who could do no wrong, for she had "single-handedly changed the configuration of Guatemalan politics." As such, a critical Daphne Patai explained, Menchú's text was "more closely akin to hagiography" than a conventional eyewitness account or biography. The lives of saints are replete with fanciful, unverifiable, and sometimes patently imaginary details.

"But to the pious reader, the historicity of these incidents is unimportant because both the lives and reading about them are acts of faith. . . . [I]t hardly matters to the devout reader whether a particular story is historically accurate or not." Under these circumstances, truth and accuracy become subservient to a higher cause.[17]

TESTIMONY AND TRUTH

For the most part, Menchú and her defenders were unfazed by what they considered to be plausible inaccuracies and modest poetic license. Stoll's exposé, the anthropologist Victoria Sanford explained, was part of a larger struggle within academia "over who will authentically represent experience: those who lived it, or 'objective' privileged, well-funded North American researchers intent on maintaining ownership of the historical record."[18] Moreover, Carol Smith argued, Stoll's nitpicking was an attempt to divert attention from his "weak scholarship on larger issues (Guatemala's guerrillas, historical memory, poverty and its causes, and multiculturalism), with spurious arguments about unrelated matters (whom Rigoberta's father battled over land, who witnessed the death of Rigoberta's brother)."[19]

For reasons born out of ignorance or politics, Stoll stood accused of trivializing the meaning of the *testimonio*—the literary format of *I, Rigoberta Menchú*. Born in the wake of the Cuban Revolution as a means of offering a voice to all sectors of politically liberated societies, the *testimonio* soon became the weapon of choice for disseminating the trials and tribulations of the dispossessed among receptive audiences in the United States and western Europe. The ultimate goal of the *testimonio* was to convey authentic eyewitness accounts of existential conditions among Latin America's subalterns, while at the same time garnering public support for the political struggles of the region's indigenous inhabitants.

Testimonio, advocates cautioned, was not to be confused with the report of a legal witness or a documentary eyewitness account. For both literary and functional reasons, this mode of expression involved a certain amount of poetic license. The *testimonio* in oral cultures and the eyewitness account of a traumatic event are more complex performances than the legalist pledge to report "just the facts." When faced with the nearly impossible task of documenting a great tragedy, ordinary rules of evidence are suspended in order to convey a terrible truth. To insist on only one standard of testimony and truth was, according to Menchú's supporters, a reductionist and historically false enterprise.

Menchú's supporters explained that there were multiple forms of bearing witness and of "truth making." Menchú was the child of a culture in which the borders separating the individual and the collective were tenuous, sometimes even nonexistent. Her appropriation of a verified story of other victims' sufferings as her own was well within the conventions of oral testimony. "Marking any expression as 'testimony' stresses its truth content, the accuracy of its rendition of something experienced or witnessed," Menchú supporter Allen Carey-Webb acknowledged. And yet, he clarified, the *testimonio* should not be narrowly construed in legalistic terms as an accurate personal account of a witness. As a "situated" act of memory, the *testimonio* "stresses the personal as reflective of a larger collective." In other words, the *testimonio* was not only a personal communicative gesture; it was also a collec-

tive performance.[20] At the very beginning of the book, Menchú
in fact acknowledges the communal nature of her testimony:

> This is my testimony. I did not learn it from a book and I
> didn't learn it alone. I'd like to stress that it's not only my life,
> and it's also the testimony of my people. It's hard to remem-
> ber everything that happened to me in my life since there
> have been many bad times, but, yes, moments of joy, as well.
> The important thing is that what has happened to me has
> happened to many other people too: my story is the story of
> all poor Guatemalans. My experience is the reality of a whole
> people.[21]

For all its authority, *testimonio*, as Menchú's advocates acknowledged, had a fundamental weakness. The *testimonio* was a
"collaborative mode of production" between a "metropolitan intellectual," the transcriber, and a usually illiterate "subaltern or
grassroots individual," the storyteller—who "are linked by shared
commitments to social justice and the radical transformation of
capitalist society." This type of communication involves translation, and often alterations, by the transcriber—a process whereby,
despite the best intentions, ideas occasionally are transformed.[22]

The conveyance of an experience between cultures inevitably
involves "systematically distorted communication." In order to
make the message coherent to metropolitan recipients, the witness of the testimony makes crucial decisions based on a partial or
sometime erroneous understanding of the mores of recipients.
Thus, guided by her somewhat flawed understanding of the
Western valorization of the personal over the collective, Menchú
"made a series of strategic, though not necessarily conscious, de-

cisions to present as her own, experiences that happened to others."[23]

Menchú's supporters acknowledged, albeit cautiously, that there were reasons other than the documentation of a tragic reality for Menchú's "authorial exaggeration and embellishment." The wrapping of certain facts "in the cover of personal memoir," Harvey Peskin explained, "stimulated more world attention . . . than had truer, less riveting accounts" disseminated by conventional means.[24] In response to the disillusionment among many who had embraced Menchú's text, both Menchú and her supporters attempted to deflect attention from herself and her text to some of the other protagonists in the debate, such as her audience and, of course, her collaborator and transcriber, Elisabeth Burgos-Debray.

Menchú and her followers attempted to assign the more glaring inaccuracies to Burgos-Debray. The ethnographer-collaborator, Menchú implied, had violated a sacred trust by recoding and reorganizing Menchú's narrative, thereby silencing her authentic voice at crucial moments. Burgos-Debray acknowledged her authorial power. She had actively participated in creating the text, she explained, for a variety of technical reasons. Splicing the various taped interviews into a coherent story was imperative because Menchú had offered a meandering narrative that followed no chronological or thematic format. The ethnographer-transcriber reiterated, however, that she had rearranged the texts but had not altered them. Moreover, her recoding of the interview had received the full approval of Menchú and her political superiors from the Guerrilla Army of the Poor (EGP) prior to publication. Language posed another challenge, inviting further changes in the original text:

> Her [Menchú's] Spanish was very basic. She translated from
> her own language [in her head]; this is what cost me a lot.
> Yes, I corrected verb tenses and noun genders, as otherwise it
> would not have made sense, but always trying to retain her
> own powerful form of expression. Rigoberta's narrative was
> anything but chronological. It had to be put in order. . . . I
> had to reorder a lot to give the text a thread, to give it the
> sense of life, to make it a story, so that it could reach the gen-
> eral public, which I did via a card file, then cutting and past-
> ing. It was hard to give it a sense of continuity in Rigoberta's
> own words.[25]

Burgos-Debray nevertheless stood accused of being the hidden manipulator, providing "incomplete explanations about what
she had eliminated from Menchú's oral account and exercising
censorship over Menchú's words in order to create the appearance of an organized and chronological life history."[26] Yet for
many observers, such accusations failed to dispel the cloud of uncertainty gathering over Menchú's narrative. Menchú had
screened the text before publication, and on Menchú's advice she
had sent the text to Guatemalan guerrilla leaders for final approval. Moreover, in subsequent publications, Menchú retracted
her insinuation and acknowledged the political underpinnings of
her biographical enterprise.

It was precisely the "force-fitting" of events and politics into
"the type of social analysis she wished to dramatize," the anthropologist Roger Lancaster observed, that actually hurt her cause.
Narrative devices such as those employed by Menchú "undercut
the authority of a text that purports to tell us the untarnished
truth—indeed, that reports to embody the truth, in a singular
persona—without proviso or caveats," he observed.[27] Such com-

ments led an enraged Arturo Arias to comment that "only the stupid Gringo of the right or the left—Puritans all—could really believe that what they were seeing [in *I, Rigoberta Menchú*] was absolute truth." At issue, he claimed, was not whether Menchú had presented an untarnished truth but rather whether one privileged the account of a "third-person anthropologist" who happens to be "white, tall, and gringo," rather than that of an oppressed eyewitness whose "only sin is to be female, short, of color, and Guatemalan."[28]

In support of the fundamental difference between "narrative truths" and "so-called 'historical truths,' " Menchú's supporters relied on Holocaust scholarship. In the construction of memory in Holocaust testimonies, scholars have long acknowledged the legitimacy of what Primo Levi defined as "blurred and stylized memories . . . influenced by information gained from later readings or the stories of others." The narrative truth of the survivor, as an amalgam of personal "lived experiences and the experiences of . . . families and communities," had not undermined the veracity of Holocaust experiences.[29] Thus, Menchú's supporters argued that her testimony, despite its flaws, should not undermine the fundamental truth of her personal experience.

By evoking Holocaust scholarship, Menchú's supporters were following the formulaic requirements of a mass-mediated society, where, in order to capture attention, victims of traumatic events adopt routinized media strategies of representation. Menchú and her adversaries understood the power of the Holocaust as a historical template in which the distinctions between good and evil are unassailable. The analogy of the Holocaust as a formula for the Maya predicament evoked profound emotional associations, precluded argument, softened inconsistencies, and privileged interpretations of the tragedy as neither inadvertent nor inevitable but, rather, a calculated act of genocide. Menchú and her supporters grasped that her mostly American audience valorized the Holocaust metaphor and approached what John McWhorter has described in another context as "victimhood not as a problem to be solved but as an identity to be nurtured."[30] Within this framework victims are assigned moral qualities by virtue of their sufferings; thus this Latin American tragedy was assimilated into the fiber of Western imageries of inhumanity. Under these circumstances the veracity of discrete incidents appeared to be a moot point.

Stoll and his allies predictably responded to this attempt to redirect the theoretical and personal aspects of the debate by reiterating the historical and technical differences between what they claimed were two different genres. To begin with, the typical Holocaust testimony did not claim a collective authority. Moreover, even when Holocaust testimonies appropriated the experiences of others, these testimonies reject as point of departure the paradigm of multiple truths. Despite the privileging of the voices of victims, the Holocaust testimony did not deny the authority of scholars to verify, measure, and assess.

Stoll also rejected accusations that he had problematized Menchú's claim to represent all poor Guatemalans in order to sustain the privileged voice of a North American anthropologist. Quite the contrary, he argued. Menchú's supporters had made the unfounded assertion that Menchú spoke for all of her Maya kin, while in fact she was the spokesperson for a specific political cause. Rather than allow the subaltern to speak, Menchú's autobiography privileged one particular voice while silencing many other Maya voices. Stoll, by contrast, claimed that in interviewing hundreds of other Maya, he—and not Menchú—had offered them voice and agency. He rejected insinuations about his interview methods, offering as proof the wide range of opinions expressed by his informants.

While acknowledging the importance of the *testimonio* for understanding Latin America, Stoll contended that Menchú's many misrepresentations went beyond the types of inconsistencies one might expect in this literary form. As far as he was concerned, Menchú's story was not an authentic *testimonio*, but rather an attempt to cram a transparent political manifesto into a format acceptable to an American public. Stoll's main contention, according to an admiring Hal Cohen, was that Menchú's book embodied "a neoromantic notion of an Indian: a subaltern noble savage. In the academic left's eagerness to amplify her voice," she produced an identity that was not hers, but rather a stereotypical portrait of the prejudices embraced by her reading public in North America.

CAN THE SUBALTERN SPEAK?

In Salman Rushdie's *Satanic Verses*, the hero, Saladin, is incarcerated in a detention center for illegal immigrants. Saladin is shocked to discover that all inmates at the center have been transformed into beasts: Saladin himself becomes a hairy goat. How did this happen? Saladin asks a fellow inmate. "They describe us," he answers, "that's all. They have the power of description and we succumb to the pictures they construct."[31]

Can the subaltern speak for herself, or are the world's subordinates destined to succumb, adapt, and behave in the manner prescribed by the metropolitan observer-incarcerator? Moreover, can the dispossessed communicate in an authentic voice that the dominant culture can comprehend? In her classic exposition, the cultural scholar Gayatri Chakravorty Spivak argued that a genuine discourse of the subaltern is impossible because of the need to translate such communication into the cultural context of the metropolis. The only manner of speaking for the subaltern is through words and meanings derived from "cherished religious, cultural, and patriotic" texts of the culture of the dominant. According to Spivak, such a strategy effectively silences the authentic voice of the subaltern. Bereft of resonant authentic texts, the subaltern uses the texts of a first world, privileged discourse, thereby supporting the very structure of dominance she seeks to dismantle. Authentic communication from the periphery to the dominant center is impossible because of the Westerner's inability or unwillingness to comprehend the indigenous texts of subalternity. Authenticity is lost in the translation.[32]

Critics have accused Stoll of taking Spivak's reservations to the extreme. As far as Stoll was concerned, Arturo Arias has argued, Menchú, as the quintessential subaltern, can never speak, not because she lacks authenticity or the command of pertinent idioms, but because she is trapped in a version of Salman Rushdie's detention center, exclusively created for her incarceration and policed by her adversary. She is "not western enough when it comes to the rigor of her logic and use of facts. . . . On the other hand, he finds her too western in her politics" and the manner of conveying her thoughts by means of a thoroughly Western discourse of liberation. Stoll "therefore claims that her ideas are not representative of what he judges to be authentic 'native' Mayan thought." According to the logic of the vicious circle proposed by Stoll, "indigenous persons who use [Western] discourse strategically either lose authenticity" or are driven by ulterior motives.[33]

When speaking for himself, Stoll phrased the issue somewhat differently. Anthropology was never threatened by the voice of the subaltern, he explained, but rather by a willful suspension of disbelief and an uncritical authentication of pseudosubaltern texts. "For scholars insecure about their moral right to depict 'the Other,' *testimonio* and related appeals to the native voice have been a godsend. By incorporating native voices into the syllabus and deferring to it on occasion, we validate our authority by claiming to abdicate it," he observed. Yet, he continued, there is no subaltern voice without rigorous scholarly validation; "there is no substitute for our capacity to judge" and "exercise our authority as scholars."[34] The willful suspension of disbelief that afflicted his colleagues when confronted by the voice of the subaltern belonged to literary criticism, not anthropology.

A whole variety of factors conspired to compromise the subaltern authenticity of Menchú's testimony—if, indeed, it ever had any. To begin with, Arias explains, her transcriber, Burgos-Debray, felt compelled to turn "the text into a hybrid Western-Mayan document with clear Western legibility."[35] Fearful that Maya concepts of time, space, community, and volition would confuse Western readers, Burgos-Debray reordered the text and, in the process, changed its meaning. Moreover, by the time Menchú related her life story to Burgos-Debray she was no longer a subaltern. Her command of Spanish, her devout Catholicism, and her identification with the guerrilla cause dictated, by default, a hybrid text. Menchú employed concepts such as Catholic liberation theology and Marxism, both Western textual traditions; in the process of transliterating her story to these idioms, the authenticity of the Maya tragedy was lost.

Menchú's advocates rejected such purism. Having reconciled

themselves to the fact that certain aspects of authenticity are lost in the process of translation, they still found redeeming qualities in her text. In contrast to Spivak's frustrating search for the authentic, Menchú's advocates claim that the subaltern indeed can speak by virtue of a creative hybridity that weaves together the familiar and the foreign. A whole variety of issues such as the Maya construction of ethnicity, gender, and sexuality; rituals of birth and death; Maya concepts of time, history, and place; and the painful search for collective identity among the fractious Maya—all of these leap out of her testimony. The *testimonio* cannot and should not represent unadulterated authenticity. It is, instead, an open-ended text, more tentative, fluid, and elusive than it is finite or static.

THE MEDIA AND THE ACADEMY

If the fundamental details of the tragedy were indeed true, why did *I, Rigoberta Menchú* encounter such hostility? In practical terms, Menchú's story had served the important function of revealing government human rights violations in Guatemala; the crux of her story concerning the Maya genocide was irrefutable. "If Rigoberta is fundamentally right about what the army did," Stoll asked rhetorically, "if her story expresses a larger truth about the violence, why dissect a personal account that is inevitably selective?"[36]

As a transparently political narrative, *I, Rigoberta Menchú* inevitably aroused an immediate, no less powerful political counterforce. An inexorable urge to dispel the romantic mythology of third world guerrilla movements, which had captivated the imagination of liberal Westerners, invited the interrogation of key portions of Menchú's life story.[37] Stoll and others were particularly committed to such investigation because many of Menchú's most ardent supporters within academia were aware of the gaping discrepancies permeating her story but chose for ulterior reasons to accept her version.

Given the growing skepticism among academics, a search for factual inconsistencies and hidden political bias was probably inevitable. The interrogation of *I, Rigoberta Menchú* was further hastened by a growing disenchantment with multiculturalism and postmodernism. The "new standard of truth" that privileged multiple versions of "truth making" and had challenged traditional, empirically based scientific inquiry had lost some of its charm by the 1990s.

Stoll's journalistic background explains why he, rather than other anthropologists who entertained similar doubts, was both willing and successful in rocking Rigoberta Menchú's pedestal. Wary of the fact that "a scholarly work would not gain nearly as much attention as an attack on the life and testimonial claims of a Nobel Prize winner," observed a disapproving Carol Smith, Stoll consciously affected the style and format of investigative journalism.[38] Moreover, Stoll's thesis placed him firmly outside the community of Latin American anthropologists, particularly Guatemalan specialists. Therefore, an exposé attacking the professional consensus from the outside was his only viable option for gaining the attention of his colleagues. Indeed, Stoll's provocative thesis placed him on the front pages of newspapers and magazines ranging from the *New York Times* and the *Washington Post* to *U.S. News and World Report* and even *Reader's Digest*. In a world in which reputation was no longer measured solely by articles in academic journals, Stoll's gamble paid off phenomenally.

Nevertheless, the discrediting of Menchú was not launched by the publication of Stoll's book; rather, it was the result of the media's validation of his findings. On December 15, 1998, reporter Larry Rohter made the front page of the *New York Times* with sensational revelations about the inconsistencies and reputed lies of a Nobel Prize laureate. Entitled "Tarnished Laureate: Nobel Winner Finds Her Story Challenged," Rohter's article was based on David Stoll's investigations. He produced no independent extension of Stoll's allegations; instead, he corroborated Stoll's material by reinterviewing some of the informants and revisiting the crucial loci where the story had transpired.[39]

Before the publication of this article, Stoll's book was on a swift route to oblivion. Despite extensive efforts to disseminate his findings through the conventional channels of academic discourse, Stoll had made only a faint impact. His validation outside the pale of academia forced his colleagues to engage his text and wrestle with his argumentation. Consequently, Claudia Ferman argues, "the controversy's inception is locked to the publication of the *Times*'s article and not the other way around."[40]

The Rohter article had an important agenda-setting function. Given the media's taste for the personalization of politics, as well as its obsession with lapsed celebrities, the story deflected attention from the actual Guatemalan tragedy and focused instead on Menchú herself. In fact, Ferman points out, once processed by the media, Stoll too lost control of the controversy's agenda.

> What then constitutes the media message that launches the controversy? What is its content? Clearly it is not Stoll's theory on Latin American guerilla movements, nor his thesis on the practice of anthropology in U.S. academe, nor his detailed investigation on Rigoberta Menchú's "autobiography"

and the possible inaccuracies portrayed in the book. . . . In my view, the mass-media message, distributed by Rohter and Stoll contains only the contention that Rigoberta Menchú "lies." . . . The mass-media message, thus, is limited to a list of misrepresentations that Menchú would have incurred in the telling of her personal life.[41]

Thus, a conservative political countercause, an ambitious anthropologist, and a scandalmongering media collectively contributed to the aggressive interrogation of *I, Rigoberta Menchú*. Nevertheless, *I, Rigoberta Menchú* invited skepticism largely because it lacked density. The book presented a heroine "edited and airbrushed into an icon," sorely lacking the complexities and petty ambiguities of real-life events.[42] The relentless probing of the book did not trivialize the horrific reality of the Maya genocide in Guatemala. In this sense, *I, Rigoberta Menchú* had accomplished its ambitious goal. The process did expose, however, the expository weaknesses of oversimplification, and the ill-advised strategy of reimagining a fascinating life story as a modern version of a passion play.

I, Rigoberta Menchú offered what Alcida Rita Ramos has called a "hyperreal Indian," an unambiguous, larger-than-life person who displays immaculately "virtuous principles, ideological purity," and Christ-like sufferings that are more a reflection of a metropolitan audience's fantasies than of reality.[43] The composite Maya of *I, Rigoberta Menchú* has only virtues and no vices; for all her sufferings, she lacks human complexity. And while such narratives may serve the cause of "rallying the faithful," they ultimately fail as comprehensive and complex ethnographic studies. A halo tends to expose blemishes as much as it illuminates virtue.

PART III

The Necessary Scandal

SEVEN

Science Fiction

Sokal's Hoax and the "Linguistic Left"

When Larry was a kid his mother . . . sometimes, out of curios-
ity, stopped the dial of the radio at the place where foreign lan-
guages came curling out of the radio's plastic grillwork: Italian
or Portuguese or Polish . . . "Jibber, jabber," Larry's father
called this talk, shaking his head, apparently convinced, despite
all reason, that these "noises" meant nothing, that they were no
more than a form of elaborate nonsense. Everything ran together; and there weren't any real words the way there were in
English. These foreigners were just pretending to talk, trying
to fool everyone.

Carol Shields, *Larry's Party*

In 1996 the trendy cultural journal *Social Text* issued a special edition dedicated to the "science wars," a highly charged debate associated with the postmodernist skepticism of the sciences' valorization of objective knowledge. Leading this attack was an
army of cultural scholars often associated with the burgeoning

science and technology studies programs—who saw the modernist pretension of pursuing a rational, scientific understanding of the natural world as a dangerous fantasy and a socially repressive enterprise. These intellectual skeptics interrogated the underpinnings of scientific objectivity, at times dismissing the achievements of science as nothing more than politically informed figments. Their alarmed adversaries—scientists from the natural and "hard sciences"—condemned these critics as ignorant, and arrogant philistines, advocates of a nihilistic relativism who willfully conflated the scientific achievements of modernism with the iniquities of capitalism.[1]

The marauding troops of the science wars emerged from different academic persuasions—philosophers, historians, sociologists—some of whom considered the laws of nature, as defined by scientists, as reflections of the subjectivity of their discoverers. They were joined by political scientists and literary critics who uncovered signs of oppression—sexism, political discrimination, and economic inequality—throughout the scientific enterprise, ranging from criteria for the selection of research topics to the very choice of words employed to define the so-called scientific laws. The critics' common denominator was the belief that all knowledge, including empirically based scientific inquiry, is produced by social interactions, is deeply influenced by social biases, and therefore is as much a social construction as it is a reflection of a verifiable reality.

As sympathizers with the rebel cause, the editors of *Social Text* assembled a prestigious group of contributors for its edition on the subject. The most conspicuous contributor was, however, a figure little known in postmodernist circles: Alan Sokal, professor of physics at New York University. Forums for critiquing the underpinnings of science were routinely shunned by practicing scientists, the ostensible victims of such assaults. Sokal's presence in this unusual company was, therefore, extraordinary. Moreover, his article was a proverbial misfit. Even in a publication not known for standardized formats of exposition, Sokal's article was wildly incoherent, rambling, and cluttered with meaningless footnotes and incomprehensible non sequiturs. But above all, Sokal's article was unusual because it was a hoax. Sokal had trundled a Trojan horse into the prestigious domain of cultural criticism.

The article, entitled "Transgressing the Boundaries: Towards a Transformative Hermeneutics of Quantum Gravity," offered a bewildering critique of the "dogma imposed by the long post-Enlightenment hegemony over the Western intellectual outlook," concerning the existence of an external world, whose properties could be deciphered by means of "the 'objective' procedures and epistemological strictures prescribed by the (so-called) scientific method."[2] In elaborately stilted prose, Sokal used the article to feign an attack on the biases of science.

His victims, the editors of *Social Text*, fell obligingly into the trap. Their faux pas resulted from error and misjudgment, as well as from a healthy dose of conceit and hubris. To begin with, they sought no peer review for Sokal's contribution. A screening of the paper by someone with even a passing knowledge of physics would have undoubtedly uncovered the many howlers scattered throughout the rambling article. Its mangled prose, observed an incredulous Paul Boghossian, was nothing more than a collection of "transparent" nonsense. Even a novice should have been able to identify the elements of parody cluttering the article.

Some of these are of a purely mathematical or scientific nature—that the well-known geometrical constant pi is a variable, that complex number theory, which dates from the nineteenth century and is taught to schoolchildren, is a new and speculative branch of mathematical physics, that the crackpot New Age fantasy of a "morphogenetic field" constitutes a leading theory of quantum gravity. Others have to do with the alleged philosophical or political implications of basic science—that quantum field theory confirms Lacan's psychoanalytic speculations about the nature of the neurotic subject, that fuzzy logic is better suited to leftist political causes than classical logic, that Bell's theorem, a technical result in the foundations of quantum mechanics, supports a claimed linkage between quantum theory and "industrial discipline in the early bourgeois epoch." Throughout, Sokal quotes liberally and approvingly from the writings of leading postmodern theorists, including several editors of *Social Text*, passages that are often breathtaking in their combination of self-confidence and absurdity.[3]

For obvious professional reasons, Sokal parodied in particular allegations about the cultural and political biases of physics. As evidence of the supposedly oppressive nature of traditional physics, Sokal trotted out the French philosopher Luce Irigaray, who claimed that even the most hallowed of modern-day physical equations, $E = mc^2$, was saturated with sexism, "as it privileges the speed of light"—a typical male preoccupation with "what goes the fastest" over other natural phenomena. Thus, he declared in a deliberately ponderous manner, scientific knowledge was not objective, but rather a reflection and justification of the social and political authority of the reigning power structure. Science ought to be liberating and therefore subordinated to progressive politics, Sokal proclaimed with panache, adding that an emancipatory scientific agenda still awaited "a profound revision of the canon of mathematics."

Soon after its publication, Sokal revealed his hoax. Troubled "by an apparent decline in the standards of intellectual rigor in certain precincts of the American academic humanities," Sokal argued that he had employed a hoax as his way of calling attention to the decline in academic discourse, in particular its attack on the hard sciences. In order to "test the prevailing intellectual standards," he had initiated "a modest (though admittedly uncontrolled) experiment: Would a leading North American journal of cultural studies—whose editorial collective includes such luminaries as Fredric Jameson and Andrew Ross—publish an article liberally salted with nonsense if (a) it sounded good and (b) it flattered the editors' ideological preconceptions?" After a few meek requests for minor corrections, the article was accepted.

Sokal explained his motivation as stemming from alarm at the spread of "subjectivist thinking."

> Intellectually the problem with such doctrines is that they are false (when not simply meaningless). There *is* a real world; its properties are *not* merely social constructions; facts and evidence *do* matter. What sane person would contend otherwise? And yet, much contemporary academic theorizing consists precisely of attempts to blur these obvious truths—the utter absurdity of it all being concealed through obscure and pretentious language.[4]

Sokal was no less concerned with the political ramifications of postmodern relativism and its alleged denial of reality. Postmodernism had eclipsed the traditional political left's recourse to science and rationality, as ways "for combating the mystifications promoted by the powerful." Sokal acknowledged that science was far from an ideologically innocent calling. But how, he wondered, would a denial of facts and reality contribute to the discovery of an effective treatment for AIDS or unmask the irrationality of racism and sexism? Subverting conventional notions of truth simply for the sake of subversion or intellectual diversion, and without providing alternatives, was, according to Sokal, a dangerous alternative to confronting the hard realities of social injustice and political irrationality.

Sokal and his allies had a field day, calling their rivals to task for their lack of standards, their boorishness, and their patronizing manner. Writing in one of the many publication forums dedicated to the hoax, Jay Rosen lashed out at the editors of *Social Text*, who apparently had few misgivings about publishing articles they did not understand, so long as they "dovetailed" with the journal's politics. Rosen accused the instigators of the science wars of promoting obscurity to conceal the fact that a once exciting and innovative intellectual trend now resorted to impenetrable jargon to conceal its inherent, self-satisfied stagnation. Publishing an incomprehensible text for ulterior motives was, Rosen announced, a sign of intellectual bankruptcy.[5]

The unwitting publication of a parody lent credence to a growing suspicion that some of the movers and shakers among the science critics neither understood science nor espoused a meaningful social critique. For Ruth Rosen, "Sokal's spoof exposed the hypocrisy practiced by these so-called cultural revolutionaries. They claim to be democratizing thought, but they purposely write in tongues for an initiated elite. They claim that their work is transformative and subversive, but they focus obsessively on the linguistic and social construction of human consciousness, not on the hard reality of people's lives."[6] Barbara Ehrenreich found the hoax to be the beginning of a long-awaited emancipation from the suffocating, dogmatic, and murky hold of postmodernism. "For over a decade, students taking courses in literature, film, 'cultural studies,' and even, in some cases, anthropology and political science, were taught that the world is just a socially constructed 'text' about which you can say just about anything you want, provided you say it murkily enough." Sokal, she claimed somewhat hyperbolically, had changed all that with a few hilarious strokes of his keyboard.[7]

The editors of *Social Text* remained unrepentant. They claimed patronizingly to have spotted Sokal's contribution as "hokey," an inarticulate attempt by a scientist to "capture the 'feel' " and bask in the approval of erudite cultural critics. Had such an awkward piece of literature been advanced by someone from the social sciences or the humanities, they commented, it would have been rejected. But coming from a repentant scientist, they felt that the piece—however sophomoric—merited publication.[8]

The defensive partisans of *Social Text* also argued rather desperately that the real culprit was Sokal himself. A hoax, they argued, constituted a fundamental breach of academic ethics. Writing in the *New York Times*, the postmodernist luminary Stanley Fish reminded his readers that the entire process of academic exchange and publication was founded upon the assumption of integrity. Perhaps forgetting that he had described the hoax as a collection of transparent inanities that reflected the author's inability to understand the field he was parodying, Fish claimed that there was no defense against Sokal, who had "carefully packaged his deception so as not to be detected except by someone who began with a deep and corrosive suspicion."[9]

Sokal, an offended Stanley Aronowitz complained, also targeted the wrong sort of journal. *Social Text*, he explained in what appeared to be a radical transformation of its public image, "has never been in the deconstructionist camp; nor do its editors . . . doubt the existence of a materialistic world. . . . *Social Text* was founded, and remains within, the Marxist project—which everyone knows, is profoundly materialistic."[10] A culturally illiterate Sokal, he lamented, could not identify a postmodernist even if she hit him in the face.

The editors of *Social Text* added the somewhat unconvincing spin that crucial parts of Sokal's article basically made sense and therefore merited publication. Bruce Robbins, one of the editors, leaned on the comfortable crutch provided by a senior writer at *Scientific American*, who claimed that Sokal's hoax had inadvertently corroborated their critique of science. Sokal had "proposed that superstring theory might help liberate science from 'dependence on the concept of objective truth.' Professor Sokal later announced that the article had been a hoax, intended to expose the hollowness of postmodernism," while in actual fact, "superstring theory is exactly the kind of science that subverts conventional notions of truth."[11]

Finally, critics chastised Sokal for aiding and abetting a common enemy. The academy in general—not just cultural studies—was under siege, a disapproving Ellen Schrecker observed. By arguing that much of what is done in an important wing of the academy was not only irrelevant but wrong, Sokal's "merry prank" had backfired and undermined the entire academic enterprise. "The battleground here is not a text but the bottom line," she argued. Populist pundits, powerful economic forces, and narrow-minded lawmakers had pounced upon the hoax in their effort to "demonize those sectors of the academic community that encourage critical thinking and offer an alternative perspective on the status quo." Such assaults on critical thinking, she feared, would eventually spread to "mainstream science" as well. By employing a hoax rather than more conventional means of criticism, Sokal had placed himself firmly with the camp of science bashers.[12]

ROOTS OF THE SCIENCE WARS

Sokal's hoax is usually interpreted as a well-aimed blow at a new and particularly dangerous assembly of subversives, the bearers of a postmodern, anti-Western, and antiscientific, "fashionable nonsense." The science wars that gave birth to the hoax, were, according to this common interpretation, symptomatic of a peculiar and novel crisis embedded in the culture and politics of the end of the twentieth century.[13] According to this view, the waning prestige of the sciences following the conclusion of the Cold War had eroded the protective walls surrounding the sciences, thereby eliciting an interrogation of its most fundamental underpinnings. The end of the twentieth century also witnessed the rise of multiculturalism, with its tendency to relativism and its hostility to the Eurocentric version of truth seeking. Contrary to previous intellectual controversies within academia, the science wars were not a dialogue; rather, the two sides in the polemic talked past each other. "To the uninitiated the language of science might just as well as well be Sanskrit or Swahili," a bemused observer noted. By the same token, cultural critics use ordinary language but bend and twist it in abnormal ways. "Deliberate obscurity, irony and metaphor are intended to discomfit the reader."[14]

In fact, the science wars revived a number of well-worn academic controversies, all of which predated postmodernism, the waning prestige of post–Cold War science, and the destabilizing influences of the late twentieth century. To begin with, the science wars bore striking resemblances to the 1950s controversy of the "two cultures," the supposedly unbridgeable rift separating scientists from intellectuals. The term was coined by the British renaissance man C. P. Snow, who identified a post–World War II culture of academic enclosures, two mutually suspicious and un-communicating fiefdoms within the university. Both subcultures suffered from what Snow defined as an abysmal ignorance of the other. By Snow's own standards, cultural scholars were oblivious to the most basic of scientific concepts. Thus, he recalled a literary gathering where he appeared to be the only person who knew anything about the second law of thermodynamics. Conversely, he wondered if the typical scientist had even a passing knowledge of the works of Shakespeare.[15]

Snow was not, however, a neutral observer. While urging scientists to broaden their cultural horizons, he denounced the gate-keepers of culture as modern-day Luddites, steeped in mythology and regressive romanticism. Quoting a string of literary figures who had espoused extreme political positions, Snow implied that the antimodern bearers of "traditional culture" were responsible for the great bloodbaths of the twentieth century. Scientists, by contrast, were democratically minded, optimistic, and forward-looking. For all their shortcomings, their quest for objectivity and informed skepticism promised to solve the practical problems of humankind in an objective and equitable manner.

Snow was not without his critics, such as the unforgiving literary scholar F. R. Leavis, who dismissed the concept of the two cultures as shallow punditry. Leavis argued that Snow had offered a confused mixing of metaphors and had misunderstood the logical division of intellectual labor that characterized the Western mode of knowledge seeking. The second law of thermodynamics was not an artifact of cultural trivia to be bandied about at soirées, but rather a specialized form of knowledge, useful for the scientist but irrelevant for the cultural scholar, whose tools were words and whose interests were mores and values. Contrary to Snow, Leavis found nothing inherently antimodern or politically regressive in the study of literature and the arts. The craft of such intellectuals was merely different from the work of scientists, not inferior; they had no need for the technical tools of science. Science, Leavis argued, was a technical enterprise aimed at improving material standards of living; it was not, as Snow implied, a guide to moral conduct. Moral issues and the interrogation of values were the province of those whom Snow had so casually trivialized as reactionaries or dead wood.[16]

The science wars permeated as well the work of Thomas Kuhn. Writing in the early 1960s, Kuhn described the development of scientific theories as a social and political process. In a counterintuitive fashion, Kuhn argued that scientific theories were not discarded because new objective knowledge or sharper forms of analysis had disproved them but rather because of what he called "paradigm shifts," fundamental changes in approach or outlook whose origins were largely social. Science, he stated, was first and foremost a sociological process, a battle in which the primacy of a paradigm or a particular school of thought was governed by political factors rather than scientific innovation.[17] The eventual codification of one particular theory as a paradigm and the attendant dismissal of competing structures was not the result of superior scientific rigor, but rather the outcome of a social struggle: which theory bearer could muster the necessary disciples to enforce acceptance. The scientific paradigm, Kuhn argued, was first and foremost a sociological construct and not necessarily the result of some innovative intellectual breakthrough. Normal science, far from seeking constant new horizons, demanded enforcement of an orthodoxy and repression of competing views, whatever their merits.

Kuhn explained that paradigm shifts occurred only in times of crisis. Confronted with repeated failures to solve scientific problems within the established framework, the ruling paradigm loses its authority, to be superseded by a new paradigm. Yet the new paradigm offers different cognitive standards, a new way of looking at familiar phenomena rather than the discovery of hitherto unavailable information. Its success hinges upon the ability to muster a critical mass of supporters. Those who espouse different ways of thinking—novel or traditional—are "simply read out of the profession."[18]

Kuhn's model of science as a social enterprise was, then, the basis for the questioning of scientific activity associated with the science wars. It was Kuhn, and not some latter-day deconstructionist, who gave birth to the idea that many of science's discoveries were not the inevitable result of objective and rigorous scientific work, but rather were related in one way or another to political and personal motives. It was from Kuhn that critics of science learned to dismiss the idea that reality had an intrinsic structure that could be deciphered only through rigorous and objective science.

Sokal's hoax had its origins not only in Kuhn but also in a new version of good old American academic parochialism. In John Sturrock's review of *Fashionable Nonsense* (1998), one of Sokal's many spinoffs from the hoax, Sturrock argued that the hoax was an instance of the periodic reaction to fears of that well-known intellectual affliction, the LFF—"the latest foreign fraud." Every now and again, he argued, the endemically provincial, Anglo academic establishment reacted against attacks on "our mental virginity" by depicting the intrusion of foreign ideas as a sort of intellectual pandemic. The vectors of the disease in Sokal's hoax were mostly French philosophers, whom Sokal regarded as the "prime source of the infection." The mesmerizing ways of these Continental poseurs had caused infinitely more damage than their American followers.[19] Bruno Latour, one of Sokal's favorite targets, responded by describing this pervasive fear of foreign infection as the work of jingoistic "theoretical physicists deprived of the fat budgets of the Cold War," who adopted the old populist refrain of pinning the blame for their misfortune on luckless foreigners. "France, in their eyes, has become another Colombia, a country of dealers who produce hard drugs—derridium, lacanium, to which American doctoral students have no more resistance than to crack."[20]

WHY A HOAX?

Foisting a hoax on unsuspecting victims was itself nothing out of the ordinary. Hoaxes offer distinct advantages over more conventional forms of criticizing the academy. Sokal would have never penetrated the bastions of his adversaries by means of a straightforward critique. Consequently, and almost inevitably, he employed a ruse rather than direct confrontation. Moreover, a gimmick was a prerequisite for media exposure. "A physicist who used the cachet of physics overtly . . . in order to mislead scholars editing a nonrefereed journal in a relatively new and experimental field . . . would not make a good story," the science historian Susan Lindee observed. In his initial marketing of the hoax, Sokal cast himself as the outsider "living by his wits," who had managed by virtue of a clever maneuver to outwit the supposedly powerful, secure, and arrogant editors of *Social Text*. This "inversion of power relations" between an influential member of a powerful discipline (Sokal) and the editors of an esoteric cultural journal catering to the initiated but nevertheless bothersome few, "provided an interesting and newsworthy transposition" of an issue that under normal circumstances would have transpired within secluded intellectual surroundings. In a strange way, Lindee observed, Sokal's hoax may have served his opponents as well. As far as she was concerned, science studies were like "a minor remote colony that has been staging ineffectual revolutions for thirty years and all of a sudden finds itself the subject of a full dreadnought attack by the Royal Navy. It's outgunned, of course, but at least the revolution has the Crown's attention."[21]

For the most part, Sokal's critics were neither amused by the hoax nor gratified by the attention. They described Sokal's ploy as an anti-intellectual weapon for silencing dissident opinion. Even though he pleaded after the fact that his hoax was a "small contribution" to reviving the dialogue "between humanists and natural scientists—'two cultures' which . . . are probably farther apart in mentality than at any time in the past 50 years," Sokal appeared, to his detractors, to have sought the converse.[22] By conflating all social critique of science with its most radical stream, Sokal effectively precluded any attempt to interrogate science's standards of truth and objectivity. Even though he claimed for himself the layman's prerogative to intelligently debate nonscientific matters—such as the root causes of World War I—he insisted in the same breath that nonscientists had no corresponding right to discuss scientific issues. Nonscientists lacked the minimal competence necessary for deciphering the specialized intricacies of physics and related fields.

Defenders of *Social Text* argued that because it attempted to silence critics through ridicule Sokal's hoax had ramifications far beyond the lampooning of pompous scholars. They rejected the assumption that a rigorous, well-applied scientific methodology filtered out political and social bias and therefore had no need for external critique. Such views struck critics as an "article of faith akin to a religious belief," or an exercise in escapism, seeking to ignore the agenda-setting priorities of government and commercial funders. A silencing-by-parody belittled critics, thereby avoiding the painful examination of "what . . . science [did] not study because of its funding sources," political biases, and social assumptions.[23]

Critics within the academy argued that the hoax was designed to revive moribund intellectual checkpoints, restrict trade routes of knowledge, and reinforce the divisionary walls of academia. Interdisciplinary inquiry such as that pursued within science and technology studies programs threatened the privileged standing of the sciences within academia. By arguing that nonscientists were, at best, incompetent to understand what scientists do, Sokal appeared to be defending his domain against trespassers. In an age of shrinking funding, researchers in a defense-related discipline such as physics felt threatened. The science wars had the potential to affect the funding of these fields by undermining their authority. Sokal and his supporters sought, therefore, authority by insularity.

THE SIGNIFICANCE OF THE SCIENCE WARS

Do the science wars matter, or are they merely another skirmish in ongoing academic turf fights? According to the University of Toronto philosopher James Robert Brown, the underlying premises of the science wars are far too important to leave in the hands of specialized practitioners. "Since much of the science wars is about how we live, the outcome will affect huge numbers of people who are not intellectually directly involved in the debate itself." Brown did not, of course, mean that the public must become experts in the machinations of supercolliders. Instead he called for greater transparency and involvement in the political, social, and economic arrangements of the scientific enterprise. Who pays for the latest scientific breakthroughs? Are minorities and women fairly represented within positions of power within the science community? Does the allocation of funds to certain projects serve the best and broadest public interest? Such crucial issues, Brown argued, cannot be left in the hands of an intellectual minority on either side of the science wars.[24]

University of Texas physicist Steven Weinberg offered a radically different opinion, calling for maintaining the autonomy of science. "If we think that the discoveries of science are flexible enough to respond to the social context of their discovery, then we may be tempted to press scientists to see nature in a way that is more proletarian, or feminine, or American or religious or whatever else it is we want." Western civilization has "been powerfully affected by the discovery that nature is strictly governed by impersonal laws." These laws were "objectively real" and had "no legitimate implications whatever for culture, or politics, or philosophy."[25]

Sokal's hoax brought to the forefront the issue of specialized language and lay audiences. Thus, literary scholar Michael Warner defended the use of jargon and specialized prose as the most functional means for creating a meaningful and practicing community of scholars. Somewhat skeptical of the benefits of translating complex issues into accessible language, Warner dismissed the common assumption that the garnering of a large audience by means of accessible prose assured greater political or social resonance.[26] Advocates of specialized prose claimed valid reasons for its use. By subverting everyday language, postmodernists strove to uncover hidden ideologies and repressive linguistic structures. The deconstruction of language—the code for deciphering everyday reality—offered an indispensable key to higher political consciousness. New linguistic terminologies and structures are imperative for the expression of radical perceptions and the subversion of the hidden yet restrictive social frameworks that permeate categories of race, class, and gender. Standardized prose, by contrast, "naturalizes" or "essentializes" crucial aspects of culture and politics that are, in actual fact, socially constructed and therefore possible to change.

By contrast, critics of such jargon-ridden discourse lamented the abandonment of an intellectual space where nonspecialists could come to terms with political and social realities. An insurmountable and deliberately high barrier of obtuse language limited access to the arguments of postmodernists. Most recourse to "pomo jargon," Ellen Willis acknowledged, was more a performative act than a radical, subversive feat. English was a rich, "supple and inventive language quite capable of subverting itself."[27] Indeed, the only meaningful lesson that *Social Text* editor Andrew Ross could extract from Sokal's mocking of his journal was the need to revive the use of standard English. "There is a high-theory ghetto," he acknowledged, "and there is a way out."[28]

Having had more than her fair share of exposure to the science wars, hoaxes and all, journalist Sheilla Jones appeared, like most of the dwindling crowd of once curious onlookers, to be fed up with the sight of intellectual elites "busy hurling glyphs and obscurationist phraseology across the abyss that divides them." Given the fact that "ordinary folk suffer little risk of being clobbered by a stray pi or fragment of ironic facetiousness," why should one care about such esoterica? Aside from the entertainment value of the hoax and the amusing sight of bickering pointed heads, she dismissed their squabbles over language as ephemeral and intellectually self-indulgent.[29]

In fact, Richard Rorty argued, the science wars were the proverbial storm in a teacup. The decline of Western civilization will not be hastened if the "not so radical, original, or relevant disciples of Foucault are taken seriously"; nor, he argued, will democracy's checks and balances crumble if positivistic supporters of Sokal's cause continue to monopolize the main media outlets. "The science wars are in part a product of deep and long-lasting clashes of intuition, but mostly they are media hype—journalists inciting intellectuals to diabolize one another. Diabolization may be helpful in keeping intellectuals aroused and active, but it need not be taken very seriously."[30]

Sokal's hoax merely ratified academia's time-honored and glib tradition of preferential treatment afforded to luminaries. Sokal's prank was accepted precisely because he was a particularly attractive "catch." Although striking the editors of *Social Text* as somewhat unusual, his article was assured publication by virtue of his professional stature. This journal was neither the first nor the last publication to accept a brand name without checking too carefully the quality of the product. Despite its espousal of critical thought and the leveling of academic discourse, *Social Text* was, and still is, a highly restrictive domain. Like most prestigious journals, it offers preferential arrangements for academic superstars, who are exempt from the exacting standards imposed on mere mortals.

If indeed the primary objective of the hoax was to silence critics, its most lasting result was precisely the opposite. The most prominent aspect of the Sokal affair is the intense level of participation in the debate and its enduring presence. The high polemic value and unusual life span of Sokal's hoax are functions of the transfer of the debate to cyberspace, where countless Web sites are still dedicated to the hoax and the science wars. Sokal himself produced an elaborate Web site to preserve his hoax.[31] However, it is precisely on the Web that his apparent triumph, which appeared to reestablish clear distinctions between science and pseudoscience, punditry and analytical rigor, has been compromised by the medium and its technology. On the Web, neither Sokal nor his critics control the nature, scope, or texture of the debate. Easy public access to the Internet has diluted Sokal's triumphant hoax with a voluminous correspondence splintering in a multitude of different directions. The Internet has enabled the curious layperson to be an equal and active creator of content and viewpoints, rather than a mere recipient of the views of Sokal or his adversaries. In a debate where there is no center or periphery, information flows in multiple directions with no central authority exercising control. Contrary to the leitmotif of the hoax, the Web sites generated by this event suggest that in the mind of a vast, inquisitive public, truth and objectivity are contestable issues.

THE BOGDANOV AFFAIR

To sum up, the chain of events able to explain the transition from the topological phase to the physical phase of the space-time might be the following:

{thermodynamical equilibrium} → *{KMS state breaking}*
→ *{imaginary time/real time decoupling}*
→ *{topological state/physical state decoupling}*
→ *{Supersymmetry breaking}*.

We have given a detailed description of such a transition in [19]. Likewise, the supersymmetry is broken in [5–6] by the finite temperature, which corresponds in our view to the decoupling between real and imaginary (topological) temperature (the topological temperature being identified, in Kounnas model, with the inverse radius of a compactified Euclidean time on $S^1 : 2\pi T = 1/R$). Applying this representation, the partition function in our case is given by the (super)trace over the thermal spectrum of the theory in 4 dimensions. According to this, supersymmetry breaking and transition from topological state to physical state might be deeply connected.[32]

The preceding quotation is not another nonsensical snippet from the feverish mind of Alan Sokal, but an excerpt from one of five peer-reviewed articles published by Grichka and Igor Bogdanov (sometimes spelled Bogdanoff), the French twins and TV personalities whose work may be described as Sokal's hoax in reverse.

Much to the embarrassment of the physics establishment, the Bogdanov brothers persuaded a number of physics journals— including the venerable, peer-reviewed *Classical and Quantum Gravity* and the *Annals of Physics*—to publish what appeared to be "a nonsensical string of trendy terms and mathematical equations" masquerading as a theory on the state of the universe on the eve of the Big Bang. Basing their work "on something called the Kubo-Schwinger-Martin condition," their theory supposedly suggested a "mathematical connection between infinite temperature and imaginary time" when, prior to the Big Bang, "all space and time were squeezed into a point without any width or duration—an infinitesimal space called singularity."[33]

The theory, deemed "intriguing" by one of the peer reviewers who later acknowledged that he had "no deep understanding of the ideas," was, according to physicist John Baez of the University of California, Riverside, a "sort of stringing together [of] plausible-sounding sentences that add up to nothing."[34] Other theoretical physicists described the brothers' collaborative brainstorming as something between "gibberish" and "nutty," perhaps even a hoax foisted upon venerable journals by a pair of suspiciously incompetent individuals.

The brothers Bogdanov, known in France primarily as the writers and producers of a pop-science TV show, describe themselves as the descendants of Russian and Austrian nobility. Born in 1949, they are graduates in applied mathematics from the École Pratiques des Hautes Études in Paris (Igor) and the University of Burgundy (Grichka). Sometime during the 1980s, the brothers began pursuing doctorates at a string of different French institutes. In 1999, approximately ten years after they began their graduate studies, Grichka received a Ph.D. in mathematics from the École Polytechnique in Paris; he was awarded the lowest possible passing grade. Igor failed to pass and was given a second chance by his committee on the condition that he publish three articles in peer-reviewed journals. His submissions included the contested articles. Igor was subsequently awarded his Ph.D. from University of Bourgogne. He, too, received the lowest possible grade. When queried by the *New York Times* about the quality of the Bogdanovs' work, one of a long string of thesis advisors, Dr. Daniel Strenheimer, explained that "these guys worked for ten years without pay. . . . They have the right to have their work recognized with a diploma, which is nothing much these days."[35] In the interim, the brothers published a book, claiming on the dust jacket that they were Ph.D.'s prior to receiving their degrees. They were sued for plagiarism (they countersued and eventually settled out of court), and continued with their TV work.

Somewhat embarrassed by the publication of an incoherent contribution that had passed peer review, the editor of the *Annals of Physics* pleaded innocence, as he had not been at the helm of the journal at the time. He somberly vowed to tighten up the journal peer-review procedures in light of the fiasco. The editor of *Classical and Quantum Gravity*, who described the article published by his journal as "a potpourri of the buzzwords of modern physics that is completely incoherent," issued an apology to his readers for the publication of the Bogdanovs' paper. The journal also vowed to improve its quality control.[36]

When pressed by journalists to explain how, indeed, the Bogdanov paper had been reviewed without requests for revisions, an MIT physicist used metaphors from the world of arts and humanities: "One person looks at a piece of [modern] art and says it is gibberish; another person looks and says it's wonderful."[37] Frank Wilczek, the editor of *Annals in Physics*, offered a less philosophical explanation. Rehearsing the types of argument offered during the Sokal debate, he explained that the peer reviewers of physics publications were reluctant to acknowledge that that they failed to understand the work of their peers, "especially if it's very fashionable."[38]

"The terrible conclusion some might draw from the episode," a bemused observer remarked, "is that string physics is no more a 'science' than" the type of social science lampooned by Alan Sokal.[39] A bristling Sokal responded that he had never "treated his hoax as demonstrating that the social sciences were fatally flawed." Backtracking furiously from his original contentions, Sokal recalled that he had already gone on record as stating that the hoax "doesn't prove that the whole field of cultural studies, or cultural studies of science—much less sociology of science—is nonsense. . . . It proves only that the editors of one rather marginal journal were derelict in their intellectual duty, by publishing an article on quantum physics that they admit they could not understand," without bothering to use a process of peer review.[40] Sokal refrained from commenting directly on the Bogdanov affair.

As for the Bogdanovs, they summarized the episode in one admirably appropriate sound bite: "Nonsense in the morning may make sense in the evening or the following day."[41]

EIGHT

What Do the Scandals Mean?

I am grateful to postmodernism for many things, especially for
giving me an alternative apprehension of the world in terms
of difference and continuity rather than binary oppositions, but
I am tired of ontological insecurity and epistemological chaos.
I need order. I miss metanarrative.

Ewa Domanska, "Hayden White: Beyond Irony"

In the early 1970s, the southern Philippine island of Mindanao
achieved brief fame when prominent media reports heralded the
"discovery" of the Tasaday people. These isolated, primitive island dwellers were reputedly one of the last extant remnants of a
Stone Age culture. The "gentle" foragers apparently had no word
for war or conflict, nor had they developed any type of weaponry
for personal safety or for hunting. They allegedly lived in total
harmony with each other and with nature, living on plants and
small animals. Dubbed by some as "palaeo-hippies," they appeared to disprove theories of genetically imprinted recourse to
violence as well as notions of "selfish genes."[1]

The "discovery" of a preagricultural human society unleashed a flurry of media interest and generated a series of studies singing the praises of "the gentle Tasaday." Such acclaim was based, however, more on a combination of conjecture, artful political spin, and wishful thinking than on verified knowledge. For the first fifteen years after their discovery, the Marcos regime had limited access to the island, ostensibly attempting to protect this remnant of pristine human culture from the iniquities of modernity. Given the Western craving for an antidote to contemporary social ailments, the Tasaday myth as a nostalgic exemplar of a time and place that ought to have existed remained undisturbed. Numerous professional anthropologists—all of whom should have known better—jumped on the media wagon and pronounced the authenticity of the Tasaday, even though they too had had limited contact with the major protagonists in this saga.

It was only after the fall of Marcos that a Swiss journalist managed to penetrate the Tasaday region, where, he claimed, he uncovered one of the scientific world's greatest hoaxes. The Tasaday, according to Oswald Iten, did not exist. A number of local residents had been hired by government officials to impersonate noble savages for the benefit of gullible consumers of the image. Caught unprepared by the arrival of journalists, the impersonators had dropped their exotic natural clothing for regular Western garb and admitted their complicity in the affair.[2]

An embarrassed Philippine government reacted to these revelations by quarantining the area and vigorously defending the authenticity of the Tasaday. Such actions did little to halt the change in the public image of the tribe and its intellectual guardians. The media unanimously presented the episode as an artful hoax while condemning the Tasaday's anthropologists as intellectual charlatans. The Tasaday affair had all the ingredients of a modern-day scandal: a narcissistic, media-savvy cadre of anthropologists who had trotted out the Tasaday as a reflection of their prejudices, even at the expense of compromising professional standards; an intrusive media responsible for both the construction and deconstruction of the myth; and, after revelations of the hoax, dire predictions of intellectual bankruptcy of a once proud intellectual enterprise.

When the dust settled, the Tasaday affair—like most academic scandals—offered multiple and mostly conflicting conclusions, ranging from painful self-flagellation to a dogged insistence that, despite overwhelming evidence to the contrary, the story might be true. As part of this ritual cycle of incrimination and counter-incrimination, anthropologists sparred over the fascination of the "primitive," and the attendant nature versus nurture controversy, while offering conflicting opinions on the ability of anthropologists to separate fact from fiction, reality from fantasy.[3]

While ostensibly a localized and well-defined dispute, the Tasaday affair produced numerous insights into the meaning of scandals in the latter-day American academy. In almost predictable fashion, the hapless Tasaday aroused heated exchanges concerning the significance of the ethnological craft suspended between textual analysis and science, the public obligations of anthropologists, and finally, the role of the media in dictating the anthropological agenda. Drawing specifically on examples related to the "gentle primitives," I seek a sense of closure for the inherently open-ended topic of academic scandal and intellectual malfeasance.

EXPLANATION 1: THE IMAGINARY SCANDAL

Perhaps there was no scandal at all.

For the postmodernist, the concept of intellectual malpractice is of limited epistemological value. Under the ironic gaze of postmodernism, the distinctions between guilt and innocence, integrity and deceit permeating the scandal debates appear irrelevant. The postmodern position argues that academic malfeasance is not an indisputable concept, but a mutable, ideologically saturated affair. Given a pervasive skepticism concerning the ability to capture reality, postmodern observers find little value in distinguishing right and wrong. Instead, they "read" all versions of academic controversies as equally valid "texts," offering insight into the ideology of the actors rather than any objective representation of historical or ethnographic "truth." The crucial issue, anthropologist Talal Asad explains, is not "whether ethnographies are fact or fiction. . . . What matters more are the kinds of political projects cultural inscriptions are imbedded in."[4]

While avoiding a rigid dismissal of either a historical or an ethnographic reality, postmodernists censure the prosecuting parties in academic scandals for confusing their linguistic encoding of reality for authenticity itself. Language has only a limited capacity to grasp reality and is mostly a reflection of the inner world of its inscribers. Thus, anthropologist Jean-Paul Dumont observes, representations of the Tasaday are mostly reflections of their ethnographers. Episodes like the Tasaday "arrive and depart, and others come to take their places, who in turn take their leave and return again." In the final analysis and at "the end of the anthropological field glasses . . . what appears is the *anthropos du jour*," an ideological construct rather than some revealing slice of reality.[5]

By the same token, the postmodernist creed assumes that both alleged wrongdoers and their accusers are engaged in equally imaginative and imaginary intellectual constructions. Disciplinary protocols do not reveal reality, but instead an intellectual variation of a "seventeenth-century garden, where nature was ruthlessly adapted to our conceptions of order, symmetry, and rationality." Much like the master gardener, ethnographers and historians remake reality in their image. Whether consciously or otherwise, they bypass "reality in their effort to domesticate it and adapt it to the restraints of their language and of the tropes inherent in it."[6]

According to Clifford Geertz, "the real is as imagined as the imaginary," by which he means that the intellectual products of the sister crafts of history and ethnography appear to be constructed rather than discovered, made rather than revealed.[7] The methods of historical research and ethnography are both prisoners of the language employed by practitioners. Far from being a technical device for the conveyance of ideas, language is theory-ridden, self-reflexive, and inherently self-limiting. Language both presupposes and creates the context of interpretation.

Thus, when confronted with two radically different versions of the Tasaday affair, the postmodernist avoids judgment, preferring instead to interrogate all texts for insights into the ethnographer's inner world. To such interrogators of the ethnographical paradigm, multiple (mis)readings of the Tasaday were inevitable because anthropologists—like all others who pretend to objectivity—reflect their own ideological concerns. Hence,

Aram Yengoyan has observed, understanding the ideological underpinnings of all representations of the "gentle" Stone Age
Tasaday is of greater interest than assessments of authenticity or
fraud.

> Exotic "others" have been similarly characterized by descrip-
> tive (usually one-word) labels that emblemize what the
> people and the society are thought to be about. Thus Kalinga
> are litigious, Samoans are sexually liberated, Tikopians are
> hierarchical, Javanese are patient, Balinese are theatrical, and
> Yanomamo are fierce. Each of these cases as caricatures
> might be blurred, over-generalized, or at odds with other de-
> scriptions, but in each case, for different reasons, the label
> seems to stick as part of ethnographic reporting as well as
> cultural translations for Western audiences.[8]

The group of about twenty-six cave dwellers captured the public imagination because their very presence drew on powerful
metaphors. In an American society scarred by the Vietnam War,
the gentle, nonviolent, and egalitarian Tasaday provided an attractive vignette of our pristine origins. As Leslie Sponsel observed, the discovery of the Tasaday in the early 1970s provided
a "source of hope—that a more peaceful world might exist."
Sponsel, who was one of Napoleon Chagnon's main prosecutors
in the Yanomami affair, was, of course, disappointed by the exposure of a fraud; a gentler and kinder primitive would have been
quite convenient for his ideological project. Nevertheless, Sponsel argued that the main reason for challenging the authenticity
of the Tasaday was not epistemological. The scandal was driven
by the pervasive cultural and political climate of the late twentieth century. In a country obsessed with a "Rambo mentality,"
there was little tolerance for narratives that conflicted with the

concept that "human aggression and territoriality are innate drives in *Homo sapiens*."[9]

EXPLANATION 2: THE SCANDAL
AS PATHOGRAPHY

In marked contradistinction to this textual approach, embattled keepers of the faith approach academic scandals as a symptom of a disease-ridden academic polity, a veritable "university in ruins." Such pessimistic viewpoints are, at times, tempered by distinctions between the scandal as an illness, a passing malaise affecting a particular individual, and the scandal as pandemic, a rampant, debilitating disease that has taken control of an entire community. Singular acts of wrongdoing are construed as symptomatic of a larger problem, a virus, passing from one infected individual to another.[10]

The disease affecting the contemporary academy is diagnosed by critics as a particularly virulent strain of narcissism. They dismiss the fixation on text-as-self-reflection as a self-centered, obsessive-compulsive disorder, in which the authorial personae of historians and anthropologists, rather than their subject matter, take center stage. While acknowledging the elusiveness of objectivity and reality, proponents of scientific methodology argue that an approximate version of reality—past or present—can be ascertained by painstaking research, dispassionate organization, and transparent explanations that acknowledge the limits of objectivity.

In fact, the controversy with adherents of the "textual approach," historian Gabrielle Spiegel explains, is not about epistemology or even methodology, as is commonly thought, but about ethics. Speaking for historians and—indirectly at least—for anthropologists, Spiegel places faith in an "ethical core," a firm belief that "arduous, often tedious labor"—documentary, ethnographic, or any combination of the two—"yields some authentic knowledge of the . . . 'other,'" whether dead or distant. While acknowledging that ethnographic or historical evidence is inevitably slanted by the "perceptions and biases" of its intellectual practitioners, she argues for "a degree of autonomy, in the sense that it cannot (putatively) be made entirely to bend to the historian's will" or the ethnographer's prejudices.[11]

Dismissing the idea that language constitutes a terminal barrier separating the interpreter from reality, Spiegel claims that whatever epistemological problems exist in its employment, language still functions "instrumentally by mediating *between* us as perceiving, knowing subjects, and the absent past" or distant present. Language, she argues, is neither "perfectly transparent [n]or completely opaque."[12] Thus, the historian E. P. Thompson wrote many years ago, one could supersede cognitive limitations by "listening" to one's "sources rather than merely giving shape to them," as well as practicing "a discipline of attentive disbelief."[13]

Hence, critics of postmodernism have argued that controversies such as the Tasaday affair had little to do with the limitations of language, the frustrations of truth seeking, or the unfathomable opaqueness of the "other." Critics claim that even a mere novice should have discovered "in a matter of hours" that the Stone Age image of the Tasaday was patently fraudulent. The Tasaday's caves were immaculately clean, with no visible evidence of midden, the layer of garbage that accumulates over the years in cave-dwelling societies. Moreover, the surrounding flora and fauna did not offer adequate sustenance for foragers. The Tasaday's tools appeared to be patently useless and most probably fake; the cave dwellers made no effort to contact or trade with nearby villages; and the size of the group was too small to sustain a population. Despite protestations to the contrary by those who embraced the Tasaday's authenticity, their language suspiciously resembled neighboring dialects, thereby contradicting the sensationalist pronouncements of hundreds of years of linguistic and cultural isolation.[14] The Tasaday affair appeared to be a prime example of what the historian Oscar Handlin condemned in another context as the inundation of the modern university by "plagiarists, loafers, incompetents, drunkards, lunatics," and the most insidious enemy of all: the glib intellectual trend-surfer.[15]

THE INDISPENSABLE SCANDAL

Curiously, both defenders of conventional professional standards and their postmodern adversaries share a viewpoint regarding academic scandals. Both acknowledge that the unitary standards of the scientific enterprise are an endangered species. The postmodernists celebrate the demise of these criteria while critics express dismay, but both assume an impending upheaval.

While wary of the dangers of trivializing either position, I find that the debates on academic impropriety discussed in this book suggest vibrancy rather than trauma. These debates may, at times, signify imminent catastrophe, the bankruptcy of scientific pretensions, or some other form of decline. Yet they may equally be part of a necessary process of reinvention.

Deviancy, Kai Erikson wrote many years ago, is "not a simple kind of leakage which occurs when the machinery of society is in poor working order." The defining of miscreant behavior is an essential community operation for marking boundaries and providing guidelines for "an orderly sense of . . . identity." Thus, Erikson explained, the demarcation of deviancy is as much a social act as it is a moral one. Aberrance "is not a property *inherent in* any particular type of behavior; it is a property *conferred upon* that behavior" for the functional purpose of inscribing rules or reassessing borders, intellectual, ideological, or otherwise.[16] The creation of deviancy is an indispensable social activity in any viable community. Scandals, in other words, reveal vital signs rather than pathogens.

With these thoughts in mind, I regard the most conspicuous accusations of academic wrongdoing in recent years as somewhat more complex than simple instances of depravity or symptoms of the unraveling of grand narratives and paradigmatic conventions, whether salutary or cataclysmic. Deviant behavior may sometimes be, in the lingo of postmodernists, an issue of positionality, or in simpler terms, in the eyes of the beholder; in other instances, it is unambiguous. Yet deviant behavior per se does not lead inevitably to a public inquest or scandal. Contrary to the implications in Erikson's study on errant faith among Puritans, the rise in accusations of deviancy within the modern academy does not necessarily reflect a community crisis. Errancy discourses are sometimes the result of a technical shift rather than an epistemological crisis.

I have argued that the surge in visible accusations of deviancy is primarily the result of the demise of conventional scholarly mediation rather than an existential crisis. Academic enclaves, such as history and anthropology, possess, in theory, mechanisms for maintaining disciplinary order that stop short of public disgrace. Disciplinary professional associations once provided the necessary apparatus for regulating deviancy. These mechanisms are now functionally obsolete. Writing in 1995, a somewhat baffled George Stocking noted that the number of "adjectival" anthropology subdivisions organized under the auspices of the AAA had reached chaotic proportions.

> There are now fifteen subsidiary "societies" (including the ethnological, humanistic, linguistic, medical, psychological, urban, visual, Latin American, and European, as well as those devoted to "consciousness" and "work"); ten "associations" (including Africanist, Black, feminist, political and legal, senior, and student), as well as several regional associations and one devoted to "the practice of anthropology"; three "councils" (education, museum, nutrition); two "sections" (biology and archeology); and one uncategorized grouping called simply "Culture and Agriculture." Finally, there is a unit devoted to "general anthropology"—the rubric which at one time might have included all the rest, but whose now residual status is appropriately marked by its denomination as a "division."[17]

Such disciplinary fragmentation led the AAA to renounce its authority as arbitrator of disciplinary disputes. This riotous assembly of incompatible faiths remains uncomfortably linked through inertia, bureaucratic entanglements, and fear of alternatives, rather than by any meaningful intellectual common denominator.

"Fin-de-siècle boundary vignettes" of fragmentation and the waning of a conventional judicial apparatus have affected history, too.[18] Over the years, the movers and shakers of the Organization of American Historians (OAH) have periodically expressed epistemological self-doubt. The criticism of disciplinary standards as politically repressive devices eventually induced a crisis in 1991, when the OAH newsletter published a call for papers from a pseudoprofessional organization dedicated to Holocaust denial. Despite OAH president Joyce Appleby's plea to reject a request that contradicted the most basic "values that bring us together as members of the OAH," the executive board voted to accept the advertisement, apparently unwilling to prescribe professional standards for separating history from pseudohistory. In seeking to accommodate historical perspectives "representing all points of view"—not only those of professional historians—the board proceeded to commit an act of professional self-immolation. A public uproar eventually led the executive board to rescind its decision and publicly condemn Holocaust denial. Nevertheless, the board continued to disclaim its prerogative to set professional standards. Decisions on the legitimacy of controversial scholarship were, according to the board, matters to be decided by the general public and not a handful of executives.[19]

Across the street, self-doubt hit the American Historical Association (AHA) as well. In May 2003, the AHA acknowledged that—willingly or otherwise—it too had lost much of its authority and was therefore terminating its procedures for investigating professional wrongdoing, because they had "proven to be ineffective for responding to misconduct in the historical profession." Citing a lack of sanctions as well a fear of lawsuits, the association decided instead to mount an educational campaign aimed at sharpening public awareness of plagiarism, falsification, and other types of violations.[20]

The professional journal, another tool for purging the deviant in a circumspect yet ruthlessly efficient manner, has suffered a similar waning of power. The conventional, peer-reviewed academic publication once possessed the technical and juridical capacity to mainstream or marginalize, embrace or ostracize. Editorial policies provided clear definitions of intellectual propriety and defined the boundaries of professional conduct; editors could literally write transgressors out of the story. Technological shifts in mediation, coupled with widespread epistemological uncertainty, have eroded the authority of such professional gatekeepers. As an indication of its waning importance, the circulation of the *American Anthropologist*, the official organ of the AAA, dropped from a peak of eleven thousand subscribers to less than eight thousand in the late 1990s.[21] As for the historical profession, no less a figure than David Thelen—at that time, editor of the flagship *Journal of American History*—questioned the authority of his own journal, calling for a transferal of the power of inventing history to nonprofessionals—"the people."[22]

The contemporary academic discourse is inattentive to conventional modes of power; an authoritative center has been overwhelmed by a privatized periphery. Yet, the radical privatization of the academic enterprise and fears of unchecked transgressions have not created a vacuum. Alternative methods of disciplinary enforcement are thriving. In other words, the public airing of deviancy occurs when the conventional means for controlling doctrinal discourse malfunction. In previous periods, cases similar to the ones analyzed here were often dealt with discreetly, usually far from the public eye, and occasionally even swept under the carpet. Alternative and highly visible forums of adjudication become visible and vocal when conventional avenues for projecting rules are contested, reassessed, reframed, or rendered obsolete by cultural and technological shifts.

The expansion of interpretive communities and the exposure

of controversy by disparate communicative formulas and disruptive technologies have challenged professional concepts of role, identity, and community. Moreover, technology and modes of dissemination have blurred distinctions between judge and jury, audience and agents. Nevertheless, the wresting of control from formal gatekeepers, and the subsequent rise in relatively unmonitored expressions of opinion, have not led, as one might expect, to turmoil or a radical rethinking of standards. To be sure, public scandals may occur more frequently, but they do not necessarily represent either disciplinary turmoil or the wholesale jettisoning of standards. In a somewhat counterintuitive manner, the modern-day version of the vox populi is decidedly averse to revisionism and intolerant of deviancy. As this book has shown, the participation of amateur scholars, graduate students, and laypersons in Internet forums and other modes of discussion suggests widespread rejection of those who seek to experiment with the canon, retool scholarly guidelines, or transgress conventional rules and regulations.

The public scandal is, then, border control by other means. It is at times a technical adjustment to changes in scholarly communication and community arrangements, and not necessarily or singularly an indication of crisis. The "discovery" of deviance is first and foremost a didactic protocol for informing and conceptualizing intellectual boundaries; it is a rhetorical device for preserving social structures and controlling ambiguity, and not a distress signal. In fact, no intellectual activity "can be wholly deviant with respect to the age in which it appeared," observes Laurence Moore. "Everything, after all, is a product of its cultural milieu and therefore, has some more or less normal meaning within the culture."[23] Hence, "there is a chilling but obvious truth in the thought that did deviance not exist, it would be necessary to invent it," historian J. C. Davis observes in his study of religious dissent in early modern England. "For it is only through deviance that we understand normality."[24] If this is indeed the case, the proliferation of disaster warnings, on the one hand, and gleeful funerals, on the other, may be somewhat premature.

NOTES

PREFACE AND ACKNOWLEDGMENTS

1. For a good survey of these issues, see Thomas Bender, ed., *Rethinking American History in a Global Age* (Berkeley, Calif.: University of California Press, 2002).

2. For a converse example of a fruitful and expansive exchange based on a meeting of Israeli and Palestinian intellectuals, see Ron Robin and Bo Stråth, eds., *Homelands: Poetic Power and the Politics of Space* (Brussels: P.I.E.–Peter Lang, 2003).

INTRODUCTION

1. George Kennan, "The Sisson Documents," *Journal of Modern History* 28 (June 1956): 130–154.

2. Ibid., 132–133.

3. Les Adler and Thomas Paterson, "Red Fascism: The Merger of Nazi Germany and Soviet Russia in the American Image of Totalitarianism," *American Historical Review* 75, no. 4 (April 1970): 1046–64.

4. Elzbieta Sklodowska, "The Poetics of Remembering, the Poetics

of Forgetting," in *The Rigoberta Menchú Controversy*, ed. Arturo Arias (Minneapolis: University of Minnesota Press, 2001), 252.

5. Alun Munslow, *Deconstructing History* (London: Routledge, 1997), 198.

6. Anna Grimshaw and Keith Hart, "Anthropology and the Crisis of the Intellectuals," *Critique of Anthropology* 14, no. 3 (1994): 228.

7. For a different opinion, see David Callahan, *The Cheating Culture: Why More Americans Are Doing Wrong to Get Ahead* (Orlando, Fla.: Harcourt, 2004).

8. Sherry Turkle, "Virtuality and Its Discontents," *American Prospect* 24, no. 7 (December 1, 1996), www.prospect.org/print/V7/24/turkle-s .html; Jimmy Dean Smith, " 'Honest about His Experience': History as Eyewitness News," *PopPolitics.com*, June 26, 2002, www.poppolitics .com/articles/2001–06–22-ellis.shtml.

9. John M. Watanabe, "Silence and Solidarity across a Watershed of War: The Heritage of U.S. Complicity in Guatemala," *American Anthropologist* (March 2002): 104, n. 1, 331.

10. Roman Jackiw, cited in Dennis Overbye, "French Physicists' Cosmic Theory Creates a Big Bang of Its Own," *New York Times*, November 9, 2002.

11. Deborah Tannen, *The Argument Culture: Changing the Way We Argue and Debate* (London: Virago Press, 1999).

12. Walter Ong, *Fighting for Life: Contest, Sexuality, and Consciousness* (Ithaca, N.Y.: Cornell University Press, 1981).

13. Deborah Tannen, "Agonism in the Academy: Surviving Higher Learning's Argument Culture," *Chronicle of Higher Education*, March 31, 2000, B7.

14. Seyla Benhabib, "Taking Ideas Seriously," *Boston Review*, December 2002–January 2003, http://bostonreview.mit.edu/BR27.6?benhabib .html; Ricoeur is cited in this article.

15. Sherry Turkle, *Life on the Screen: Identity in the Age of the Internet* (New York: Simon and Schuster, 1995).

CHAPTER 1. PLAGIARISM AND THE
DEMISE OF GATEKEEPERS

1. Both the mainstream and academic media in the United States and elsewhere provided continuous coverage of the Oates controversy. See, for example, "The Case of the Lincoln Book," editorial, *Washington Post,* May 30, 1992; Denise Magner, "Stephen Oates Again Is Accused of Plagiarism," *Chronicle of Higher Education,* April 14, 1993, A19; "Scientific Fraud," *Economist,* June 19, 1993, 88.

2. Doris Kearns Goodwin, cited in Bo Crader, "A Historian and Her Sources," *Weekly Standard,* January 28, 2002, www.weeklystandard.com/Content/Public/Articles/000/000/000/793ihurw.asp. For a summary of the Goodwin case, see History News Network Staff, "How the Goodwin Story Developed," History News Network (HNN), http://hnn.us/articles/590.html. For another prominent case of plagiarism, involving historian Ann Lane, see Nathan Williams, "Ann Lane's Dissertation," HNN, November 11, 2002, http://hnn.us/articles/1097.html.

3. See, for example, Jonathan Ned Katz, "Stephen Ambrose and Plagiarism," *New York Times,* January 12, 2002, a brief response to David D. Kirkpatrick's front-page article "As Historian's Fame Grows, So Do Questions on Methods," *New York Times,* January 11, 2002; Associated Press, "Home Town Stands by Beleaguered Historian," *Australian,* January 23, 2002; Toby Hamden, "Alarm and Plague of Plagiarism," *Daily Telegraph* (London), March 23, 2002; Lance Gould, "Historian Ambrose: 'I'm No Plagiarist,' " *New York Daily News,* May 9, 2002.

4. Exchange of accusation and defense between James Morris and Philip Foner, in "Philip Foner and the Writing of the Joe Hill Case: An Exchange," *Labor History* 12, no. 1 (1971): 81–114.

5. Ibid.

6. Recently, labor historian Melvin Dubofsky and others have offered incriminating evidence of additional instances of plagiarism committed by Philip Foner. See "Was Philip Foner Guilty of Plagiarism?" HNN, June 2, 2003, http://hnn.us/articles/1481.html.

7. For a summary of the Oates saga, including Oates's version and re-

sponses from the instigators of the accusations, see Stephen Oates, "I Stood Accused of Plagiarism," HNN, April 15, 2002, http://hnn.us/articles/658.html.

8. Stephen Oates, "A Horse Chestnut Is Not a Chestnut Horse: A Refutation of Bray, Davis, MacGregor, and Wollan," *Journal of Information Ethics*, 3, no. 1 (Spring 1994): 26–27.

9. Jones, cited in Denise Magner, "History Group Says Professor Gave Inadequate Credit," *Chronicle of Higher Education*, May 27, 1992, A15. See also Robert Jones, "Popular Biography, Plagiarism, and Persecution," *Journal of Information Ethics* 3, no. 1 (Spring 1994): 80–82.

10. Hans L. Trefouse, "The Oates Case," *Journal of Information Ethics* 3, no. 1 (Spring 1994): 76–77.

11. John Swan, "Sharing and Stealing: Persistent Ambiguities," *Journal of Information Ethics* 3, no. 1 (Spring 1994): 43.

12. Robert Bray, "Reading between the Texts: Benjamin Thomas's *Abraham Lincoln* and Stephen Oates's *With Malice to None*," *Journal of Information Ethics* 3, no. 1 (Spring 1994): 21.

13. On Stewart's and Feder's involvement in this and other cases of scientific misconduct, see "Walter Stewart's Site of Scientific Misconduct," http://home.t-online.de/home/Bernhard.Hiller/wstewart/main.html.

14. Michael Burlingame, " 'A Sin against Scholarship': Some Examples of Plagiarism in Stephen B. Oates's Biographies of Abraham Lincoln, Martin Luther King Jr., and William Faulker," *Journal of Information Ethics* 3, no. 1 (Spring 1994): 48–49.

15. David Wheeler, "NIH Reassigns 2 Researchers," *Chronicle of Higher Education*, April 21, 1993, A16; David Wheeler, "Did 2 Who Fought Research Fraud for NIH Go Too Far?" *Chronicle of Higher Education*, May 12, 1993, A16; Stephen Burd, "Fraud Office in Trouble," *Chronicle of Higher Education*, November 24, 1993, A21.

16. Louis D. Rubin, "Binges and Trysts," *New York Times*, September 20, 1987.

17. Oates, cited in Bray, "Reading between the Texts," 21.

18. Eric Foner, "The Man Who Had a Dream," *New York Times*, September 12, 1982.

19. Stephen Oates, *A Woman of Valor: Clara Barton and the Civil War* (New York: New Press, 1994).

20. Andrew Delbanco, "The Angel of the Battlefield," *New York Times*, June 12, 1994.

21. Davis, cited in Denise Magner, "Professor Did Not Adequately Attribute Material in Book, History Group Says," *Chronicle of Higher Education*, May 27, 1992, A15.

22. AHA decision cited in Denise Magner, "Verdict in a Plagiarism Case," *Chronicle of Higher Education*, January 5, 1994, A17.

23. Fred Barnes, "Stephen Ambrose, Copycat," *Weekly Standard*, January 14, 2002, 27.

24. Mark Lewis, "Did Ambrose Write Wild Blue, or Just Edit It?" *Forbes.com*, February 27, 2002, www.forbes.com/home/2002/02/27/0227ambrose.html.

25. Ibid.

26. Balkoski, cited in Mark Lewis, "More Controversy for Stephen Ambrose," *Forbes.com*, September 1, 2002, www.forbes.com/2002/01/09/0109ambrose.html.

27. Mark Lewis, "Nothing Like It in the World? Hardly," *Forbes.com*, January 17, 2002, www.forbes.com/2002/01/17/0117ambrose.html.

28. Mark Lewis, "Dueling D-Day Authors: Ryan versus Ambrose," *Forbes.com*, January 29, 2002, www.forbes.com/2002/01/29/0129ambrose.html.

29. Copies of the exchange of letters between Ryan and Ambrose appear in ibid.

30. Kia Shant'e Breaux, "Historian Stephen Ambrose Addresses Plagiarism Charges," *Nando Times*, February 1, 2002, www.nando.net/entertainment/story/235707p-2256415c.html (defunct Web site).

31. Lewis, "Dueling D-Day Authors."

32. Rosenthal, cited in Wendy Kaminer, "Heavy Lifting," *American Prospect* 13, no. 4 (February 25, 2002): 9.

33. Ambrose, cited in Kirkpatrick, "As Historian's Fame Grows."

34. George McGovern, "Letter of Support from WWII Veteran George McGovern," January 23, 2002, www.stephenambrose.com/ g_mcgovern.html.

35. David Lavender, cited in Lewis, "Nothing Like It in the World?"

36. Eric Foner, cited in Hillel Italie, "Historian Stephen Ambrose Faces More Allegations of Lifting Material," Associated Press, January 9, 2002.

37. Kolleen Guy, cited in Samar Farah, "Taking a Page out of Another's Book," *Christian Science Monitor,* January 31, 2002.

38. Thomas Preston, cited in Tan Vinh, "Plagiarism Scandal Puts Schools in Bind," *Seattle Times,* February 2, 2002.

39. Jackson Lears, cited in Jay Tolson, "Whose Own Words?" *U.S. News and World Report,* January 21, 2002, 52.

40. James McPherson, cited in David Robinson, "Ambrose Bestsellers Questioned for Citation Methods," *Daily Princetonian,* February 4, 2002.

41. Ken Ringle, "Stephen Ambrose and the Rights of Passage," *Washington Post,* January 11, 2002.

42. The Takiff story appears in David Plotz, "The Plagiarist: Why Stephen Ambrose Is a Vampire," *Slate,* January 11, 2002, http:// slate.msn.com/id/2060618/sidebar/2060623.

43. Stephen Ambrose, "Beware the Fury of an Aroused Democracy," *Wall Street Journal,* October 1, 2001.

44. Robinson, "Ambrose Bestsellers Questioned," 3.

45. Nicholas Confessore, "Selling Private Ryan," *American Prospect* 12, no. 17 (September 24–October 8, 2001): 21.

46. Michael Manville, "Private Ryan, Amnesiac," September 6, 2001, www.freezerbox.com/archive/2001/10/war.

47. Thomas Nutter, "Citizen Soldiers," H-WAR, *Freezerbox Magazine,* February 18, 2002.

48. Ambrose, cited in Confessore, "Selling Private Ryan," 21.

49. Kaminer, "Heavy Lifting," 9.

50. Ibid.

51. Plotz, "The Plagiarist."

52. Breaux, "Historian Stephen Ambrose Addresses Plagiarism Charges."

53. Thomas Mallon, *Stolen Words: Forays into the Origins and Ravages of Plagiarism* (New York: Penguin Books, 1989).

54. Peter Morgan and Glenn Reynolds, *The Appearance of Impropriety: How the Ethics Wars Have Undermined American Government, Business, and Society* (New York: Free Press, 1997), 149.

CHAPTER 2. THE NOBLE LIE

1. José Saramago, *The History of the Siege of Lisbon*, trans. Giovanni Pontiero (New York: Harcourt Brace, 1997).

2. Michael Bellesiles, *Arming America: The Origins of a National Gun Culture* (New York: Alfred A. Knopf, 2000), 4.

3. Ibid., 14.

4. Ibid., 103, 297.

5. Ibid., 258.

6. Ibid., 80.

7. Roger Lane, review of *Arming America*, by Michael Bellesiles, *Journal of American History* 88, no. 2 (September 2001): 614–615; Edmund Morgan, "In Love with Guns," *New York Review of Books*, October 19, 2000, 30; Richard Slotkin, "The Fall into Guns," *Atlantic Monthly*, November 2000, 114–118; Garry Wills, "Spiking the Gun Myth," *New York Times*, September 10, 2000.

8. Bellesiles, *Arming America*, 262.

9. Morgan, "In Love with Guns," 30.

10. Wills, "Spiking the Gun Myth."

11. Jack Rakove, "Words, Deeds, and Guns: *Arming America* and the Second Amendment," *William and Mary Quarterly* 59, no. 1 (January 2002): 207.

12. Ibid.

13. Michael Bellesiles, "Disarming Early American History," *Common-Place*, September 2000, www.common-place.org/vol-01/no-01/arming.

14. Michael Bellesiles, "Disarming the Critics," *OAH Newsletter*, November 2001, www.oah.org/pubs/nl/2001nov/bellesiles.html.

15. The most persistent and ultimately the most successful of these Web scholars was Clayton Cramer. See his Web site at www.claytoncramer.com.

16. Bellesiles, *Arming America*, 22, 41.

17. Robert O'Connell, review of *Arming America*, by Michael Bellesiles, *Armed Forces and Society* 27, no. 3 (Spring 2000): 487–491.

18. Comment by Andy Frechting, January 24, 2002, in *OAH Newsletter*, November 2001, www.oah.org/cgi-data/view.html.

19. Comment by Don Williams, January 24, 2002, in *OAH Newsletter*, November 2001, www.oah.org/cgi-data/view.html

20. Michael Bellesiles, "Silenced: Is Civil Discourse Quelling Scholarship on Controversial Issues?" cited in *Academic Exchange*, Emory University, February 18, 2002, www.emory.edu/ACAD_EXCHANGE/2002/decjan/silenced.html.

21. Michael Bellesiles, interview by Brooke Gladstone, *On the Media*, National Public Radio, August 25, 2001, www.wnyc.org/onthemedia/transcripts_082501_guns.html.

22. Daniel Justin Herman, "Michael A. Bellesiles's *Arming America: The Origins of a National Gun Culture*," History News Network (HNN), June 17, 2001, http://hnn.us/articles/99.html.

23. James Lindgren and Justin Lee Heather, "Counting Guns in Early America," *William and Mary Law Review* 43, no. 2 (2002): 1781. See also James Lindgren, "Fall from Grace: *Arming America* and the Bellesiles Scandal," *Yale Law Journal* 111 (2002): 2195–2249.

24. Herman, "Michael A. Bellesiles's *Arming America*." See also Joyce Lee Malcolm, "Arming America," *Texas Law Review* 79, no. 6 (May 2001): 1657–1676.

25. Jackson Lears, "The Shooting Game," *New Republic*, January 22, 2001, 30; Bellesiles, *Arming America*, 15.

26. Kevin Hardwick, comments in response to colloquy on *Arming America*, February 4, 2002, *Chronicle of Higher Education* Web site, http://chronicle.com/colloquy/2002/guns/88.htm.

27. Michael Bellesiles, cited in Danney Postel, "Did the Shootouts from *Arming America* Divert Attention from the Real Issues?" *Chronicle of Higher Education*, February 1, 2002, A12.

28. Bellesiles, cited in Jen Sansbury, "Scholar under Heavy Fire for Book on Gun Culture," *Atlanta Journal-Constitution*, January 20, 2002.

29. Bellesiles, "Disarming the Critics."

30. Kevin Hardwick, comments in response to colloquy on *Arming America, Chronicle of Higher Education* Web site.

31. David Skinner, "The Historian Who Couldn't Shoot Straight," *Weekly Standard*, February 25, 2002, 31.

32. Statement by OAH Executive Board, *OAH Newsletter*, November 2001, www.oah.org/pubs/nl/2001nov/newsorg.html#Anchor-36501.

33. Statement by Chairman Bruce Cole on Newberry Library Fellowship Award, HNN, May 21, 2002, http://hnn.us/articles/691.html.

34. Gloria Main, "Many Things Forgotten: The Use of Probate Records in Arming America," *William and Mary Quarterly* 59, no. 1 (January 2002): 212.

35. Ibid., 213.

36. Ira Gruber, "Of Arms and Men: Arming America and Military History," *William and Mary Quarterly* 59, no. 1 (January 2002): 220.

37. Randolph Roth, "Guns, Gun Culture, and Homicide: The Relationship between Firearms, the Uses of Firearms, and Interpersonal Violence," *William and Mary Quarterly* 59, no. 1 (January 2002): 234.

38. Michael Bellesiles, "Exploring America's Gun Culture," *William and Mary Quarterly* 59, no. 1 (January 2002): 262.

39. A refutation of Bellesiles's flood defense appears in Jerome Sternstein, " 'Pulped' Fiction: Michael Bellesiles and His Yellow Note Pads," HNN, May 20, 2002, http://hnn.us/articles/742.html.

40. Bellesiles, "Exploring America's Gun Culture," 262.

41. Emory University, "Report of the Investigative Committee in the Matter of Professor Michael Bellesiles," July 10, 2002, www.emory.edu/central/NEWS/Releases/Final_Report.pdf.

42. Michael Bellesiles, "Statement on Emory University's Inquiry of

Arming America," Emory University Web site, www.emory.edu/central/NEWS/Releases/B_statement.pdf.

43. Ibid.

44. "Michael Bellesiles Resigns from Emory Faculty," *NewsEmory*, October 25, 2002, www.emory.edu/central/NEWS/General_archive.html.

45. Announcement of Columbia University Board of Trustees, HNN, December 13, 2002, http://hnn.us/articles/1157.html.

46. Knopf decision, released on January 8, 2003, is cited in HNN, http://hnn.us/articles/691.html#latest.

47. This felicitous phrase belongs to Jerome Sternstein, in " 'Pulped' Fiction."

48. James Lindgren, "Mr. Bellesiles's Emails," HNN, April 15, 2002, http://hnn.us/articles/678.html; Andrew Ackerman, "E-mails May Include Lies," *Emory Wheel*, April 25, 2002, www.emorywheel.com/vnews/display.v/ART/2002/04/25/3cc89bcfe177d.

49. Bellesiles, *Arming America*, 11.

50. Melissa Seckora, "Disarming America," *National Review*, October 15, 2001, www.nationalreview.com/15octo1/seckora101501.shtml.

51. Lindgren and Heather, "Counting Guns in Early America," 1832.

52. Bellesiles, *Arming America*, 262.

53. Roth, "Guns, Gun Culture, and Homicide," 227.

54. See, for example, Judith McGraw, *Early American Technology: Making and Doing Things, from the Colonial Era to 1850* (Chapel Hill: University of North Carolina Press, 1994); Gloria Main, *Tobacco Colony: Life in Early Maryland, 1650–1720* (Princeton, N.J.: Princeton University Press, 1982); Anna Hawley, "The Meaning of Absence: Household Inventories in Surry County, Virginia, 1690–1715," in *Early American Probate Inventories*, ed. Peter Benes and Jane Benes (Boston: Boston University Press, 1987), 27–28; Alice Hanson Jones, *Wealth of a Nation to Be: The American Colonies on the Eve of the Revolution* (New York: Columbia University Press, 1980).

55. Hardwick, February 4, 2002, comments in response to colloquy on *Arming America*.

56. Sanford Levinson, "The Embarrassing Second Amendment," *Yale Law Journal* 99 (1989): 648, n. 54.

57. Gruber, "Of Arms and Men," 217.

58. Lears, "The Shooting Game," 30.

59. O'Connell, review of *Arming America*, 487.

60. Lindgren and Heather, "Counting Guns in Early America," 1841.

61. Bellesiles's response to James Lindgren, HNN, April 17, 2002, http://hnn.us/articles/678.

62. Clayton Cramer, "What Clayton Cramer Saw and (Nearly) Everybody Else Missed," HNN, January 6, 2003, http://hnn.us/articles/1185.html.

63. See, for example, Michael Bellesiles's review of *The Deadly Ethnic Riot*, by Donald Horowitz, *Journal of the West* 42, no. 3 (Summer 2003): 103; and his review of *American Law in the Twentieth Century*, by Lawrence Friedman, *Journal of American Studies* 37, no. 2 (August 2003): 325.

64. History News Service, "Statement of Purpose," January 4, 2004, www.h-net.org/%7Ehns.

65. See, for example, Michael Bellesiles, "Captive Scholarship Serves Nobody Well," *Charleston Gazette*, January 11, 2004; Michael Bellesiles, "In Technology We Shouldn't Trust (War): Shock and Awe Have Their Limits, as History Has Shown," *St. Louis Post-Dispatch*, December 8, 2003.

66. Letter from James Banner to the editors of History News Network, November 11, 2003, http://hnn.us/articles/1794.html.

CHAPTER 3. "A SELF OF MANY POSSIBILITIES"

1. Milton Cohen, "Fitzgerald's Third Regret: Intellectual Pretense and the Ghost of Edmund Wilson," *Texas Studies in Literature and Language* 33, no. 1 (Spring 1991): 64.

2. Ellis, cited in "At War with Truth," editorial, *Boston Globe*, June 20, 2001, A12.

3. Walter Robinson, "Professor's Past in Doubt," *Boston Globe*, June 18, 2001.

4. Jack Thomas, "The Road to the Ellis Story," *Boston Globe*, July 2, 2001.

5. Ana Marie Cox, "In Wake of the Scandal over Joseph Ellis, Scholars Ask 'Why?' and 'What Now?' " *Chronicle of Higher Education*, July 13, 2001, O10.

6. President Joanne Creighton of Mount Holyoke College, cited in ibid.

7. Statement by Joanne Creighton, August 17, 2001, www .danford.net/prexy.htm.

8. Joseph Ellis, "Further Statement of Joseph J. Ellis," Mount Holyoke College, August 17, 2001, www.mtholyoke.edu/offices/comm/news/ellisstatement.html.

9. Peg Tyre and Brian Braiker, "Improving on History," *Newsweek*, July 2, 2001, 34; John Omicinski, "The Unmasking of Phony War Heroes," *Denver Post*, September 9, 2001; Kenneth Bredemeier, "Another Defeat in the Lying Game," *Washington Post*, December 23, 2001.

10. Richard John Neuhaus, "The Tangled Web," *First Things*, November 2001, 67–70.

11. Ramesh Ponnuru, "Liars for the Cause: When Scholars Ditch the Truth," *National Review*, August 6, 2001, 24–25.

12. Joan Cocks, cited in Patrick Healy, "A War with Truth," *Boston Globe*, June 28, 2001; Joan Cocks, letter to the editor, *Boston Globe*, July 8, 2001.

13. Donal O'Shea, cited in Josh Tyrangiel, "A History of His Own Making," *Time*, July 2, 2001, 52.

14. Richard Jensen, in History News Network, "Readers Sound Off about Joe Ellis's Suspension," HNN, August 18, 2001, http://hnn.us/articles/205.html.

15. David Nyberg, cited in Bredemeier, "Another Defeat in the Lying Game."

16. Howard Segal, "What's Lesson of Ellis Affair?" *Boston Globe*, August 21, 2001.

17. Michael Burlingame, in "Readers Sound Off about Joe Ellis Suspension."

18. David Garrow, cited in Lynn Smith and Tim Rutten, "For Historian's Students, a Hard Lesson in Lying," *Los Angeles Times*, June 22, 2001. Garrow would later find himself embroiled in a nonacademic scandal of his own. See Arielle Kass, "Professor Suspended after Alleged Assault," *Emory Wheel*, January 23, 2003, 1.

19. Jim Sleeper, cited in Smith and Rutten, "For Historian's Students, a Hard Lesson in Lying."

20. Scott Gac, in "Readers Sound Off about Joe Ellis Suspension."

21. Doris Kearns Goodwin, cited in Healy, "A War with Truth."

22. Ann Lane, in "Readers Sound Off about Joe Ellis's Suspension"; on Ann Lane's plagiarism ordeal see the exchange between Lane and the editors of the HNN, in Nathan Williams, "Ann Lane's Dissertation," November 11, 2002, http://hnn.us/articles/1097.html.

23. Joseph Ellis, *American Sphinx: The Character of Thomas Jefferson* (New York: Alfred A. Knopf, 1997), 97.

24. Joseph Ellis and Eugene Foster, "When a Saint Becomes a Sinner," *U.S. News and World Report*, November 9, 1998, 67.

25. Joseph Ellis, "Jefferson: Post-DNA," *William and Mary Quarterly* 57, no. 1 (January 2000): 126.

26. Joseph Ellis, "The Magnificent Seven: An Interview with Pulitzer Prize Winning Historian Joseph J. Ellis," interview by David Tebaldi, *Mass Humanities* (Spring 2001), www.mfh.org/newsandevents/newsletter/MassHumanities/Spring2001/ellisprt.html.

27. Joseph Ellis, "Role of a Lifetime," review of *Dutch: Role of a Lifetime*, by Edmund Morris, *Washington Post*, October 3, 1999.

28. Ibid.

29. Mark Oppenheimer, "Legends (in Their Own Minds)," *Pittsburgh Post-Gazette*, June 24, 2001.

30. Peter Rollins, "Joe Ellis: The Danger of Playing a Role as a Public Intellectual," HNN, June 17 2002, http://hnn.us/articles/789.html.

31. Geoffrey Wheatcroft, "Not So Macho," *Guardian*, June 22, 2001. See also Steven Gorelick, "Vietnam Fantasies Trouble a Veteran Non-combatant," *International Herald Tribune*, June 27, 2001.

32. Ben Macintyre, "Top US Scholar Invented Role in Vietnam," *London Times*, June 20, 2001.

33. Editorial Desk, "The Lies of Joseph Ellis," *New York Times*, August 21, 2001.

34. Andrew Burstein, "The Politics of Memory: Taking Measure of the Ever More Popular Demand for Historical Greatness," *Washington Post*, October 14, 2001.

35. Joseph Ellis, "American Sphinx: The Contradictions of Thomas Jefferson," Library of Congress, *American Memory*, http://memory.loc.gov/ammem/mtjhtml/mtjessay1.html.

36. Ibid.

37. Ibid.

38. Ellis, "Jefferson: Post-DNA," 132.

39. Erik Erikson, *Dimensions of a New Identity*, 1973 Jefferson Lectures in the Humanities (New York: W. W. Norton, 1974), 107–108.

40. Quote from Ellis, *American Sphinx*, 123; Merrill Peterson, *Thomas Jefferson and the New Nation: A Biography* (New York: Oxford University Press, 1970).

41. Ellis, *American Sphinx*, 90.

42. Ellis, "American Sphinx" (Web site article).

43. Joseph Ellis, "Man of Character," interview by David Gergen, *PBS Newshour*, August 11, 1997, www.pbs.org/newshour/gergen/august97/ellis_8–11.html.

44. Ellis, *American Sphinx*, 3.

45. Joseph Ellis, "Man of Character."

46. Benjamin Schwarz, "American Sphinx: The Character of Thomas Jefferson," *Nation*, May 26, 1997, 29–32.

47. Ellis, "American Sphinx" (Web site article), quoting Salter.

48. Ellis, *American Sphinx*, 271, 297.

49. Ibid., 22.

50. Joseph Ellis, interview by *PBS Frontline*, n.d., www.pbs.org/wgbh/pages/frontline/shows/jefferson/interviews/ellis.html.

51. Emily Eakin, letter to the editor, *New York Times*, June 24, 2001.

52. Edmund Morris, "Just Our Imaginations, Running Away," *New York Times*, June 22, 2001. For readers' response to Morris's defense, see readers' letters in "Joseph Ellis: History and Fiction," *New York Times*, June 23, 2001.

53. Alison Landsberg, cited in Robert Burgoyne, "Prosthetic Memory / Traumatic Memory: *Forrest Gump* (1994)," *Screening the Past*, April 1999, www.latrobe.edu.au/screeningthepast/firstrelease/fr0499/rbfr6a.htm.

54. Burgoyne, "Prosthetic Memory / Traumatic Memory."

55. Student cited in Robinson, "Professor's Past in Doubt."

56. Jimmy Dean Smith, " 'Honest about His Experience': History as Eyewitness News," *PopPolitics.com*, June 26, 2001, http://www.poppolitics.com/articles/2001-06-22-ellis.shtml.

57. Turkle, "Virtuality and Its Discontents."

58. George Will and Joyce Appleby, cited in Scott Casper, "Going Dutch," *Common Place* 1, no. 1 (September 2000), http://www.common-place.org/vol-01/no-01/dutch.

59. Carlin Romano, "The Dirty Little Secret about Publicity Intellectuals," *Chronicle of Higher Education*, February 19, 1999, B4–B5.

60. David Samuels, "Edmund Wilson and the Public Intellectuals," *Wilson Quarterly* 20, no. 1 (1996): 102–112.

61. Jean Bethke Elshtain, cited in "The Future of the Public Intellectual," *Nation*, February 12, 2001, 25–35.

62. Richard Posner, *Public Intellectuals: A Study of Decline* (Cambridge, Mass.: Harvard University Press, 2002).

63. Scott Gac, in "Readers Sound Off about Joe Ellis's Suspension."

64. Rollins, "Danger of Playing a Role"; Garrow, cited in Smith and Rutten, "For Historian's Students, a Hard Lesson Lying."

65. Joseph Ellis, *"What Kind of Nation:* Clash of the Titans," *New York Times*, March 10, 2002, review of *Thomas Jefferson, John Marshall, and the Epic Struggle to Create a United States*, by James Simon.

66. "In Memory of Sergeant Harry Joseph Ellis," Path of Jesus Web Services, http://tanaya.net/vmw/E/rec-14908.html.

CHAPTER 4. THE GHOST OF CALIBAN

The quotation in the chapter title comes from Derek Freeman, *The Fateful Hoaxing of Margaret Mead: A Historical Analysis of Her Samoan Research* (Boulder, Colo.: Westview Press, 1999).

1. Nancy Scheper-Hughes, "The Margaret Mead Controversy: Culture, Biology, and Anthropological Inquiry," *Human Organization* 43, no. 1 (Spring 1984): 85.

2. Margaret Mead, *Coming of Age in Samoa: A Psychological Study of Primitive Youth for Western Civilization* (New York: William Morrow, 1928), 132.

3. Ibid., 76, 102–103, 107.

4. Mead, *Coming of Age in Samoa*, 136.

5. Scheper-Hughes, "Margaret Mead Controversy," 85; emphasis in the original.

6. Peter Worsley, foreword to *Confronting the Margaret Mead Legacy: Scholarship, Empire, and the South Pacific*, ed. Lenora Foerstal and Angela Gilliam (Philadelphia: Temple University Press, 1992), x; Worsley, "Margaret Mead: Science or Science Fiction," *Science and Society* 21, no. 2 (1975): 122–134. See also, William Mitchell, "Communicating Culture: Margaret Mead and the Practice of Popular Anthropology," in *Popularizing Anthropology*, ed. Jeremy MacClancy and Chris McDonaugh (New York: Routledge, 1996), 122–135.

7. Derek Freeman, "My Relations with Margaret Mead," in *The Samoa Reader: Anthropologists Take Stock*, ed. Hiram Caton (Lanham, Ma.: University Press of America, 1990), 201–202.

8. Ibid., 204.

9. George Appell, "The Discouragement of Criticism," in *The Samoa Reader*, ed. Caton, 275.

10. Derek Freeman, "Historical Glosses," in *The Samoa Reader*, ed. Caton, 192.

11. Ibid., 193.

12. Franz Boas, cited in Derek Freeman, "On Franz Boas and the Samoan Researches of Margaret Mead," *Cultural Anthropology* 32, no. 3 (June 1991): 324.

13. Derek Freeman, "Fa'apua'a Fa'amū and Margaret Mead," *American Anthropologist* 91 (1989): 1017.

14. Derek Freeman, *Margaret Mead and Samoa: The Making and Unmaking of an Anthropological Myth* (Cambridge, Mass.: Harvard University Press, 1983), 238–240.

15. Ibid., 241–244.

16. Ibid., 201.

17. Ibid., 203.

18. Derek Freeman, "Inductivism and the Test of Truth," in *The Samoa Reader*, ed. Caton, 82.

19. Derek Freeman, "Rejoinder to Patience and Smith," *American Anthropologist* 88 (1986): 165.

20. Freeman, *Margaret Mead and Samoa*, 302.

21. All quotations in this passage are from Lowell Holmes, "A Sad Day for Anthropology," in *The Samoa Reader*, ed. Caton, 225.

22. Richard Handler, "Ruth Benedict, Margaret Mead, and the Growth of American Anthropology," *Journal of American History* 71, no. 1 (September 1984): 366.

23. Lowell Holmes, "The Margaret Mead Vendetta, Round Two," *The World and I* 14, no. 5 (May 1999): 262–266.

24. Allan Patience and Joseph Wayne Smith, "Derek Freeman and Samoa: The Making and Unmaking of a Biobehavioral Myth," *American Anthropologist* 88 (1986): 161.

25. Richard Feinberg, "Margaret Mead and Samoa: *Coming of Age* in Fact and Fiction," *American Anthropologist* 90 (1988): 661.

26. Deborah Gordon, "The Unhappy Relationship of Feminism and Postmodernism in Anthropology," *Anthropological Quarterly* 66, no. 3 (1993): 111; George Marcus, "One Man's Mead: Margaret Mead and Samoa," *New York Times Book Review*, March 27, 1983, 3, 22, 24.

27. Bonnie Nardi, "The Height of Her Powers: Margaret Mead's Samoa," *Feminist Studies* 10 (1984): 323–337.

28. Derek Freeman, "Paradigms in Collision: Margaret Mead's Mistake and What It Has Done to Anthropology," *Skeptic* 5, no. 3 (1997): 66–73.

29. Virginia Yans-McLaughlin, "Inquisition and Appreciation: Two Approaches to the Study of Anthropology," *American Anthropology* 36 (Summer 1984): 320.

30. Roy Rappaport, "The Oracle Profaned," in *The Samoa Reader*, ed. Caton, 224.

31. Scheper-Hughes, "Margaret Mead Controversy," 446.

32. Mead, *Coming of Age in Samoa*, 7.

33. Martin Orans, *Not Even Wrong: Margaret Mead, Derek Freeman, and the Samoans* (Novato, Calif.: Chandler and Sharp Publishers, 1996), 132.

34. Derek Freeman, "Was Margaret Mead Misled or Did She Mislead on Samoa?" *Current Anthropology* 41, no. 4 (August–October, 2000): 609–614.

35. Yans-McLaughlin, "Inquisition and Appreciation," 320–321.

36. Karl Heider, "The Rashomon Effect: When Ethnographers Disagree," *American Anthropologist* 90 (1988): 73–81; Derek Freeman, "Comment on Heider's 'The Rashomon Effect,' " *American Anthropologist* 91 (1989): 169–171; John Rhoades, "The 'Rashomon Effect' Reconsidered," *American Anthropologist* 91 (1989): 171.

37. Martin Orans, "Hoaxing, Polemics, and Science," *Current Anthropology* 41, no. 4 (August–October 2000): 615–616.

38. Paul Shankman, "The History of Samoan Sexual Conduct and the Mead-Freeman Controversy," *American Anthropologist* 98 (1996): 557.

39. James Côté, "Was Mead Wrong about Coming of Age in Samoa? An Analysis of the Mead/Freeman Controversy for Scholars of Adolescence and Human Development," *Journal of Youth and Adolescence* 21, no. 5 (1992): 507.

40. Marcus, "One Man's Mead," 22.

41. Roy Wagner, *The Invention of Culture* (Englewood Cliffs, N.J.: Prentice-Hall, 1975), 10.

42. Eleanor Leacock, "Anthropologists in Search of a Culture: Mar-

garet Mead, Derek Freeman, and All the Rest of Us," in *Confronting the Margaret Mead Legacy*, ed. Foerstal and Gilliam, 10–11.

43. F. Wendt, cited in Côté, "Was Mead Wrong about Coming of Age?" 524.

44. Frank Miele, "The Shadow of Caliban: An Introduction to the Tempestuous History of Anthropology," *Skeptic* 9, no. 1 (2001): 22.

45. Paul Ehrlich, *The Population Bomb* (New York: Ballantine Books, 1968).

46. Paul Ehrlich and Anne Ehrlich, *The Population Explosion* (New York: Hutchinson, 1990).

47. Paul Ehrlich, *Human Natures: Genes, Cultures, and the Human Prospect* (New York: Island Press, 2000), 87.

48. Paul Ehrlich and Marcus Feldman, "Genes and Cultures: What Creates Our Behavioral Phenome?" *Current Anthropology* 44, no. 1 (February 2003): 87.

49. See, for example, Steven Pinker, *How the Mind Works* (New York: W. W. Norton, 1997), and *The Blank Slate: The Modern Denial of Human Nature* (New York: Viking Press, 2002).

50. Kenan Malik, "Human Conditions," review of *The Blank Slate*, by Steven Pinker, and *Straw Dogs*, by John Gray, Kenan Malik Web page, October 2002, www.kenanmalik.com/essays/pinker_gray.html.

51. Kenan Malik, "Genes, Environment, and Human Freedom," Kenan Malik Web page, March 2001, www.kenanmalik.com/essays/genes_freedom.html.

52. John Dupre, "Making Hay with Straw Men," *American Scientist* 91, no. 1 (January–February 2003): 69.

CHAPTER 5. VIOLENT PEOPLE AND GENTLE SAVAGES

The Yanomami are also called Yanomamo or Yanomama. Originally the spellings indicated different groups among the Yanomami, but the various terms are now used interchangeably. The word *Yanomami* means "human being."

1. Terry Turner and Leslie Sponsel, "Scandal about to Be Caused by Book by Patrick Tierney," ANTHRO-L archives, September 22, 2000, http://listserv.acsu.buffalo.edu/cgi-bin/wa?A2 = ind0009&L = anthro-l&F = &S = &P = 15000.

2. Patrick Tierney, *Darkness in El Dorado: How Scientists and Journalists Devastated the Amazon* (New York: W. W. Norton, 2001), 59.

3. Ibid., 30.

4. Turner and Sponsel, "Scandal about to Be Caused."

5. Ibid.

6. Tierney, *Darkness in El Dorado*, 8.

7. Napoleon Chagnon, "Life Histories, Blood Revenge, and Warfare in a Tribal Population," *Science*, February 26, 1988, 985.

8. Napoleon Chagnon, "Is Reproductive Success Equal in Egalitarian Societies?" in *Evolutionary Biology and Human Social Behavior: An Anthropological Perspective*, ed. Napoleon Chagnon and William Irons (North Scituate, Mass.: Duxbury Press, 1979), 374–401.

9. Ibid., 377.

10. Clifford Geertz, "Life among the Anthros," *New York Review of Books*, February 8, 2001, 18.

11. Tierney, *Darkness in El Dorado*, 114–121.

12. Jack Snyder, "Anarchy and Culture: Insights from the Anthropology of War," *International Organizations* 56, no. 1 (Winter 2002): 7.

13. Chagnon, "Life Histories, Blood Revenge, and Warfare," 985.

14. Doyne Dawson, "The Origins of War: Biological and Anthropological Theories," *History and Theory* 35, no. 1 (February 1996): 8.

15. Leslie Sponsel, "Response to Otterbein," *American Anthropologist* 102 (2000): 837–841.

16. Ruth Benedict, *Patterns of Culture* (Boston: Houghton Mifflin, 1934), 32.

17. American Anthropological Association (AAA), *El Dorado Task Force Papers*, vol. 1, 21–30, AAA Web site, May 2002, www.aaanet.org/edtf.

18. Susan Lindee, "Perspectives on *Darkness in El Dorado*," *Current Anthropology* 42, no. 2 (April 2001): 272–274.

19. AAA, *El Dorado Task Force Papers*, vol. 1, 44.

20. James Neel, "On Being a Headman," *Perspectives in Biology and Medicine* 23 (1980): 283.

21. John Tooby, "Executive Summary," in "Preliminary Report on Neel/Chagnon Allegations," 26, University of California, Santa Barbara, Department of Anthropology, October 11, 2001, www.anth.ucsb .edu/ucsbpreliminaryreport.pdf.

22. Tooby, "Executive Summary," 29.

23. Chagnon, cited in Tooby, "Executive Summary," 7.

24. Tooby, "Executive Summary," 8.

25. "E-mail from Peter Biella on 'Staged' Films" (September 19, 2000), in Tooby, "Executive Summary," 67.

26. AAA, *El Dorado Task Force Papers*, vol. 2, 85.

27. Ibid., vol. 1, 31.

28. Ibid., 32.

29. AAA, *El Dorado Task Force Papers*, vol. 1, 32.

30. Chagnon, "Life Histories, Blood Revenge, and Warfare," 985.

31. Ferguson, cited in AAA, *El Dorado Task Force Papers*, vol. 2, 88, 98; Brian Ferguson, *Yanomami Warfare* (Santa Fe: School of American Research Press, 1995), 169, 348.

32. Judith Shulevitz, "Is Anthropology Evil?" *Slate*, December 8, 2000, http://slate.msn.com/id/1006646.

33. Quote from R. Brian Ferguson, "10,000 Years of Tribal Warfare: History, Science, Ideology, and 'The State of Nature,' " *Journal of the International Institute* 8, no. 3 (2002), www.umich.edu/~iinet/ journal/vol8no3/ferguson.html. See also Ferguson, "Materialist, Cultural, and Biological Theories on Why Yanomami Make War," *Anthropological Theory* 1, no. 1 (March 2001): 99–116; Keith Otterbein, "A History of Research on Warfare in Anthropology," *American Anthropologist* 101 (1999): 794–805; and various responses to Otterbein in *American Anthropologist* 102 (2000). See also exchange between Ferguson and Azar Gat, in *Anthropological Quarterly* 73, no. 3 (July 2000): 159–168.

34. Lindee, "Perspectives on *Darkness in El Dorado*," 273.

35. Thomas Gregor and Daniel Gross, "Anthropology and the

Search for the Enemy Within," *Chronicle of Higher Education,* July 26, 2002, B11.

36. AAA, *El Dorado Task Force Papers,* vol. 1, 9.

37. Joe Watkins, "Roles, Responsibilities, and Relationships between Anthropologists and Indigenous People," in AAA, *El Dorado Task Force Papers,* vol. 2, 64–79.

38. Gregor and Gross, "Anthropology and the Search for the Enemy Within," B11.

39. Ibid.

40. David Stoll, "Science Attacks Amazon Tribe," *New Republic,* March 19, 2001, 38.

41. Florinda Donner, *Shabono* (New York: Delacorte Press, 1982). For criticism of Donner's work, see Rebecca De Holmes, "Shabono: Scandal or Superb Social Science?" *American Anthropologist* 85 (1983): 664–667, as well as Debra Picchi's review of *Shabono* in the same issue of *American Anthropologist,* 674–675. For a lively defense of Donner's work, see Alcida Rita Ramos, "Reflecting on the Yanomami: Ethnographic Images and the Pursuit of the Exotic," in *Rereading Cultural Anthropology,* ed. George Marcus (Durham, N.C.: Duke University Press, 1992), 48–68. Some primary examples of "fictocriticism" in anthropology are Michael Taussig, *The Magic of the State* (New York: Routledge, 1997), as well as the most famous early exemplar of this genre, Carlos Castaneda, *Journey to Ixtlan: The Lessons of Don Juan* (New York: Simon and Schuster, 1972).

42. Mark Ritchie, *Spirit of the Rainforest: A Yanomamö Story* (Chicago: Island Lake Press, 1996); Frank Salamone, *The Yanomami and Their Interpreters: Fierce People or Fierce Interpreters?* (Lanham, Md.: University Press of America, 1997). See also Linda Rabben, *Unnatural Selection: The Yanomami, the Kayapo, and the Onslaught of Civilisation* (Seattle: University of Washington Press, 1998). The AAA confrontation is discussed in Neil Whitehead, "Yanomamology, Missiology, and Anthropology," *American Anthropologist* 100 (1998): 517–519.

43. Alcida Rita Ramos, "Perspectives on Tierney's *Darkness in El Dorado,*" *Current Anthropology* 42, no. 1 (April 2000): 275.

44. Geertz, "Life among the Anthros," 18.

45. D. W. Miller, "Academic Scandal in the Internet Age," *Chronicle of Higher Education*, January 12, 2001, A14.

46. Ramos, "Perspectives on Tierney's *Darkness in El Dorado*," 275.

47. Fernando Coronil, introduction to "Perspectives on Tierney's *Darkness in El Dorado*," *Current Anthropology* 42, no. 2 (April 2001): 265–266.

48. AAA, *El Dorado Task Force Papers*, vol. 1, 9.

49. Zygmunt Bauman, *Modernity and the Holocaust* (Ithaca, N.Y.: Cornell University Press, 1989), 8.

50. See, for example, Chagnon and Irons, *Evolutionary Biology and Human Social Behavior*; Leonard Lieberman, "A Discipline Divided: Acceptance of Human Sociobiological Concepts in Anthropology," *Current Anthropology* 30, no. 5 (December 1989): 676–682; Johan van der Dennen and Vincent Falger, eds., *Sociobiology and Conflict* (Bristol, U.K.: Kluwer Academic Publishers, 1990).

51. Bill Durham, cited in Michael Shermer, "Spin-Doctoring the Yanomamo: Science as a Candle in the Darkness of the Anthropology Wars," *Skeptic* 9, no. 1 (2001): 39.

52. Ullica Segerstrale, "The Sociobiology of Conflict and the Conflict about Sociobiology," in van der Dennen and Falger, *Sociobiology and Conflict*, 273.

53. Ibid., 279.

54. Lindee, "Perspectives on Tierney's *Darkness in El Dorado*," 274.

CHAPTER 6. THE WILLFUL SUSPENSION OF DISBELIEF

1. This summary of the curriculum changes at Stanford is based on Mary Louise Pratt, "*I, Rigoberta Menchú* and the 'Culture Wars,' " in *The Rigoberta Menchú Controversy*, ed. Arturo Arias (Minneapolis: University of Minnesota Press, 2001), 29–48.

2. All quotes in the preceding passage are from ibid., 34–37.

3. "The Stanford Mind," editorial, *Wall Street Journal*, December 22, 1988.

4. Dinesh D'Souza, *Illiberal Education: The Politics of Race and Sex on Campus* (New York: Free Press, 1991), 67.

5. Ibid., 72.

6. C. Vann Woodward, cited in Patricia Aufderheide, *Beyond PC: Towards a Politics of Understanding* (St. Paul, Minn.: Graywolf Press, 1992), 148–154.

7. Larry Rohter, "Rigoberta Menchú, Tarnished Laureate," *New York Times*, December 15, 1998. Stoll later added a correction, acknowledging that Menchú had two brothers by the name of Nicolas. The first died as a baby, long before Rigoberta was born.

8. Jan Rus, introduction to "If Truth Be Told: A Forum on David Stoll's *Rigoberta Menchú and the Story of All Poor Guatemalans*," *Latin American Perspectives* 26, no. 6 (November 1999): 6.

9. David Stoll, *Rigoberta Menchú and the Story of All Poor Guatemalans* (New York: Westview Press, 1999), viii.

10. Ibid., xii.

11. Ibid., 235.

12. David Stoll, reply to Peter Canby, "The Truth about Rigoberta Menchú," *New York Review of Books*, October 21, 1999, www.nybooks.com/articles/353.

13. David Stoll, "The Battle of Rigoberta," in *The Rigoberta Menchú Controversy*, ed. Arias, 398.

14. Stoll, *Rigoberta Menchú*, xiii.

15. Daphne Patai, "Whose Truth? Iconicity and Accuracy in the World of Testimonial Literature," in *The Rigoberta Menchú Controversy*, ed. Arias, 279–280.

16. Elisabeth Burgos-Debray, "Testimonio and Transmission," *Latin American Perspectives* 26, no. 6 (November 1999): 86.

17. Patai, "Whose Truth?" 270–271.

18. Victoria Sanford, "The Silencing of Maya Women from Mama Maquin to Rigoberta Menchú," *Social Justice* 27, no. 1 (Spring 2000): 136.

19. Carol Smith, "Why Write an Exposé of Rigoberta Menchú," *Latin American Perspectives* 26, no. 6 (November 1999): 26.

20. Allen Carey-Webb, "Transformative Voices," in *Teaching and Testimony: Rigoberta Menchú and the North American Classroom*, ed. Allen Carey-Webb and Stephen Benz (New York: State University of New York Press, 1996), 6–7.

21. Rigoberta Menchú, *I, Rigoberta Menchú: An Indian Woman in Guatemala*, ed. and intro. Elisabeth Burgos-Debray, trans. Ann Wright (London: Verso, 1984), 1.

22. Mary Louise Pratt, "Me llamo Rigoberta Menchú," in *Teaching and Testimony*, ed. Carey-Webb and Benz, 65.

23. Mary Louise Pratt, "*I, Rigoberta Menchú*, and the 'Culture Wars,' " in Arias, *The Rigoberta Menchú Controversy*, 43.

24. Harvey Peskin, "Memory and Media: 'Cases' of Rigoberta Menchú and Benjamin Wilkomirski," *Society* (November–December 2000): 40.

25. Burgos-Debray, cited in Stoll, *Rigoberta Menchú*, 185.

26. Rino Avellaneda, Ksenija Bilbija, Laura Gutiérrez, Myriam Osorio, Stacey Skar, and Angela Wasia, "Testimonial Dictionary to the Reading of *Me llamo Rigoberta Menchú*," in *Teaching and Testimony*, ed. Carey-Webb and Benz, 209.

27. Roger Lancaster, "Rigoberta's Testimonio," *NACLA Report on the Americas* 32, no. 6 (May–June 1999): 4–5.

28. Arturo Arias, cited in Hal Cohen, "The Unmaking of Rigoberta Menchú," *Lingua Franca* (July–August 1999): 52.

29. Primo Levi, *The Drowned and the Saved*, trans. Raymond Rosenthal (New York: Summit Books, 1988), 19.

30. McWhorter, cited in Damon Linker's review of *Losing the Race: Self-Sabotage in Black America*, by John McWhorter, *Commentary* (October 2000): 75.

31. Salman Rushdie, *The Satanic Verses* (London: Viking Press, 1988), 167–168.

32. Gayatri Chakravorty Spivak, "Can the Subaltern Speak?" in

Marxism and the Interpretation of Culture, ed. Cary Nelson and Larry Grossberg (Chicago: University of Illinois Press, 1988), 271–313.

33. Arturo Arias, "Authoring Ethnicized Subjects: Rigoberta Menchú and the Performative Production of the Subaltern Self," *Publications of the Modern Language Association of America* 116, no. 1 (January 2001): 75–76.

34. Stoll, *Rigoberta Menchú*, 277.

35. Arias, "Authoring Ethnicized Subjects," 81.

36. Stoll, *Rigoberta Menchú*,viv.

37. Ibid., xiv–xv.

38. Carol Smith, "Stoll as a Victim," *Latin American Perspectives* 26, no. 6 (November 1999): 81–82.

39. Larry Rohter, "Tarnished Laureate: Nobel Winner Finds Her Story Challenged," *New York Times*, December 15, 1998; reprinted in *The Rigoberta Menchú Controversy*, ed. Arias, 58–65.

40. Claudia Ferman, "Textual Truth, Historical Truth, and Media Truth: Everybody Speaks about the Menchús," in *The Rigoberta Menchú Controversy*, ed. Arias, 159.

41. Ibid., 161.

42. Lancaster, "Rigoberta's Testimonio," 5.

43. Alcida Rita Ramos, "The Hyperreal Indian," *Critique of Anthropology* 14, no. 2 (1994): 171.

CHAPTER 7. SOKAL'S HOAX AND THE "LINGUISTIC LEFT"

1. Among the many contributions to this fray, see Paul Gross and Norman Levitt, *Higher Superstition: The Academic Left and Its Quarrels with Science* (Baltimore: Johns Hopkins University Press, 1998); Steven Weinberg, *Facing Up: Science and Its Cultural Adversaries* (Cambridge, Mass.: Harvard University Press, 2001); James Robert Brown, *Who Rules in Science? An Opinionated Guide to the Wars* (Cambridge, Mass.: Harvard University Press, 2001). The *Social Text* contribution to the culture wars was mostly a response to *Higher Superstition*.

2. Alan Sokal, "Transgressing the Boundaries: Towards a Transformative Hermeneutics of Quantum Gravity," *Social Text* 46–47 (Spring–Summer 1996): 217–252. Among the many publications devoted to the Sokal affair, see the collection of articles published by the editors of *Lingua Franca, The Sokal Hoax: The Sham That Shook the Academy* (Lincoln, Nebr.: University of Nebraska Press, 2000), and a forum of responses published in *Social Text* 50 (Spring 1997).

3. Paul A. Boghossian, "What the Sokal Hoax Ought to Teach Us: The Pernicious Consequences and Internal Contradictions of 'Postmodernist' Relativism," *Times Literary Supplement*, December 13, 1996, 14–15.

4. Alan Sokal, "A Physicist Experiments with Cultural Studies," *Lingua Franca* (May–June 1996); reprinted in Editors of *Lingua Franca, The Sokal Hoax*, 51.

5. Jay Rosen, "Swallow Hard: What *Social Text* Should Have Done," *Tikkun* (September–October 1996): 59–61.

6. Ruth Rosen, "A Physics Prof Drops a Bomb on the Faux Left," *Los Angeles Times*, May 23, 1996.

7. Barbara Ehrenreich, "Farewell to a Fad," *Progressive*, March 1999, 17–18.

8. Bruce Robbins and Andrew Ross, "Response: Mystery Science Theater," *Lingua Franca* (July–August 1996): 55; reprinted in Editors of *Lingua Franca, The Sokal Hoax*, 51.

9. Stanley Fish, "Professor Sokal's Bad Joke," *New York Times*, May 21, 1996.

10. Stanley Aronowitz, "Alan Sokal's 'Transgression,'" *Dissent* 44, no. 1 (Winter 1997): 107–110.

11. John Horgan, cited in Bruce Robbins, "Anatomy of a Hoax," *Tikkun* (September–October 1996): 58–59. Robbins misidentifies the writer as Paul Horgan.

12. Letter from Ellen Schrecker, *Lingua Franca* (July–August 1996); reproduced in Alan Sokal's Web site, http://physics.nyu.edu/~as2/mstsokal.html.

13. See, for example, Paul R. Gross, "The So-Called Science Wars

and Sociological Gravitas," *Scientist*, April 28, 1997, 8; Sheila Jasanoff, "Is Science Socially Constructed?" *Science and Engineering Ethics* 2 (1996): 263–76.

14. Sheilla Jones, "The Culture Wars Reach the Heavens," *Globe and Mail* (Toronto), February 9, 2002.

15. Charles Percy Snow, *The Two Cultures* (London: Cambridge University Press, 1963).

16. For the Leavis-Snow controversy, see Frank Raymond Leavis, *Two Cultures? The Significance of C. P. Snow* (New York: Pantheon, 1963); Roger Kimball, " 'The Two Cultures' Today," *New Criterion*, February 1994, www.newcriterion.com/archive/12/feb94/cultures.htm.

17. Thomas Kuhn, *The Structure of Scientific Revolutions* (Chicago: University of Chicago Press, 1962).

18. Ibid., 19.

19. John Sturrock, "Le Pauvre Sokal," *London Review of Books*, July 16, 1998, www.lrb.co.uk/v20/n14/stur01_.html.

20. Bruno Latour, "Is There Science after the Cold War?" *Le Monde*, January 3, 1997; reprinted in Editors of *Lingua Franca, The Sokal Hoax*, 124.

21. Susan Lindee, "Wars of Out-Describing," *Social Text* 50 (1997): 139.

22. Alan Sokal, "Transgressing the Boundaries: An Afterword," *Dissent* 43, no. 1 (Fall 1996): 93.

23. Aronowitz, "Alan Sokal's 'Transgression,' " 108.

24. James Robert Brown, *Who Rules in Science? A Guide to the Wars* (Cambridge, Mass.: Harvard University Press, 2001), 5.

25. Steven Weinberg, "Sokal's Hoax," *New York Review of Books*, August 8, 1996, 11–15.

26. Michael Warner, *Publics and Counterpublics* (New York: Zone Books, 2002).

27. Ellen Willis, "My Sokaled Life; or, Revenge of the Nerds," in Editors of *Lingua Franca, The Sokal Hoax*, 136.

28. Andrew Ross, "Reflections on the Sokal Affair," *Social Text* 50 (Spring 1997): 151.

29. Jones, "The Culture Wars Reach the Heavens."

30. Richard Rorty, "Phony Science Wars," *Atlantic Monthly*, November 1999, 120–122.

31. For Sokal's Web site, see http://physics.nyu.edu/~as2.

32. Grichka Bogdanoff and Igor Bogdanoff, "Spacetime Metric and the KMS Condition at the Planck Scale," *Annals of Physics* 296 (2002): 96.

33. Dennis Overbye, "French Physicists' Cosmic Theory Creates a Big Bang of Its Own," *New York Times*, November 9, 2002; Richard Monastersky, "The Emperor's New Science: French TV Stars Rock the World of Theoretical Physics," *Chronicle of Higher Education*, November 15, 2002, A16.

34. Roman Jackiw, cited in Overbye, "French Physicists' Cosmic Theory"; John Baez, cited in Andrew Orlowski, "Wine Bores Discover Physics," *Register*, December 13, 2003, www.theregister.co.uk/content/28/27963.html.

35. Daniel Strenheimer, cited in Overbye, "French Physicists' Cosmic Theory."

36. Journal editors cited in John Baez, "The Bogdanov Affair," John Baez's Web site, November 11, 2002, http://math.ucr.edu/home/baez/bogdanov.html.

37. Jackiw, cited in Overbye, "French Physicists' Cosmic Theory."

38. Frank Wilczek, cited in Monastersky, "The Emperor's New Science."

39. Andrew Orlowski, "Physics Hoaxers Discover Quantum Bogosity," *Register*, November 1, 2002, www.theregister.co.uk/content/6/27894.html.

40. John Baez, "Re: Physics Bitten by Reverse Alan Sokal Hoax?" in sci.physics.research newsgroup, October 31, 2002, www.lns.cornell.edu/spr/2002-10/msg0045241.html.

41. Grichka Bogdanov and Igor Bogdanov, cited in Overbye, "French Physicists' Cosmic Theory."

CHAPTER 8. WHAT DO THE SCANDALS MEAN?

1. John Nance, *The Gentle Tasaday: A Stone Age People in the Philippine Rain Forest* (London: Harcourt Brace Jovanovich, 1975), was the first

major book to bring the Tasaday to the attention of Western readers. The quoted phrase is from Walter Goldschmidt, "An Anthropological View of the Counter-Culture Movement," in *Exploring the Ways of Mankind: A Text-Casebook*, ed. Walter Goldschmidt (New York: Holt, Rinehart, and Winston, 1977), 538.

2. Oswald Iten, "The Tasaday and the Press," in *The Tasaday Controversy: Assessing the Evidence*, ed. Thomas Headland (Washington, D.C.: American Anthropological Association, 1992).

3. Among the many autopsies of the Tasaday affair, see Bruce Bower, "The Strange Case of the Tasaday: Were They Primitive Hunter-Gatherers or Rain-Forest Phonies?" *Science News*, May 6, 1989, 280–283; Eliot Marshall, "Anthropologists Debate Tasaday Hoax Evidence," *Science*, December 1, 1989, 1113–1117; Allan Palmer, "Primitives among Us," *Science Communication* 21, no. 3 (March 2000): 223–243; Robin Hemley, *Inventing Eden: The Elusive, Disputed History of the Tasaday Controversy* (New York: Farrar, Straus, and Giroux, 2003).

4. Talal Asad, "Ethnography, Literature, and Politics: Some Readings and Uses of Salman Rushdie's *The Satanic Verses*," *Cultural Anthropology* 5, no. 3 (August 1990): 260.

5. Jean-Paul Dumont, "The Tasaday: Which and Whose? Toward the Political Economy of an Ethnographic Sign," *Cultural Anthropology* 3, no. 3 (August 1988): 273.

6. F. R. Ankersmit, "Hayden White's Appeal to Historicism," *History and Theory* 37, no. 2 (May 1998): 189–190.

7. Clifford Geertz, *Negra: The Theatre State in Nineteenth Century Bali* (Princeton, N.J.: Princeton University Press, 1980), 136.

8. Aram Yengoyan, "Shaping and Reshaping the Tasaday: A Question of Cultural Reality—A Review Article," *Journal of Asian Studies* 50, no. 3 (August 1991): 565.

9. Leslie Sponsel, "Ultraprimitive Pacifists: The Tasaday as a Symbol of Peace," *Anthropology Today* 6, no. 1 (February 1990): 3–5.

10. See, for example, Jerold Auerbach, "The Corruption of Historians," *Society* (November–December 2002): 38–42; Ralph Luker, "The

Year We Got Caught," History News Network, December 30, 2002, http://hnn.us.articles/1184.html.

11. Gabrielle Spiegel, "History and Postmodernism," *Past and Present* 135 (May 1992): 196.

12. Ibid., 201.

13. E. P. Thompson, *The Poverty of Theory and Other Essays* (London: Monthly Review Press, 1978), 27–29.

14. Jonathan Benthal, "The Tasaday Drama as Docu-Drama," *Anthropology Today* 6, no. 1 (February 1990): 16–18.

15. Oscar Handlin, "The Vulnerability of the American University," *Encounter* 35 (July 1970): 25.

16. Kai Erikson, *Wayward Puritans: A Study in the Sociology of Deviance* (New York: John Wiley, 1966), 6, 13; emphasis in the original.

17. George Stocking, "Delimiting Anthropology: Historical Reflections on the Boundaries of a Boundless Discipline," *Social Research* 62, no. 4 (Winter 1995): 933–934.

18. Ibid., 933.

19. Joyce Appleby, letter to the editor, *OAH Newsletter* (November 1991): 4; David Thelen, Mary Frances Berry, Dan Carter, Cullom Davis, Sara Evans, Linda Gordon, Lawrence Levine, Mary Ryan, letter to the editor, *OAH Newsletter* (November 1991): 5.

20. American Historical Association, "AHA Announces Changes in Efforts Relating to Professional Misconduct," May 5, 2003, www.theaha.org/press/PR_Adjudication.htm.

21. Stocking, "Delimiting Anthropology," 933.

22. David Thelen, "Making History and Making the United States," *Journal of American Studies* 32, no. 1 (April 1998): 373–397; Roy Rozenzweig and David Thelen, *The Presence of the Past: Popular Uses of History in American Life* (New York: Columbia University Press, 1998).

23. R. Laurence Moore, "Insiders and Outsiders in American Historical Narrative and American History," *American Historical Review* 87, no. 2 (April 1982): 390.

24. J. C. Davis, *Fear, Myth, and History: The Ranters and the Historians* (London: Cambridge University Press, 1986), 111.

INDEX

sexuality: anthropologists among
Yanomami, 141, 158; Nussbaum
misrepresentation, 89–90; presi-
dential lapses, 93–94; primitive
societies, 144–45; Samoan,
12–13, 113–37; Yanomami, 144,
149
Shabono (Donner), 157–58
Shakespeare, William, 133, 170
Sherry, Michael, 45–46
Shields, Carol, 195
Simon and Schuster, 47
Sisson, Edgar, 1
Sisson documents, 1–3
Sklodowska, Elzbieta, 4
Sleeper, Jim, 92
Smith, Carol, 179, 190
Snow, C.P., 204–5
"The Social Structure of a Samoan
Village Community" (Freeman),
118
Social Text, 19–20, 195–213
Soft Skull Press, New York, 83
Sokal, Alan, 19–21, 195–218
Spiegel, Gabrielle, 225–26
Spivak, Gayatri Chakravorty, 187,
189
Sponsel, Leslie, 138, 139, 147, 160,
162, 224
Stanford University, 134, 163,
169–72
Stephen Ambrose Enterprises, 47,
49–50
Stevenson, Robert Louis, 113
Stewart, Walter, 38, 39
Stocking, George, 229
Stoll, David, 17–19, 157, 166,
172–92, 258n7
Strenheimer, Daniel, 216
Sturrock, John, 207

subalterns, 170, 171, 177, 178, 180,
181, 185–89
subjectivist thinking, science wars
and, 5, 196, 199
The Supreme Commander (Ambrose), 47

Takiff, Michael, 51
Tannen, Deborah, 22
"Tarnished Laureate: Nobel Win-
ner Finds Her Story Chal-
lenged" (Rohter), 191
Tasaday people, 219–27
The Tempest (Shakespeare), 133,
170
testimonio, Menchú, 18–19,
179–86, 188–89
Thatcher, Laurel, 75–76
Thelen, David, 231
Thomas, Benjamin, 36–45, 56
Thompson, E.P., 226
Tierney, Patrick, 14–16, 138–63
Tooby, John, 149–51
totalitarianism, government-
academic conflation, 2–3, 39
"Transgressing the Boundaries: Towards a Transformative
Hermeneutics of Quantum
Gravity" (Sokal), 197–218
truths, 27; Ellis and, 90, 94, 95–96,
101, 102, 106; historical/narra-
tive, 184; media historian and,
108–9; Menchú scandal and, 17,
19, 166, 174, 177, 178–86, 189,
190; Samoa scandal and, 123,
126, 131–32; science wars and,
4, 200, 202, 203, 209. See also
realism/imagination
Turkle, Sherry, 11, 24, 85, 106
Turner, Terry, 138, 139, 160, 162

Compositor:	Binghamton Valley Composition
Indexer:	Barbara Roos
Text:	10/15 Janson
Display:	Janson
Printer and Binder:	Maple-Vail Manufacturing Group

CPSIA information can be obtained
at www.ICGtesting.com
Printed in the USA
JSHW052244101120
9478JS00001B/13